Bedside Companion for Travel Lovers

Bedside Companion
for Travel Lovers

EDITED BY JANE MCMORLAND HUNTER

ILLUSTRATIONS BY ELEN WINATA

BATSFORD

First published in the United Kingdom in 2024 by
Batsford
43 Great Ormond Street
London
WC1N 3HZ

An imprint of B. T. Batsford Holdings Ltd

ISBN 978 184994 919 4

A CIP catalogue record for this book is available from the
British Library.

10 9 8 7 6 5 4 3 2 1

Reproduction by Mission Productions, Hong Kong
Printed and bound by Dream Colour, China
Illustrations by Elen Winata

This book can be ordered direct from the publisher at
www.batsfordbooks.com, or try your local bookshop

CONTENTS

To John Hare, founder of the Wild Camel Protection Foundation,
To the wild camels of the Gobi desert,
And to Matilda, paperweight and armchair companion,
With all my love

Acknowledgements

As always huge thanks to Hatchards, in Piccadilly, St Pancras and
Cheltenham, for all their support. Thanks to Julie Apps, Francis
Cleverdon, Sally Hughes, Adam Nagy, John Peatfield, Julia Schaper
and Harper Stringer for suggestions and research. Thanks to Kate
Rae, Benedict Allen, Robin Hanbury-Tenison, Barry Lewis, Anna
Bramwell, Mark Staples and Jana Synková for permission to include
works and, last but definitely not least, thanks to all at Batsford, in
particular my wonderful editor, Nicola Newman.

About the editor

Jane McMorland Hunter has compiled anthologies for Batsford
and the National Trust including collections on gardening, books,
food, nature, friendship, London, England and the First World
War. She has also worked as a gardener, potter and quilter, writes
nature, gardening, cookery and craft books and works at Hatchards
bookshop in Piccadilly. She was brought up in the country but now
lives happily in London in a house overflowing with books and a
small garden overflowing with plants.

Jane is a patron of the Wild Camel Protection Foundation and a
percentage of the proceeds of this book will be given to the charity to
help pay for the breeding centre for the wild Bactrian camels living
in the Gobi desert.
wildcamels.com

Introduction

I went on a camping holiday when I was 18 and endured three weeks of failing to learn how to put up a tent. We moved around a lot and, every night, my friend and I would stand holding a piece of kit (always a different piece) and look ruefully at our pitiful effort at tent construction. All the other tents in the field stood proud; ours sagged sadly, as if it knew it had been put up by a pair of incompetents. Ever since then I have been an armchair traveller.

Travel narratives allow the reader to travel anywhere, under any circumstances, at any time. Add in fiction, poetry and children's stories and the choice is endless. The simple act of sitting comfortably and opening a book can transport you wherever you wish, be it a ship on the high seas, a remote grassy plain or into someone else's charming life abroad. Books have the ability to take you back, or even forwards, in time, down the deepest cave or up the highest mountain and beyond, to the stars.

As well as choosing a variety of destinations and modes of transport, the travellers themselves form a wide-ranging collection. Almost everyone who travels has their own view of the journey. Twenty people viewing the same monument or scene would all write different descriptions, and in this collection I hope to encompass that variety, with extracts from books of explorers to those of hedonists chasing the good life. There are shipwrecked sailors, time travellers, drunkards, merchants and holidaymakers.

In historical times exploration was necessary – people needed to know whether they were in danger of falling off the edge of the world and, if not, what delights or dangers awaited them beyond the horizon in the empty spaces on the maps. Even now, with most of the gaps filled in, exploration can still have a purpose, helping us to better understand our planet and its many inhabitants. Gradually people became travellers, journeying bravely but not usually intrepidly, and then tourists, the slightly despised group who want to see the world but free of hassle. Greed, science and latterly conservation are motives for travel. As are relaxation, exercise and pleasure. Many travelled to improve themselves: pilgrims often journeying in hardship, the rich of the Renaissance and the Grand Tour in comfort. In most journeys the motives are blurred. Most probably travel for the experience, which obviously means different things to different people. Some liked 'abroad' so much that they settled there. All these people wrote, and still write, books describing their experiences: good, bad, hilarious or life-threatening. From the point of view of the reader it is often the mishaps which make the best stories: wayward pack animals, recalcitrant builders, broken bridges or avalanches, but there are also moving descriptions and inspiring people to discover.

As well as those who travel for knowledge or pleasure there are vast numbers, both past and present, who travel because they have no choice. Unfortunately many early explorers exploited what they found – pillaging treasures and regarding the indigenous people as a commodity to make use of. Alexander Maitland makes the point in his book *Exploring the World* that most 'discoveries' were actually 'first sightings by a European', which completely ignored the local guides who helped them or the people who may have lived there for hundreds of years, unknown to the rest of the world. Though few have left written descriptions, thousands of people have been forcibly displaced: as enslaved people, migrant workers or prisoners. In turn some of these made their own journeys, escaping to better lives, often in distant lands. As well as those who were forced to undertake journeys against their will, a great many people did, and still do, travel for their livelihoods. Farmers following their flocks according to the seasons and migrant workers chasing harvests. Merchants, soldiers, sailors, spies and diplomats all travel as the needs of their work dictates.

Many of these various travellers kept diaries or wrote about their travels afterwards, in the comfort of their homes. Gradually the professional travel writer emerged. Many of these explorers and travellers were products of their time and expressed opinions which we now recognize as insensitive, self-aggrandizing and plainly wrong; this is not to condone what they said and did, but if they lived today, one would hope their attitudes might be very different. In the extracts I have chosen I have tried to concentrate on descriptions of place, transport or people rather than the political or sociological aspects of the journeys. I have purposefully not included the writings of missionaries as their aim was to convert and teach rather than entertain. For the same reason the writings of many eminent explorers and scientists have been left out. Copyright constraints and, the common enemy in all my anthologies, space, or rather lack of it, have resulted in more omissions.

The defining factor for me in deciding what to include and what to leave out was the writing rather than the destination. Avoiding divisions by continent or even country, I have aimed to create a random patchwork of destinations, transports and opinions. I would be the first to admit that this is not a balanced patchwork; from my armchair I am drawn to inhospitable deserts, snowy mountain passes and Parisian cafés and I am afraid these destinations have a disproportionately high number of entries. I also appreciate not everyone lives in south-west London, but I do and to me it is home. Try as I might, I failed to compile this anthology with an international mind-set. So if you are reading this in America, Australia or in fact anywhere other than south-west London, I can only apologize. I may well have regarded the place you call 'home' as a far-distant destination.

In terms of posterity, most journeys are nothing without some sort of record – in word, paint, picture or, more recently, film. Only then are we, the ones who stayed at home, for whatever reason, able to appreciate what the traveller saw.

JANUARY

The Magnificence of the View

Traditional Gaelic Blessing

Anon

May the road rise up to meet you.
May the wind be always at your back.
May the sun shine warm upon your face,
And rains fall soft upon your fields.
And until we meet again,
May God hold you in the palm of his hand.

1 January

Ten Minutes

From *The Happy Traveller: A Book for Poor Men, 1923*

Rev. Frank Tatchell, Vicar of Midhurst (1906–1935)

Alternate town and country, because a constant length of either
soon palls. This you can do by walking from place to place, or,
if that is too arduous, sometimes leave the train a station or two
before reaching your destination and walk into the town so as to get
a view of it from a distance. A railway seldom approaches a town in
the best way, and, by following this plan, you get a first sight of the
place as generations of former travellers have seen it. The quiet of the
countryside is an admirable foil to the bustle of towns, and to rush
about by train from one famous city to another is not travelling.
For the same reason, vary your mode of journeying, walking for
a week or two, and then using trains or coasting steamers. I also have
a secret liking for being a poor man most of the time, with
an occasional week as a rich man.

The Ambition

From *Explorer*, 2022 | Benedict Allen (1960–)

I was ten before I told my father.

. . . .

'An explorer?' Dad said. 'I think that's a wonderful thing to want
to be!'

I still recall standing by the door of what we called the drawing
room – the brass handle like an apple in my hand, the carpet a
mustard yellow, the thick linen curtains a burgundy red. And
everywhere in that room the silence. At last I'd made my intent
known.

'I expect he'll grow out of it,' my grannie sad.

But my mum sighed, because she knew. Deep down, I think
they all knew.

I went outdoors, pleased to have made my announcement.
I strode back and forth along the herbaceous border, for the first
time wondering about the practicalities of becoming 'an explorer'.

The Panorama of Stars From the Equator

From *The Beauties of Scenery, 1943* | Vaughan Cornish (1862–1948)

Those who live near the Equator have the unique advantage of seeing all the constellations. Not only is the panorama complete in the course of the year, but the long interval between sunset and sunrise and the shortness of evening and morning twilight make the views at the beginning and end of the night almost complementary. Thus on every night throughout the year the panorama of the constellations is very nearly complete. The picture thus provided of the whole circle of the Milky Way is a special advantage, for this marks the plane about which the stars within the range of human eyesight are symmetrically grouped. Moreover, this is the world of stars to which our sun belongs.

The rotation of the constellations round the northern and southern pole cannot be seen from the Equator, but a compensation for this loss in scenery is afforded by the impression of swift revolution which is given by the vertical ascent and descent of the stars. This rapid change of altitude makes the spectator realize that the Earth is a spinning ball.

The Great Rivers of the World

From *Travels, 1325–1354* | Ibn Battuta (1304–1368/9 or 1377)

Translated by Samuel Lee (1783–1852)

At Cairo:

The Nile, which runs through this country, excels all other rivers in the sweetness of its taste, the extent of its progress, and the greatness of the benefits it confers. It is one of the five great rivers of the world, which are, itself, the Euphrates, the Tigris, the Sīhūn, the Jaihūn (or Gihon). Five other rivers too may be compared with them, namely, the river of Sindia, which is called the Panj āb (or five waters), the river of India, which is called the Gung (or Ganges), to which the Indians perform their pilgrimages, and into which they throw the ashes of their dead when burnt: they say it descends from Paradise; also the river Jūn (or Jumna): the river Athil (Volga) in the desert of Kifhāk, and the river Sarv in Tartary, upon the bank of which is the city of Khān Bālik, and which flows from that place to El Khansā, and thence to the city of Zaitūn in China.

The Golden Journey to Samarkand

James Elroy Flecker (1884–1915)

Prologue

We who with songs beguile your pilgrimage
    And swear that Beauty lives though lilies die,
We Poets of the proud old lineage
    Who sing to find your hearts, we know not why, –

What shall we tell you? Tales, marvellous tales
    Of ships and stars and isles where good men rest,
Where nevermore the rose of sunset pales,
    And winds and shadows fall towards the West:

And there the world's first huge white-bearded kings
    In dim glades sleeping, murmur in their sleep,
And closer round their breasts the ivy clings,
    Cutting its pathway slow and red and deep.

Cold Tea

From *Ice Bird, 1975* | David Lewis (1917–2002)

'Is anyone awake? Do you mind if I tie up alongside?' The saloon door crashed open and a very startled figure appeared. I threw him a line and made fast. The first single-handed voyage to Antarctica had been accomplished.

Calypso's sleepy and startled crew popped out of their cabins like gophers, to help moor up *Ice Bird* and to ply me with steaming black coffee and crisp rolls. My urgent preoccupation, though, was to have a radio message sent off to report my safe arrival and a tall, lean Frenchman, who seemed to be in charge, promised to see to this immediately. I had recognized the ship's name, *Calypso*. It was on the tip of my tongue to ask him if he had bought her from Cousteau when I realized that he *was* the celebrated scuba-diving pioneer and marine publicist. He would hardly, I think, have been amused at not being recognized.

Gibraltar

Jana Synková (1968–)

The Rock stands ominous above the town,
With vertiginous aspect to the sea.
Macaque monkeys command the higher ground;
An edginess denies tranquillity.
In the Alameda Botanic Park,
Cactuses put forth alien flowers;
Pine processionary caterpillars stalk
Paths walked by the unwary visitor;
Subtropical blooms of vermillion
Blaze unabashedly, in mid-winter.
Here we'd landed, ingénues, thrust upon
This odd promontory: mother and daughter
On our first cruise, 'Atlantic Adventure';
We'd sought Spain; and they gave us Gibraltar.

The Lubéron in Winter

From *A Year in Provence, 1989* | Peter Mayle (1939–2018)

The drive had turned into a miniature mountainscape where wind
had drifted the snow into a range of knee-deep mounds, and the only
way out was on foot. Buying a loaf of bread became an expedition
lasting nearly two hours – into Ménerbes and back without seeing
a single moving vehicle, the white humps of parked cars standing
patiently as sheep by the side of the hill leading up to the village.
The Christmas-card weather had infected the inhabitants who
were greatly amused by their own efforts to negotiate the steep and
treacherous streets, either teetering precariously forward from the
waist or leaning even more precariously backward, placing their feet
with the awkward deliberation of intoxicated roller-skaters.

The municipal cleaning squad, two men with brooms, had cleared
the access routes to essential services – butcher, baker, *épicerie*
and café – and small knots of villagers stood in the sunshine
congratulating each other on their fortitude in the face of calamity.
A man on skis appeared from the direction of the Mairie and,
with marvellous inevitability, collided with the only other owner
of assisted transport, a man on an ancient sled. It was a pity the
journalist from *Le Provençal* wasn't there to see it: SNOW CLAIMS
VICTIMS IN HEAD-ON COLLISION, he could have written, and
he could have watched it all from the steamy comfort of the café.

The Joy of Flying

From *The Fun of It, 1932* | Amelia Earhart (1897–disappeared 1937)

Perhaps the greatest joy of flying is the magnificence of the view.
If visibility is good, the passenger seems to see the whole world.
Colors stand out and shades of the earth, unseen from below, form
an endless magic carpet. If anyone really wishes to see the seasons'
changes, he should fly. Autumn turns its most flaming leaves
upwards and spring hints its coming first for birds and aviators.

I have spoken of the effect of height in flattening the landscape,
always a phenomenon in the eyes of the air novitiate. Even mountains
grow humble and really rough terrain appears comparatively smooth.
Trees look like bushes and automobiles like flat-backed bugs.
A second plane which may be flying a few hundred feet above the
ground, seen from a greater altitude looks as if it were just skimming
the surface. All vertical measurement is foreshortened.

The world seen from the air is laid out in squares. Especially
striking is the checker board effect whenever one looks down on what
his brother man has done. Country or city, it is always the same –
only the rectangles are of different sizes. The city plays its game
of checkers in smaller spaces than the country, and divides its area
more minutely.

Ballade of an Omnibus

Amy Levy (1861–1889)

To see my love suffices me.
 – *Ballades in Blue China*

Some men to carriages aspire;
On some the costly hansoms wait;
Some seek a fly, on job or hire;
Some mount the trotting steed, elate.
I envy not the rich and great,
A wandering minstrel, poor and free,
I am contented with my fate –
An omnibus suffices me.

In winter days of rain and mire
I find within a corner strait;
The 'busmen know me and my lyre
From Brompton to the Bull-and-Gate.
When summer comes, I mount in state
The topmost summit, whence I see
Crœsus look up, compassionate –
An omnibus suffices me.

I mark, untroubled by desire,
Lucullus' phaeton and its freight.
The scene whereof I cannot tire,
The human tale of love and hate,
The city pageant, early and late
Unfolds itself, rolls by, to be
A pleasure deep and delicate.
An omnibus suffices me.

Princess, your splendour you require,
I, my simplicity; agree
Neither to rate lower nor higher.
An omnibus suffices me.

Troy

From *The Glorious Adventure, 1927*

Richard Halliburton (1900–1939: disappeared while attempting to sail a Chinese
junk across the Pacific Ocean from Hong Kong to San Francisco)

If you had to choose the most romantic corner in the world, what
corner would you choose? I know mine. It is a corner that has fired
imagination for three thousand years. It is a corner packed with
stirring drama, touched by pathos and deluged with poetry. Such
bitter tragedy it has known; such vivid personalities. It is the corner
that Homer has immortalized in the first great masterpiece of
European literature. It is Troy.

How many a night, as a very small boy, I was rocked to sleep in
my father's lap to the romantic tales of this romantic city. Hector
and Paris, Ajax and Achilles and the crafty Ulysses were my intimate
childhood companions. A hundred times and more I heard the story
of the wooden horse, until, if my father failed to recite every smallest
word in the telling, I would know it and solemnly correct him.

. . . .

How vividly my five-year-old eyes saw it all from the high
battlements of my father's lap. How many beastly Greeks (before
I went to sleep) I pursued in wild flight across the Trojan plain, back
to their ships at the edge of the Hellespont! I never grew tired of Troy
and its bloody drama. *These* stories had guts. Peter Rabbit! Uncle
Remus! Bah! They were for idiot children.

Coming in to Land

From *A Dragon Apparent: Travels in Cambodia, Laos and Vietnam, 1951* | Norman Lewis (1909–1979)

In the middle of January 1950, deciding to risk no further delays,
I caught an Air France plane at Paris, bound for Saigon:
On the morning of the fourth day the dawn light daubed our faces
as we came down the skies of Cochin-China. The passengers were
squirming in their seats, not sleeping and not waking, and the air-
hostess's trained smile came stiffly. With engines throttled back the
plane dropped from sur-Alpine heights in a tremorless glide, settling
in the new, morning air of the plains, like a dragonfly on the surface
of a calm lake. As the first rays of the sun broke through the magenta
mists that lay along the horizon, the empty sketching of the child's
painting book open beneath us received a wash of green. Now
lines were ruled lightly across it. A yellow penciling of reds and
blue canals.

Travelling With a Bicycle Named Roz

From *Full Tilt: Ireland to India with a Bicycle, 1965*

Dervla Murphy (1931–2022)

On my tenth birthday a bicycle and an atlas coincided as presents and a few days later I decided to cycle to India. I've never forgotten the exact spot on a hill near my home at Lismore, County Waterford, where the decision was made and it seemed to me then, as it still seems to me now, a logical decision, based on the discoveries that cycling was a most satisfactory method of transport and that (excluding the USSR for political reasons) the way to India offered fewer watery obstacles than any other destination at a similar distance.

However I was a cunning child so I kept my ambition to myself, thus avoiding the tolerant amusement it would have provoked among my elders. I did not want to be soothingly assured that this was a passing whim because I was quite confident that one day I would cycle to India.

That was at the beginning of December 1941, and on 14 January 1963, I started to cycle from Dunkirk towards Delhi.

The preparations had been simple; one of the advantages of cycling is that it automatically prevents a journey from becoming an Expedition. I already possessed an admirable Armstrong Cadet man's bicycle named Rozinante, but always known as 'Roz'. By a coincidence I had bought her on 14 January 1961, so our journey started on her second birthday.

The Inn at Sestri di Levante

From *Travels Through France and Italy, 1766*

Tobias Smollett (1721–1771)

Letter XXVI

Nice, January 15, 1765

The house was tolerable, and we had no great reason to complain
of the beds: but, the weather being hot, there was a very offensive
smell, which proceeded from some skins of beasts new killed,
that were spread to dry on an out-house in the yard. Our landlord
was a butcher, and had very much the looks of an assassin. His
wife was a great masculine virago, who had all the air of having
frequented the slaughter-house. Instead of being welcomed with
looks of complaisance, we were admitted with a sort of gloomy
condescension, which seemed to say, 'We don't much like your
company; but, however, you shall have a night's lodging in favour of
the *patron of the gondola*, who is our acquaintance.' In short, we had
a very bad supper, miserably dressed, passed a very disagreeable
night, and payed a very extravagant bill in the morning, without
being thanked for our custom. I was very glad to get out of the house
with my throat uncut.

Unhappy Travellers

From *A Sentimental Journey, 1768* | Laurence Sterne (1713–1768)

The learned Smelfungus* travelled from Boulogne to Paris, – from Paris to Rome, – and so on; – but he set out with the spleen and jaundice, and every object he pass'd by was discoloured or distorted. – He wrote an account of them, but 'twas nothing but the account of his miserable feelings.

. . . .

Mundungus**, with an immense fortune, made the whole tour; going on from Rome to Naples, – from Naples to Venice, – from Venice to Vienna, – to Dresden, to Berlin, without one generous connection or pleasurable anecdote to tell of; but he had travell'd straight on, looking neither to his right hand nor his left, lest Love or Pity should seduce him out of his road.

Peace be to them! if it is to be found; but heaven itself, were it possible to get there with such tempers, would want objects to give it – every gentle spirit would come flying upon the wings of Love to hail their arrival. – Nothing would the souls of Smelfungus and Mundungus hear of, but fresh anthems of joy, fresh raptures of love, and fresh congratulations of their common felicity. I heartily pity them: they have brought up no faculties for this work; and was the happiest mansion in heaven to be allotted to Smelfungus and Mundungus, they would be so far from being happy, that the souls of Smelfungus and Mundungus would do penance there to all eternity!

*Smelfungus: Tobias Smollett
**Mundungus: Dr Samuel Sharp

Qualifications for a Traveller

From *The Art of Travel or Shifts and Contrivances Available in Wild Countries, 1872* | Sir Francis Galton (1822–1911)

If you have health, a great craving for adventure, at least a moderate fortune, and can set your heart on a definite object, which old travellers do not think impracticable, then – travel by all means. If, in addition to these qualifications, you have scientific taste and knowledge, I believe that no carer, in time of peace, can offer you more advantages than that of a traveller. If you have not independent means, you may still turn travelling to excellent account; for experience shows it often leads to promotion, nay, some men support themselves by travel. They explore pasture land in Australia, they hunt for ivory in Africa, they collect specimens of natural history for sale, or they wander as artists.

Marmalade

From *Childe Harold's Pilgrimage* | George Gordon, Lord Byron (1788–1824)

Canto the First, IV

'Adieu, adieu! my native shore
Fades o'er the water blue;
The Night-winds sigh, the breakers roar,
And shrieks the wild sea-mew.
Yon Sun that sets upon the sea
We follow in his flight;
Farewell awhile to him and thee,
My native Land – Good Night!

'A few short hours and He will rise,
To give the Morrow birth;
And I shall hail the main and skies,
But not my mother earth.
Deserted is my own good hall,
Its hearth is desolate;
Wild weeds are gathering on wall,
My dog howls at the gate.

Landfall and Departure

From *The Mirror of the Sea, 1906* | Joseph Conrad (1857–1924)

Landfall and Departure mark the rhythmical swing of a seaman's life and of a ship's career. From land to land is the most concise definition of a ship's earthly fate.

A 'Departure' is not what a vain people of landsmen may think. The term 'Landfall' is more easily understood; you fall in with the land, and it is a matter of a quick eye and of a clear atmosphere. The Departure is not the ship's going away from her port any more than the Landfall can be looked upon as the synonym of arrival. But there is this difference in the Departure: that the term does not imply so much a sea event as a definite act entailing a process – the precise observation of certain landmarks by means of the compass card.

19 January

The Voyage

From *The Story of Dr Dolittle, 1922* | Hugh Lofting (1886–1947)

They were just going to start on their journey, when the Doctor said he would have to go back and ask the sailor the way to Africa.

But the swallow said she had been to that country many times and would show them how to get there.

So the Doctor told Chee-Chee to pull up the anchor and the voyage began.

. . . .

Now for six whole weeks they went sailing on and on, over the rolling sea, following the swallow who flew before the ship to show them the way. At night she carried a tiny lantern, so they should not miss her in the dark; and the people on the other ships that passed said that the light must be a shooting star.

A Wanderer

From *Persian Pictures: From the Mountains to the Sea*, 1894

Gertrude Bell (1868–1926)

Every man, says a philosopher, is a wanderer at heart. Alas! I fear
the axiom would be truer if he had confined himself to stating that
every man loves to fancy himself a wanderer, for when it comes to
the point there is not one in a thousand who can throw off the ties of
civilized existence – the ties and the comforts of habits which have
become easy to him by long use, of the life whose security is ample
compensation for its monotony. Yet there are moments when the
cabined spirit longs for liberty. A man stands a-tiptoe on the verge
of the unknown world which lures him with its vague promises; the
peaceful years behind lose all their value in his dazzled eyes; like him,
'qui n'a pas du ciel que ce qui brille par le trou du volet,' he pines to
stand in the great free sunlight, the great wide world which is all too
narrow for his adventurous energy. For one brief moment he shakes
off the traditions of a lifetime, swept away by the mighty current
which silently, darkly, goes watering the roots of his race. He, too, is
a wanderer like his remote forefathers; his heart beats time with the
hearts long stilled that dwelt in their bosoms, who came sweeping
out of the mysterious East, pressing ever resistlessly onward till the
grim waste of Atlantic waters bade them stay. He remembers the look
of the boundless plain stretching before him, the nights when the
dome of the sky was his ceiling, when he was awakened by the cold
kisses of the wind that flies before the dawn. He cries for space to
fling his fighting arm; he burns to measure himself unfettered with
the forces of God.

A Flattering Description

From *A Tour Through the Whole Island of Great Britain,*
1724–1726 | Daniel Defoe (1660–1731)
Preface to the First Volume

If this work is not both pleasant and profitable to the reader, the
author most freely and openly declares the fault must be in his
performance, and it cannot be any deficiency in the subject. As
the work it self is a description of the most flourishing and opulent
country in the world, so there is a flowing variety of materials;
all the particulars are fruitful of instructing and diverting objects.

Stranded

From 'The Name-Day', *Beasts and Super Beasts, 1914*

Saki (H. H. Munro) (1870–1916)

'Snow comes,' said the train official to the station officials; and
they agreed that snow was about to come. And it came, rapidly,
plenteously. The train had not been more than an hour on its journey
when the cotton-wool clouds commenced to dissolve in a blinding
downpour of snowflakes. The forest trees on either side of the line
were speedily coated with a heavy white mantle, the telegraph
wires became thick glistening ropes, the line itself was buried more
and more completely under a carpeting of snow, through which
the not very powerful engine ploughed its way with increasing
difficulty. The Vienna-Fiume line is scarcely the best equipped of
the Austrian State railways, and Abbleway began to have serious
fears for a breakdown. The train had slowed down to a painful and
precarious crawl and presently came to a halt at a spot where the
drifting snow had accumulated in a formidable barrier. The engine
made a special effort and broke through the obstruction, but in
the course of another twenty minutes it was again held up. The
process of breaking through was renewed, and the train doggedly
resumed its way, encountering and surmounting fresh hindrances
at frequent intervals. After a standstill of unusually long duration
in a particularly deep drift the compartment in which Abbleway
was sitting gave a huge jerk and a lurch, and then seemed to remain
stationary; it undoubtedly was not moving, and yet he could hear the
puffing of the engine and the slow rumbling and jolting of wheels.
The puffing and rumbling grew fainter, as though it were dying away
through the agency of intervening distance. Abbleway suddenly gave
vent to an exclamation of scandalised alarm, opened the window, and
peered out into the snowstorm. The flakes perched on his eyelashes
and blurred his vision, but he saw enough to help him to realise what
had happened. The engine had made a mighty plunge through the
drift and had gone merrily forward, lightened of the load of its rear
carriage, whose coupling had snapped under the strain.

A Very Long Way

From *In Xanadu, 1989* | William Dalrymple (1965–)

I got out the maps and drew a black line between Jerusalem and
Acre. It was about a quarter of an inch long. Lahore was three feet
away at the edge of the map. Peking lay halfway across the room on
an entirely different sheet. It seemed a very long way indeed.

In Seventy-Two Days

From *Around the World in Seventy-Two Days, 1890*

Nellie Bly (1864–1922)

In Chicago, a cable which afforded me much pleasure reached me, having missed me at San Francisco.

'Mr. Verne wishes the following message to be handed to Nellie Bly the moment she touches American soil: M. and Mme. Jules Verne address their sincere felicitations to Miss Nellie Bly at the moment when that intrepid young lady sets foot on the soil of America.'

. . . .

Almost before I knew it I was at Philadelphia, and all too soon to please me, for my trip was so pleasant I dreaded the finish of it. A number of newspaper men and a few friends joined me at Philadelphia to escort me to New York. Speech-making was the order from Philadelphia on to Jersey City. I was told when we were almost home to jump to the platform the moment the train stopped at Jersey City, for that made my time around the world. The station was packed with thousands of people, and the moment I landed on the platform, one yell went up from them, and the cannons at the Battery and Fort Greene boomed out the news of my arrival. I took off my cap and wanted to yell with the crowd, not because I had gone around the world in seventy-two days, but because I was home again.

A Schloss

From *A Time of Gifts, 1977* | Patrick Leigh Fermor (1915–2011)

January 1934

(Things were beginning to look up! I would have given anything to
know what my kind sponsor in Munich had written. It was a change
to have favourable reports circulating.) As a result, after a second
cow-shed sojourn near Riedeau, I found myself in the corner tower
of another castle two evenings later, wallowing in a bath of ancient
shape, enclouded by the scent of the cones and the pine-logs that
roared like caged lions in the huge copper stove.

The word 'schloss' means any degree of variation between a
fortified castle and a baroque palace. This one was a fair sized manor
house. I had felt shy as I ploughed through the snow of the long
avenue late that afternoon; quite baselessly. To go by the solicitude of
the trio at the stove-side in the drawing room – the old Count and
his wife and their daughter-in-law – I might, once again, have been
a schoolboy asked out for a treat, or, better still, polar explorer on
the brink of expiring. 'You must be *famished* after all that walking!'
the younger Gräfin said, as a huge tea appeared: she was a beautiful
dark-haired Hungarian and she spoke excellent English. 'Yes,' said
the elder, with an anxious smile, 'We've been told to feed you up!'
Her husband radiated silent benevolence as yet another silver dish
appeared. I spread a third hot croissant with butter and honey and
inwardly blessed my benefactor in Munich.

Travel

From *The Tale of Nur Al-Din Ali and His Son Badr Al-Din Hasan, Tales from the Arabian Nights, 1885*

Translated by Sir Richard Burton (1821–1890)

Travel! and thou shalt find new friends for old ones left behind;
Toil! for the sweets of human life by toil and moil are found:
The stay-at-home no honour wins nor aught attains buant;
So leave thy place of birth and wander all the world around!
I've seen, and very oft I've seen, how standing water stinks,
And only flowing sweetens it and trotting makes it sound:
And were the moon for ever full and ne'er to wax or wane,
Man would not strain his watchful eyes to see its gladsome round:
Except the lion leave his lair he ne'er would fell his game;
Except the arrow leave the bow ne'er had it reached its bound:
Gold-dust is dust the while it lies untravelled in the mine,
And aloes-wood mere fuel is upon its native ground:
And gold shall win his highest worth when from his goal ungoal'd;
And aloes sent to foreign parts grows costlier than gold.

A Life Well Lived

John Hare (1934–2022)

Founder of the Wild Camel Protection Foundation

'My camels are saddled, the harness bells are tinkling in the breeze and I am ready now for my last expedition.'

A Good Thick Skirt

From *Travels in West Africa, 1897* | Mary Kingsley (1862–1900)

About five o'clock I was off ahead and noticed a path which I had
been told I should meet with, and, when met with, I must follow.
The path was slightly indistinct, but by keeping my eye on it I could
see it. Presently I came to a place where it went out, but appeared
again on the other side of a clump of underbush fairly distinctly.
I made a short cut for it and the next news was I was in a heap,
on a lot of spikes, some fifteen feet or so below ground level, at the
bottom of a bag-shaped game pit.

It is at these times you realise the blessing of a good thick skirt.
Had I paid heed to the advice of many people in England, who ought
to have known better, and did not do it themselves, and adopted
masculine garments, I should have been spiked to the bone, and
done for. Whereas, save for a good many bruises, here I was with the
fulness of my skirt tucked under me, sitting on nine ebony spikes
some twelve inches long, in comparative comfort, howling lustily to
be hauled out. The Duke came along first, and looked down at me.
I said, 'Get a bush-rope, and haul me out.' He grunted and sat down
on a log. The Passenger came next, and he looked down. 'You kill?'
says he. 'Not much,' say I; 'get a bush-rope and haul me out.' 'No fit,'
says he, and sat down on the log. Presently, however, Kiva and Wiki

came up, and Wiki went and selected the one and only bush-rope suitable to haul an English lady, of my exact complexion, age, and size, out of that one particular pit. They seemed rare round there from the time he took; and I was just casting about in my mind as to what method would be best to employ in getting up the smooth, yellow, sandy-clay, incurved walls, when he arrived with it, and I was out in a twinkling, and very much ashamed of myself, until Silence, who was then leading, disappeared through the path before us with a despairing yell. Each man then pulled the skin cover off his gun lock, carefully looked to see if things there were all right and ready loosened his knife in its snake-skin sheath; and then we set about hauling poor Silence out, binding him up where necessary with cool green leaves; for he, not having a skirt, had got a good deal frayed at the edges on those spikes.

The Rolling English Road

G. K. Chesterton (1874–1936)

Before the Roman came to Rye or out to Severn strode,
The rolling English drunkard made the rolling English road.
A reeling road, a rolling road, that rambles round the shire,
And after him the parson ran, the sexton and the squire;
A merry road, a mazy road, and such as we did tread
The night we went to Birmingham by way of Beachy Head.

I knew no harm of Bonaparte and plenty of the Squire,
And for to fight the Frenchman I did not much desire;
But I did bash their baggonets because they came arrayed
To straighten out the crooked road an English drunkard made,
Where you and I went down the lane with ale-mugs in our hands,
The night we went to Glastonbury by way of Goodwin Sands.

His sins they were forgiven him; or why do flowers run
Behind him; and the hedges all strengthening in the sun?
The wild thing went from left to right and knew not which was which,
But the wild rose was above him when they found him in the ditch.
God pardon us, nor harden us; we did not see so clear
The night we went to Bannockburn by way of Brighton Pier.

My friends, we will not go again or ape an ancient rage,
Or stretch the folly of our youth to be the shame of age,
But walk with clearer eyes and ears this path that wandereth,
And see undrugged in evening light the decent inn of death;
For there is good news yet to hear and fine things to be seen,
Before we go to Paradise by way of Kensal Green.

Hardship

From *The Worst Journey in the World, 1922*

Apsley Cherry-Garrard (1886–1939)

Polar exploration is at once the cleanest and most isolated way of having a bad time which has been devised. It is the only form of adventure in which you put on your clothes at Michaelmas and keep them on until Christmas, and, save for a layer of natural grease of the body, find them as clean as though they were new. It is more lonely than London, more secluded than any monastery, and the post comes but once a year. As men will compare the hardships of France, Palestine, or Mesopotamia, so it would be interesting to contrast the rival claims of the Antarctic as a medium of discomfort. A member of Campbell's party tells me that the trenches at Ypres were a comparative picnic. But until somebody can evolve a standard of endurance I am unable to see how it can be done. Take it all in all, I do not believe anybody on earth has a worse time than an Emperor penguin.

FEBRUARY

Set Adrift by Pyrates

Reading the Travels of Ibn Battutah

From *Travels with a Tangerine: A Journey in the Footnotes of Ibn Battutah, 2001* | Tim Mackintosh-Smith (1961–)

It was a world of miracles and mundanities, of sultans, scholars, saints and slave-girls, in which outrageous fortune and dubious dragomen – the sort Pegolotti warned against – steered a course that lurched between luxury and poverty, asceticism and hedonism. IB [Ibn Battutah], I discovered, had a penchant for the picaresque and a storyteller's delight in close shaves, honed along the way by constant recounting in princely courts and caravanserais. He escaped pirates, storms and shipwrecks; he dodged the Black Death, purged himself of a fever with an infusion of tamarinds, survived the near-fatal consequences of undercooked yams and endured diarrhoea caused by a binge on melons; he worked for the Sultan of Delhi – 'of all men the most addicted to the making of gifts and the shedding of blood', who had bumped off his father in a Buster Keaton-style collapsing pavilion operated by elephants – and lived to tell the tale.

. . . .

It had become addictive. What would I do when I finished? I could start at the beginning again. But I knew that cerebral travel was not enough; from those very first words – 'My departure from Tangier ...' my feet had been itching for the physical, visitable past. The more I read of the Travels, the stronger became the itch. There was only one way to cure it.

It would be an enormous undertaking. But I felt certain that the remains of IB's world were out there to be tracked down – not just the great buildings of Mamluk Cairo or Palaeologue Constantinople, but also the minor monuments: a scholar's pen box, houses of fishes' bones, half-forgotten graves, buffalo-milk puddings, smells, sounds. And people.

Khavārezm

From *Travels, 1325–1354* | Ibn Battuta (1304–1368/9 or 1377)

Translated by Samuel Lee (1783–1852)

This is the largest city the Turks have, and is very much crowded, on account of the multitude of its inhabitants. It is subject to the sultan Uzbek Khān, and is governed on his part by a great Emīr, who resides within it. I have never seen better bred, or more liberal, people than the inhabitants of Khavārezm, or those who are more friendly to strangers. They have a very commendable practice with regards to their worship, which is this: When anyone absents himself from his place in the mosque, he is beaten by the priest in the presence of the congregation; and, moreover, fined five dinars, which go towards repairing the mosque. In every mosque, therefore, a whip is hung up for this purpose.

Playing the Trip to Canton by Ear

From *Slow Boats to China, 1981* | Gavin Young (1928–2001)

There was no point relying on elusive dates and problematical itineraries subject to whimsical change. I would take what came along the way, trusting to luck that any delay would not be horrendously long. I had taken leave of absence from the *Observer* telling Donald Trelford, the editor, that the journey shouldn't take me more than four months; that seemed a longish time as I pored over my maps in London. I would board any vessel moving in the right direction: a tanker, a freighter, a dhow, a junk – anything. Nothing that went too far at one time; that would reduce the number of ports of call – and I wanted to see a good number of ports.

I was embarking, in fact, on a game of traveller's roulette. I bought a cheap atlas and marked with a ballpoint pen a number of ports either because I liked the sound of them or because I'd been there before as a foreign correspondent: Smyrna, Alexandria, Port Said, Suez, Jedda, Dubai, Karachi, Bombay, Cochin, Colombo, Calcutta, Madras, Singapore, Brunei, Bangkok, Manila, Hong Kong, Macao, Canton. As an afterthought, though without much hope, I added the Andaman Islands, in the Bay of Bengal; the sombre vision of a tropical penal settlement and sudden and agonizing death from native poisoned darts had lodged in my mind since my first reading of Conan Doyle's Sherlock Holmes thriller *The Sign of Four*.
[The trip took seven months.]

Heaven-Haven

Gerard Manley Hopkins (1844–1889)

A nun takes the veil

I have desired to go
    Where springs not fail,
To fields where flies no sharp and sided hail
    And a few lilies blow.

And I have asked to be
Where no storms come,
    Where the green swell is in the havens dumb,
    And out of the swing of the sea.

4 February

The Sights

From *The Towers of Trebizond, 1956* | Rose Macaulay (1881–1958)

Turks, like Russians and Israelites, seem to want you to see the things that show how they have got on since Atatürk, or the Bolshevik revolution, or since they took over Palestine. But how people have got on is actually only interesting to the country which has got on. What foreign visitors care about are the things that were there before they began to get on. I dare say foreigners in England really only want to see Stonehenge and Roman walls and villas, and the field under which Silchester lies buried, and Norman castles and churches, and the ruins of medieval abbeys, and don't care a bit about Sheffield and Birmingham, or our model farms and new towns and universities and schools and dams and aerodromes and things. For that matter, we don't care a bit about them ourselves. But foreigners in their own countries (Russians are the worst, but Turks are bad too) like to show off these dreadful objects, and it is hard not to let them see how very vile and common we think them, compared with what was in the country before they got there. We did not like to tell the Turkish students, whom we liked very much, that the most interesting things in Turkey were put there before it was Turkey at all, when Turks were roaming about mountains and plains in the East (which perhaps they should not really have left, but this was another thing we did not like to tell the students, who did not know where they truly belonged, and perhaps actually few of us do).

The Taklamakan Desert

From *Foreign Devils on the Silk Road, 1980* | Peter Hopkirk (1930–2014)

Surrounding the Taklamakan on three sides are some of the highest
mountain ranges in the world, with the Gobi desert blocking the
fourth. Thus even the approaches to it are dangerous. Many travellers
have perished on the icy passes which lead down to it from Tibet,
Kashmir, Afghanistan and Russia, either by freezing to death or
by missing their foothold and hurtling into a ravine below. In one
disaster, in the winter of 1839, an entire caravan of forty men was
wiped out by an avalanche, and even now men and beasts are lost
each year.

No traveller has a good word to say for the Taklamakan.
Sven Hedin, one of the few Europeans to have crossed it, called
it 'the worst and most dangerous desert in the world'. Stein, who
came to know it even better, considered the deserts of Arabia
'tame' by comparison.

. . . .

Ancient Han records show that two thousand years ago the Chinese
knew the Taklamakan as the Liu Sha, or 'Moving Sands', for its
yellow dunes are ever in motion, driven by the relentless winds that
scour the desert. Present-day hydrographers and climatologists refer
to it more tamely as the Tarim Basin after the glacier-fed river which
flows eastwards across it to shallow Lop-nor lake, the mystery of
whose apparent 'wandering' would finally be solved by Sven Hedin.
On the map of modern China the Taklamakan (meaning, in Turki,
'go in and you won't come out') is shown by a large egg-shaped blank
in the heart of what is now officially termed the Sinkiang-Uighur
Autonomous Region.

Reading on a Journey

From *The Lawless Roads, 1939* | Graham Greene (1904–1991)

What books to take on a journey? It is an interesting – and important – problem. In West Africa once I had made the mistake of taking the *Anatomy of Melancholy*, with the idea that it would, as it were, match the mood. It matched all right, but what one really needs is contrast, so I surrendered perhaps my only hope of ever reading *War and Peace* in favour of something overwhelmingly national. And one did want, I found, an *English* book in this hating and hateful country. I am not sure how the sentiment of *Dr Thorne* – of Frank Gresham divided from Mary by his birth and by the necessity of marrying money if Greshambury were to be maintained, and of Mary's rich inheritance from her scoundrelly uncle after he had drunk himself to death – I am not sure how it would have gone down at home. I think there would have been mental reservations before one surrendered to the charm, but here – in this hot, forgotten tropic town, among the ants and the beetles – the simplicity of the sentiment did literally fill the eyes with tears. It is a love story and there are few love stories in literature; love in fiction is so often now – as Hemingway expresses it – what hangs up behind the bathroom door. *Dr Thorne*, too, is the perfect 'popular' novel – and when one is lonely one wants to claim kinship with all the simple friendly people turning the pages of their *Home Notes*.

Trespassers in Fairyland

From *Brazilian Adventure, 1933* | Peter Fleming (1907–1971)

Enchantment has, I suppose, its drawbacks; there are penalties for dealing in magic. On the whole the Tapirapé let us off very lightly. Trespassers in fairyland, we were cautioned and discharged.

When I say fairyland, I mean the antique fairyland. Make no mistake about that. I mean a green, an old-established, an incalculable place. Not the choice glades of Spenser, laid out in an allegorical design which no one who follows them is minded to decipher: not Milton's formal lawns, curiously haunted though they are by the truth so high-mindedly travestied upon them: not (above all) that insipid Tom Tiddler's Ground whereon the artfully inconsequent fancies of the moderns can pick up gold and silver royalties to their publishers' content and the corruption of our nurseries. I mean a haunted, lovely, formidable place in which man is always an intruder, never a patron. I mean a place which is the very opposite of unearthly, seeing that it had all the qualities of the earth before it came to be exploited by us.

Travel

Edna St Vincent Millay (1892–1950)

The railroad track is miles away,
    And the day is loud with voices speaking,
Yet there isn't a train goes by all day
    But I hear its whistle shrieking.

All night there isn't a train goes by,
    Though the night is still for sleep and dreaming,
But I see its cinders red on the sky,
    And hear its engine steaming.

My heart is warm with the friends I make,
    And better friends I'll not be knowing;
Yet there isn't a train I wouldn't take,
    No matter where it's going.

Set Adrift by Pyrates

From *Gulliver's Travels, 1726* | Jonathan Swift (1667–1745)

When I was at some Distance from the Pyrates, I discovered, by my
Pocket-Glass, several Islands to the South-East. I set up my Sail, the
Wind being fair, with a design to reach the nearest of those Islands,
which I made a Shift to do, in about three Hours. It was all rocky:
however I got many Birds' Eggs; and, striking Fire, I kindled some
Heath and dry Sea Weed, by which I roasted my Eggs. I ate no other
Supper, being resolved to spare my Provisions as much as I could.
I passed the Night under the Shelter of a Rock, strewing some Heath
under me, and slept pretty well.

The next Day I sailed to another Island, and thence to a third and
fourth, sometimes using my Sail, and sometimes my Paddles. But,
not to trouble the Reader with a particular Account of my Distresses,
let it suffice, that on the 5th day I arrived at the last Island in my
Sight, which lay South-South-East to the former.

This Island was at a greater Distance than I expected, and I did
not reach it in less than five Hours. I encompassed it almost round,
before I could find a convenient Place to land in; which was a small
Creek, about three Times the Wideness of my Canoe. I found the
Island to be all rocky, only a little intermingled with Tufts of Grass,
and sweet smelling Herbs. I took out my small Provisions and after
having refreshed myself, I secured the Remainder in a Cave, whereof
there were great Numbers. I gathered plenty of Eggs upon the Rocks,
and got a Quantity of dry Sea-weed, and parched Grass, which
I designed to kindle the next Day, and roast my Eggs as well as I
could. (For I had about me my Flint, Steel, Match, and Burning-
glass.) I lay all Night in the Cave where I had lodged my provisions.
My Bed was the same dry Grass and Sea-weed which I intended for
Fewel. I slept very little, for the Disquiets of my Mind prevailed over
my Wearyness, and kept me awake. I considered how impossible it
was to preserve my Life in so desolate a Place, and how miserable my
End must be.

Mapping With Your Feet

From *Flâneuse, 2016* | Lauren Elkin (1978–)

Nearly two decades after those first early experiments in *flâneuserie* I still live and walk in Paris, after having walked in New York, Venice, Tokyo and London, all places I've lived in temporarily for work or love. It's a hard habit to shake. Why do I walk? I walk because I like it. I like the rhythm of it, my shadow always a little ahead of me on the pavement. I like being able to stop when I like, to lean against a building and make a note in my journal, or read an email, or send a text message, and for the world to stop while I do it. Walking, paradoxically, allows for the possibility of stillness.

Walking is mapping with your feet. It helps you piece a city together, connecting up neighbourhoods that might otherwise have remained discrete entities, different planets bound to each other, sustained yet remote. I like seeing how in fact they blend into one another, I like noticing the boundaries between them. Walking helps me feel at home. There's a small pleasure in seeing how well I've come to know the city through my wanderings on foot, crossing through different neighbourhoods of the city, some I used to know quite well, others I may not have seen in a while, like getting reacquainted with someone I once met at a party.

Reading Poetry on the Move

From *Other Men's Flowers, 1944* | A. P. Wavell (1883–1950)

It amused me to set down in a notebook – mainly with a view to discussion with my son, who shares my liking for poetry – the poems I could repeat entire or in great part. I have now collected and arranged the poems.

. . . .

Driving a motor car alone or riding a horse I often declaim out loud; but not when walking, walking for me is somehow a more serious business and does not seem to loosen my memory to verse; perhaps pace is required as an incentive. I neither sing nor recite poetry in my bath. I have never piloted an aeroplane alone, but I feel it would move me to declaim in the skies.

Neighbours Across the Valley

From *Driving over Lemons: An Optimist in Andalucía*, 1999

Chris Stewart (1951–)

Chris meets Bernardo, his Dutch neighbour from Rotterdam who is leading several goats, a mule and a sheep:

'You must be the lunatic who's bought El Valero. We've heard about you,' he said with a chuckle, attempting to hold out his right hand but failing. 'Welcome to the valley. Wait while I put these creatures away and I can greet you properly.'

. . . .

13 February

They told me how pleased Romero was to sell the place and I began to put them right, explaining how he was forever moaning about how much he loved the place and hated to be parted from it – and 'especially for the misery of money I paid him.'

Bernardo looked in danger of choking on his wine. 'He and his people have been desperate to sell that place for years,' he said, 'and they couldn't get to town quick enough. He was about to give it to Domingo for a million – then you came along and gave him five. He must have thought you fell off a Christmas tree. I mean who the hell was going to buy a place that has no access, no running water, no electricity – and that huge patch of land to work? I must say I think it very bold of you to have bought it. Or maybe you are a complete lunatic?'

'I'm at least half-lunatic,' I volunteered. 'But we'll manage somehow. It's an exciting challenge, and anyway, it beats being an insurance clerk working in an office.'

'Yes, but you don't look to me like an insurance clerk.'

'No, but I might have been …' and I recalled with a shudder the six months I'd once spent in an office.

On Honeymoon

From *There's Rosemary, There's Rue*, 1939

Winifred Fortescue (1888–1951)

After the register had been signed by everybody, and Consuela had decorated us all with tiny waxen sprays of orange blossom, John and I drove with her to Sunderland House for a quick luncheon before catching our train to Devonshire.

. . . .

It was evening when we drove up to Castle Hill. The approach to the great white house, which was built in the style of a French *Château* – a central block with two long wings extending on either side – did not greatly impress me, for the drive swept up to the back of the house. But once inside, I could admire the beautiful staircase, one of the proud features of the house, rising from the midst of a lofty flower-filled hall; the gracious curves of the circular library, where a great fire blazed a welcome and the warm air was scented by burning logs of pine and bowls of lilies-of-the-valley, and, as John quietly led me to one of the French windows, opened it and ushered me out onto the terrace in front of the house, I was struck dumb by the beauty of the view before me.

The Aurora Borealis

From *Himalayan Journals, 1855* | Joseph Dalton Hooker (1817–1911)

Baroon, February 1848

During the night of the 14th of February, I observed a beautiful display of the Aurora borealis. It commenced at 9 p.m., with about thirty lancet beams rising in the north-west from a low luminous arch, which crossed the zenith, and converged towards the opposite quarter of the heavens. All moved and flashed slowly, occasionally splitting and forking, fading and brightening; they were clearly defined, though the milky way and zodiacal light could not be discerned, and the stars and planets were very pale. When this display had lasted about an hour, the light became more diffused, the beams lessened by degrees, and a dark belt appeared in the luminous arch, gradually breaking it up, and appearing to disperse the beams, of which, however, a few faint ones continued to appear occasionally until midnight.

On First Looking into Chapman's Homer

John Keats (1795–1821)

Much have I travelled in the realms of gold,
    And many goodly states and kingdoms seen;
    Round many western islands have I been
Which bards in fealty to Apollo hold.
Oft of one wide expanse had I been told
    That deep-browed Homer ruled as his demesne;
    Yet did I never breathe its pure serene
Till I heard Chapman speak out loud and bold:
Then felt I like some watcher of the skies
    When a new planet swims into his ken;
Or like stout Cortez when with eagle eyes
    He stared at the Pacific – and all his men
Looked at each other with a wild surmise –
    Silent, upon a peak in Darien.

At Entry of the Haven

From *Odyssey, 8–7th century* BC | Homer (8th century BC)

Translated by George Chapman (c. 1559–1634)

At entry of the haven, a silver ford
   Is from a rock-impressing fountain pour'd,
All set with sable poplars. And this port
Were we arrived at, by the sweet resort
Of some God guiding us, for 'twas a night
So ghastly dark all port was past our sight,
Clouds hid our ships, and would not let the moon
Afford a beam to us; the whole isle won
By not an eye of ours. None thought the blore
That then was up, shov'd waves against the shore,
That then to an unmeasured height put on;
We still at sea esteem'd us, till alone
Our fleet put in itself. And then were strook
Our gather'd sails; our rest ashore we took,
And day expected. When the morn gave fire,
We rose, and walk'd, and did the isle admire.

An Inn Near Chioggia

From *The Life of Benvenuto Cellini, Written by Himself,*
1558–1562 | Benvenuto Cellini (1500–1571)

Translated by John Addington Symonds (1840–1893)

Book First, LXXIX

We lay one night at a place on this side Chioggia, on the left hand as
you go toward Ferrara. Here the host insisted upon being paid before
we went to bed, and in his own way; and when I observed that it was
the custom everywhere else to pay in the morning, he answered:
'I insist on being paid overnight, and in my own way.' I retorted that
men who wanted everything their own way ought to make a world
after their own fashion, since things were differently managed here.
Our host told me not to go on bothering his brains, because he was
determined to do as he had said. Tribolo stood trembling with fear,
and nudged me to keep quiet, lest they should do something worse
to us; so we paid them in the way they wanted, and afterwards we
retired to rest. We had, I must admit, the most capital beds, new
in every particular, and as clean as they could be. Nevertheless I did
not get one wink of sleep, because I kept on thinking how I could
revenge myself.

The Sea Cave

From *Moonfleet, 1898* | John Meade Falkner (1858–1932)

It was on a ledge of that rock-face that our cave opened, and
sometimes on a fine day Elzevir would carry me out thither, so that
I might sun myself and see all the moving Channel without myself
being seen. For this ledge was carved out something like a balcony,
so that when the quarry was in working they could lower the stone
by pulleys to boats lying underneath, and perhaps haul up a keg or
two by the way of ballast, as might be guessed by the stanchions still
rusting in the rock.

Such was this gallery; and as for the inside of the cave, 'twas a
great empty room, with a white floor made up of broken stone-dust
trodden hard of old till one would say it was plaster: and dry, without
those sweaty damps so often seen in such places – save only in one
corner a land-spring dropped from the roof trickling down over spiky
rock-icicles, and falling into a little hollow in the floor. This basin
had been scooped out of set purpose, with a gutter seaward for the
overflow, and round it and on the wet patch of the roof above grew
a garden of ferns and other clinging plants.

The Worth of a Journey

From *Arabian Sands, 1959* | Wilfred Thesiger (1910–2003)

For me, exploration was a personal venture. I did not go to the
Arabian desert to collect plants nor to make a map; such things
were incidental. At heart I knew that to write or even talk of my
travels was to tarnish the achievement. I went there to find peace
in the hardship of desert travel and the company of desert peoples.
I set myself a goal on these journeys, and, although the goal itself
was unimportant, its attainment had to be worth every effort and
sacrifice. Scott had gone to the South Pole in order to stand for a few
minutes on one particular and almost inaccessible spot on the earth's
surface. He and his companions died on their way back, but even as
they were dying he never doubted that the journey had been worth
while. Everyone knew that there was nothing to be found on the top
of Everest, but even in this materialistic age few people asked, 'What
point is there in climbing Everest? What good will it do anyone when
they get there?' They recognized that even today there are experiences
that do not need to be justified in terms of raw profit.

No, it is not the goal but the way there that matters, and the
harder the way the more worth while the journey.

North Labrador

Hart Crane (1899–1932)

A land of leaning ice
Hugged by plaster-grey arches of sky,
Flings itself silently
Into eternity.

'Has no one come here to win you,
Or left you with the faintest blush
Upon your glittering breasts?
Have you no memories, O Darkly Bright?'

Cold-hushed, there is only the shifting moments
That journey toward no Spring –
No birth, no death, no time nor sun
In answer.

Small Towns in America

From *The Lost Continent: Travels in Small-Town America, 1989*

Bill Bryson (1951–)

About all that separates them are their names. They always have
a gas station, a grocery store, a grain elevator, a place selling
farm equipment and fertilisers, and something improbable like a
microwave oven dealer or a dry cleaner's, so you can say to yourself
as you glide through town, 'Now what would they be doing with
a dry cleaner's in Fungus City?' Every fourth or fifth community
will be a county town, built around a square. A handsome brick
court-house with a Civil War cannon and a monument to the dead
of at least two wars will stand on one side of the square and on the
other side will be businesses: a five and dime, a luncheonette, two
banks, a hardware store, a Christian bookstore, a barber's, a couple
of hairdressers, a place selling the sort of men's clothing that only
someone from a very small town would wear. At least two businesses
will be called Vern's. The central area of the square will be a park,
with fat trees and a bandstand and a pole with an American flag and
scattered benches full of old men in John Deere caps sitting around
and talking about the days when they had something else to do other
than sit around and talk about the days when they had something
else to do. Time in these places creaks along.

Narratives of Travellers Considered

From *The Idler, No. 97, 23 February 1760*

Samuel Johnson (1709–1784)

It may, I think, be justly observed, that few books disappoint their readers more than the narrations of travellers. One part of mankind is naturally curious to learn the sentiments, manners, and condition of the rest; and every mind that has leisure or power to extend its views, must be desirous of knowing in what proportion Providence has distributed the blessings of nature, or the advantages of art, among the several nations of the earth.

This general desire easily procures readers to every book from which it can expect gratification. The adventurer upon unknown coasts, and the describer of distant regions, is always welcomed as a man who has laboured for the pleasure of others, and who is able to enlarge our knowledge and rectify our opinions; but when the volume is opened, nothing is found but such general accounts as leave no distinct idea behind them, or such minute enumerations as few can read with either profit or delight.

Every writer of travels should consider, that, like all other authors, he undertakes either to instruct or please, or to mingle pleasure with instruction. He that instructs must offer to the mind something to be imitated, or something to be avoided; he that pleases must offer new images to his reader, and enable him to form a tacit comparison of his own state with that of others.

How to Make a Living

From *A General History of the Pyrates, from the first Rise and Settlement in the Island of Providence, to the present Time. With the remarkable Actions and Adventures of the two female Pyrates Mary Read and Anne Bonny, 1724*

Captain Charles Johnson: identity unknown. Thought by some to be a pseudonym for Daniel Defoe (166o–1731) or the journalist and printer Nathaniel Mist (d. 1737)

To seek her fortune, Mary Read (yet again) assumes man's apparel and ships herself on board of a vessel bound for the West Indies:

It happen'd this Ship was taken by *English* Pyrates, and *Mary Read* was the only *English* Person on Board, they kept her amongst them, and having plundered the Ship, let it go again; after following this Trade for some Time, the King's Proclamation came out, and was publish'd in all Parts of the *West-Indies*, for pardoning such Pyrates, who should voluntarily surrender themselves by a certain Day therein mentioned. The Crew of *Mary Read* took the Benefit of this Proclamation, and having surrender'd, liv'd quietly on Shore; but Money beginning to grow short, and hearing that Captain *Woods Rogers*, Governor of the Island of *Providence*, was fitting out some Privateers to cruise against the *Spaniards*, she with several others embark'd for that Island, in order to go upon the privateering Account, being resolved to make her Fortune one way or other.

A New Type of Traveller: Paterfamilias

From *Labels: A Mediterranean Journal, 1930*

Evelyn Waugh (1903–1966)

By about 1860 middle-class prosperity and mechanical transport had produced a new type; the Jones, Brown and Robinson of the picture books, the Paterfamilias of Punch. Paterfamilias, as a rule, travels with his wife and without his children; often there are other adult members of his family with him – a sister or brother-in-law; he wears a heavy tweed overcoat and a tweed cap with ear flaps in winter; in summer he gets very hot; he has lived all his life in England and has worked very hard and done well; he is very jealous of his country's prestige, but he thinks it is better preserved by a slightly blustering manner with hotel proprietors and a refusal to be 'done' than by his predecessor's scrupulous observance of etiquette; he is very suspicious of foreigners, chiefly on the grounds that they do not have baths, disguise their food with odd sauces, are oppressed by their rulers and priests, are dishonest, immoral, and dangerous, and talk a language no one can make head or tail of; he is made to ride upon a donkey far too small for him and suffer other similar indignities; the question of cigar smoke in railway carriages is with him one of particular cogency; with his arrival he begins the ignoble trade of manufacturing special trinkets for tourists, horrible paperweights of wood or stone, ornaments of odious design, or bits of cheap jewellery for him to take back as souvenirs. The noble products of his age and Baedeker's guide books and Cook's travel agency.

Jet-lagged Prophets

John Agard (1949–)

When Jesus landed at Gatwick
his style was far from three-piece slick.
So they sniffer-dogged his hippy hair
and sandalled feet in need of washing.

When Buddha showed up at Heathrow
he was taken in for questioning.
He said he had nothing to declare
but his passport had a suspicious glow.

When Mohammed made it to Dover
they thought to themselves: asylum seeker,
though his papers were in order
and Dover not his idea of Mecca.

O jet-lagged prophets who come in peace
what made you think it legal to be meek?
Your restless feet will know no resting ground,
when even prayers are frisked for a weapon.

An Ambitious Plan

From *The Cosmography and Geography of Africa, 1526*

Leo Africanus (Al-Hassan Ibn-Mohammed Al-Wezaz Al-Fasi) (1494?–1552)

Translated by John Pory (1572–1636) as *The History and Description of Africa and of the Notable Things Therein Contained*, 1600

Having in my first booke made mention of the cities, bounds, divisions, and some other notable and memorable things contained in Africa; we will in this second part more fully, particularly, largely, and distinctly describe sundrie provinces, townes, mountaines, situations of places, lawes, rites, and customes, of people. Insomuch that we will leave nothing untouched, which may any way serve to the illustrating and perfecting of this our present discourse. Beginning therefore at the west part of Africa, we will in this our geographicall historie proceede eastward, till we come to the borders with Aegypt. And all this our narration following we will divide into seven bookes; whereunto (God willing) we purpose to annexe the eighth, which shall intreat of rivers, of living creatures, of trees, of plants, of fruits, of shrubs, and of such other most delightfull matters.

The Caves of the Thousand Buddhas

From *Ruins of Desert Cathay, Vol II, 1912* | Sir Marc Aurel Stein
(1862–1943)

After less than a mile they came in view as we turned into the silent
valley by the side of a shallow little stream just freed from the grip of
winter. There was not a trace of vegetation on the curiously eroded
grey slopes which the spurs of the low hill range eastwards send
down to the debouchure of the stream. But all thought of slowly
dying nature reflected in these shrivelled barren ridges and hillocks
passed from me when, on the almost perpendicular conglomerate
cliffs rising on our right, I caught sight of the first grottoes.

A multitude of dark cavities, mostly small, was seen here,
honeycombing the sombre rock faces in irregular tiers from the foot
of the cliff, where the stream almost washed them, to the top of the
precipice. Here and there the flights of steps connecting the grottoes
still showed on the cliff face. But in front of most the conglomerate
mass had crumbled away, and from a distance it looked as if
approach to the sanctuaries would be possible only to those willing
to be let down by ropes or to bear the trouble and expense of
elaborate scaffolding.

. . . .

The fine avenues of trees, apparently elms, which extended along the foot of the honeycombed cliffs, and the distant view of some dwellings farther up where the river bank widened, were evidence that the cave-temples had still their resident guardians. Yet there was no human being about to receive us, no guide to distract one's attention. In bewildering multitude and closeness the lines of grottoes presented their faces, some high, some low, perched one above the other without any order or arrangement in stories. In front of many were open verandah-like porches carved out of the soft rock with walls and ceilings bearing faded frescoes. Rough stairs cut into the cliff and still rougher wooden galleries served as approaches to the higher caves. But many of these seemed on the point of crumbling away, and high up in the topmost rows there were manifestly shrines which had become quite inaccessible.

The Luxuriance of the Vegetation

From *Voyage of the Beagle, 1831–1836* | Charles Darwin (1809–1882)

Bahia, or San Salvador, Brazil, Feb 29th

The day has passed delightfully. Delight itself, however, is a weak
term to express the feelings of a naturalist who, for the first time, has
wandered by himself in a Brazilian forest. Among the multitude of
striking objects, the general luxuriance of the vegetation bears away
the victory. The elegance of the grasses, the novelty of the parasitical
plants, the beauty of the flowers, the glossy green of the foliage.

A most paradoxical mixture of sound and silence pervades the shady
parts of the wood. The noise from the insects is so loud, that it may
be heard even in a vessel anchored several hundred yards from the
shore; yet within the recesses of the forest a universal silence appears
to reign. To a person fond of natural history, such a day as this brings
with it a deeper pleasure than he can ever hope again to experience.
After wandering about for some hours, I returned to the landing-
place; but, before reaching it, I was overtaken by a tropical storm.
I tried to find shelter under a tree, which was so thick that it would
never have been penetrated by common English rain; but here, in a
couple of minutes, a little torrent flowed down the trunk. It is to this
violence of the rain that we must attribute the verdure at the bottom
of the thickest woods: if the showers were like those of a colder
climate, the greater part would be absorbed or evaporated before it
reached the ground.

MARCH

A Mountain Chalet

Arrival

From *English Hours, 1905* | Henry James (1843–1916)

There is a certain evening that I count as virtually a first impression,
– the end of a wet, black Sunday, twenty years ago, about the first
of March. There had been an earlier vision, but it had turned to grey,
like faded ink, and the occasion I speak of was a fresh beginning.
No doubt I had mystic prescience of how fond of the murky modern
Babylon I was one day to become; certain it is that as I look back
I find every small circumstance of those hours of approach and
arrival still as vivid as if the solemnity of an opening era had breathed
upon it. The sense of approach was already almost intolerably strong
at Liverpool, where, as I remember, the perception of the English
character of everything was as acute as a surprise, though it could
only be a surprise without a shock. It was expectation exquisitely
gratified, superabundantly confirmed. There was a kind of wonder
indeed that England should be as English as, for my entertainment,
she took the trouble to be; but the wonder would have been greater,
and all the pleasure absent, if the sensation had not been violent.
It seems to sit there again like a visiting presence, as it sat opposite to
me at breakfast at a small table in a window of the old coffee-room of
the Adelphi Hotel – the unextended (as it then was), the unimproved,
the unblushingly local Adelphi. Liverpool is not a romantic city, but
that smoky Saturday returns to me as a supreme success, measured by
its association with the kind of emotion in the hope of which, for the
most part, we betake ourselves to far countries.

The Departure

Henry David Thoreau (1817–1862)

Verses 1–4

In this roadstead I have ridden,
In this covert I have hidden;
Friendly thoughts were cliffs to me,
And I hid beneath their lea.

This true people took the stranger,
And warm hearted housed the ranger;
They received their roving guest,
And have fed him with the best;

Whatsoe'er the land afforded
To the stranger's wish accorded;
Shook the olive, stripped the vine,
And expressed the strengthening wine.

And by night they did spread o'er him
What by day they spread before him,
That good-will which was repast
Was his covering at last.

The Ruins of Lou-Lan

From *My Life as an Explorer, 1925* | Sven Hedin (1865–1952)

On March 3 we camped at the base of a clay tower, twenty-nine feet high. We stowed our ice in the shadow of a clay ridge and sent a man back to the spring with all the camels. These were to return to us again in six days with a further supply of ice. We promised to have a beacon fire burning on the sixth day.

We were now cut off from the world. I felt like a king in his own country, in his own capital. No one else on earth knew of the existence of this place. But I had to make good use of my time. First I located the place astronomically. Then I drew plans of the nineteen houses near our camp. I offered a tempting reward to the first man who discovered human writing in any form. But they found only scraps of blankets, pieces of red cloth, brown human hair, boot-soles, fragments of skeletons of domestic animals, pieces of rope, an ear-ring, Chinese coins, chips of earthenware and other odds and ends.

Nearly all the houses had been built of wood, the walls of bunched osiers or clay-covered wicker. In three places the door frames still remained upright. One door actually stood wide open, just as it must have been left by the last inhabitant of this ancient city, more than fifteen hundred years ago.

The Rhone

From *Praeterita*, 1885–1889 | John Ruskin (1819–1900)

For all other rivers there is a surface, and an underneath, and
a vaguely displeasing idea of the bottom. But the Rhone flows
like one lambent jewel; its surface is nowhere, its ethereal self is
everywhere, the iridescent rush and translucent strength of it blue
to the shore, and radiant to the depth.

Fifteen feet thick, of not flowing, but flying water; not water,
neither, – melted glacier, rather, one should call it; the force of the ice
is with it, and the wreathing of the clouds, the gladness of the sky,
and the continuance of Time.

Waves of clear sea are, indeed, lovely to watch, but they are always
coming or gone, never in any taken shape to be seen for a second.
But here was one mighty wave that was always itself, and every
fluted swirl of it, constant as the wreathing of a shell. No wasting
away of the fallen foam, no pause for gathering of power, no helpless
ebb of discouraged recoil; but alike through bright day and lulling
night, the never-pausing plunge, and never-fading flash, and never-
hushing whisper, and, while the sun was up, the ever-answering
glow of unearthly aquamarine, ultramarine, violet-blue, gentian-
blue, peacock-blue, river-of-paradise blue, glass of a painted window
melted in the sun, and the witch of the Alps flinging the spun tresses
of it for ever from her snow.

A Stranger in the Desert

From *Eothen, 1844* | A. W. Kinglake (1809–1891)

At first there was a mere moving speck on the horizon. My party of course became all alive with excitement, and there were many surmises. Soon it appeared that three laden camels were approaching, and that two of them carried riders. In a little while we saw that one of the riders wore European dress, and at last the travellers were pronounced to be an English gentleman and his servant. By their side there were a couple, I think, of Arabs on foot, and this was the whole party.

. . . .

5 March

When you have travelled for days and days over an Eastern desert without meeting the likeness of a human being, and then at last see an English shooting-jacket and his servant come listlessly slouching along from out of the forward horizon, you stare at the wide unproportion between this slender company and the boundless plains of sand through which they are keeping their way. This Englishman, as I afterwards found, was a military man returning to his country from India, and crossing the Desert at this part in order to go through Palestine. As for me, I had come pretty straight from England, and so here we met in the wilderness at about half-way from our respective starting-points. As we approached each other it became with me a question whether we should speak. I thought it likely that the stranger would accost me, and in the event of his doing so I was quite ready to be as sociable and chatty as I could be according to my nature; but still I could not think of anything particular that I had to say to him. Of course, among civilised people the not having anything to say is no excuse at all for not speaking, but I was shy and indolent, and I felt no great wish to stop and talk like a morning visitor in the midst of those broad solitudes. The traveller perhaps felt as I did, for except that we lifted our hands to our caps and waved our arms in courtesy, we passed each other as if we had passed in Pall Mall. Our attendants, however, were not to be cheated of the delight that they felt in speaking to new listeners and hearing fresh voices once more. The masters, therefore, had no sooner passed each other than their respective servants quietly stopped and entered into conversation. As soon as my camel found that her companions were not following her she caught the social feeling and refused to go on. I felt the absurdity of the situation, and determined to accost the stranger if only to avoid the awkwardness of remaining stuck fast in the Desert whilst our servants were amusing themselves. When with this intent I turned round my camel I found that the gallant officer who had passed me by about thirty or forty yards was exactly in the same predicament as myself. I put my now willing camel in motion and rode up towards the stranger, who seeing this followed my example and came forward to meet me. He was the first to speak.

The Little Châlet

From *Mountain Madness, 1943* | Winifred Fortescue (1888–1951)

We had just decided to explore the neighbourhood on foot, to see if
there were any likely châlets for hire, as camping would be impossible
in such uncertain weather, when suddenly I espied another huge
telescope at the end of the terrace, pointing towards the glacier.

I went to it at once and started making funny faces into it,
screwing up first one eye and then the other, but seeing, at first,
nothing but a coloured blur. Persevering and screwing, and adjusting
this Spier of Secrets, I at last managed to focus it, and swivelled it
from right to left triumphantly, hoping frantically to see a chamois
perched on a peak. When, suddenly, I ceased swivelling, for, framed
in the luminous lens before me, I saw a little wooden house, built
in the style of a Swiss châlet, with a peaked central gable, a wooden
balcony, and a flight of steps leading up to the front door. The little
house was surrounded, and seemed half submerged by a sea of white
narcissi, which washed down to it from the foot of the glittering blue
glacier; swirled around a forest of dark pine trees until it reached the
châlet where it divided into encircling white rivers which met again
at the foot of the wooden steps and then flowed down in a rolling
flood of blossom to the river bank in the valley.

A New Type of Traveller: Writers

From *Labels: A Mediterranean Journal, 1930*

Evelyn Waugh (1903–1966)

There is a new type of traveller which is represented by nearly all
the young men and women who manage to get paid to write travel
books. One comes into frequent and agreeable contact with him in
all parts of the world; his book, if finished, is nearly always worth
reading. It is his duty, he feels, to the publisher who has advanced his
expenses, to have as many outrageous experiences as he can. He holds
the defensible, but not incontrovertible, opinion that poor and rather
disreputable people are more amusing and representative of national
spirit than rich people. Partly for this reason and partly because
publishers are, by nature, unwilling to become purely charitable,
he travels and lives cheaply and invariably runs out of money. But
he finds a peculiar relish in discomfort. Bed bugs, frightful food,
inefficient ships and trains, hostile customs, police and passport
officers, consuls who will not cash cheques, excesses of heat and
cold, night club champagne, and even imprisonment are his peculiar
delights. I have done a certain amount of this kind of travelling, and
the memory of it is wholly agreeable. With the real travel-snobs I
have shuddered at the mention of pleasure cruises or circular tours or
personally conducted parties, of professional guides and hotels under
English management. Every Englishman abroad, until it is proved to
the contrary, likes to consider himself a traveller and not a tourist.

No Excuse

Phillis Wheatley (c. 1753–1784)

> 'Twas mercy brought me from my Pagan land,
> Taught my benighted soul to understand
> That there's a God – that there's a Saviour too;
> Once I redemption neither sought nor knew.
> Some view our sable race with scornful eye –
> 'Their colour is a diabolic die.'
> Remember, Christians, Negros, black as Cain,
> May be refined, and join the angelic train.

Marco Polo

From *In Xanadu, 1989* | William Dalrymple (1965–)

Polo was not the romantic gallant that legend has made him out to be; he was a hard-headed merchant's son taking a calculated risk on a potentially lucrative expedition. The Venetians were always lukewarm about the concept of crusading and the Polos seem to have soon forgotten the original purpose of their journey. One can only judge Polo from the evidence of *The Travels* and in this light his motive for continuing east from Ayas was simple: profit. Nor was he heading into the unknown. The elder Polos, like, no doubt, many before them, had already made the journey to China, and knew that the risks were not too great; indeed once out of Cilician Armenia and the reach of the armies of the Sultan Baibars, the journey would probably be relatively easy. The Mongols had built caravanserai along the length of the trading routes and had made safe the roads, *Pax Mongolia* ruled. They also had the additional boon of the Gold Tablet from Kubla Khan, a safe conduct from the Supreme Khan himself. There were some dangers certainly – a party of Frankish merchants had been pillaged near Amassya only a few years before. But the mediaeval merchant had always to take risks, and travel within the Mongol empire was probably considerably safer than in Europe. Fifteen years later when they returned to Venice they were rich men (so much so that in 1362, nearly one hundred years later, Polo's descendants were still arguing over the ownership of the palace which had been acquired with the profits of their forefather's China expedition). The Polos certainly took a gamble when they watched their friars flee back to Acre, and loaded up their caravan for the long journey to Xanadu, but it was a calculated gamble – and it paid off.

Xanadu

From *The Travels, 1271–1295, published c. 1300* | Marco Polo
(1254–1324), co-written by Rustichello da Pisa (fl. late 13th century)
Translated as *The Book of Ser Marco Polo, the Venetian*, 1871 by
Colonel Henry Yule (1820–1889)

And when you have ridden three days from the city last mentioned,
between north-east and north, you come to a city called Chandu*
which was built by the Kaan now reigning. There is at this place a
very fine marble Palace, the rooms of which are all gilt and painted
with figures of men and beasts and birds, and with a variety of trees
and flowers, all executed with such exquisite art that you regard them
with delight and astonishment.

. . . .

Moreover at a spot in the Park where there is a charming wood he has
another Palace built of cane, of which I must give you a description.
It is gilt all over, and most elaborately finished inside. It is stayed on
gilt and lackered columns, on each of which is a dragon all gilt, the
tail of which is attached to the column whilst the head supports the
architrave, and the claws likewise are stretched out right and left to
support the architrave. The roof, like the rest, is formed of canes,

covered with a varnish so strong and excellent that no amount of rain will rot them. These canes are a good 3 palms in girth, and from 10 to 15 paces in length. They are cut across at each knot, and then the pieces are split so as to form from each two hollow tiles, and with these the house is roofed; only every such tile of cane has to be nailed down to prevent the wind from lifting it. In short, the whole Palace is built of these canes, which (I may mention) serve also for a great variety of other useful purposes. The construction of the Palace is so devised that it can be taken down and put up again with great celerity; and it can all be taken to pieces and removed whithersoever the Emperor may command. When erected, it is braced against mishaps from the wind by more than 200 cords of silk.

*Chandu, also Shangdu, Xanadu.

Differing Views

From *As You Like It, 1599* | William Shakespeare (1564–1616)

Act II, Scene IV

Rosalind: Well, this is the Forest of Arden.

Touchstone: Ay, now I am in Arden; the more fool I: when I
was at home I was in a better place but travellers must be content.

Rosalind: Ay, be so, good Touchstone.

. . . .

Celia: I like this place,
And willingly could waste some time in it.

Musicians and Dancers

From *Polynesia Researches; Hawaii, 1829* | William Ellis (1794–1872)

In the afternoon, a party of strolling musicians and dancers arrived at Kairua. About four o'clock they came, followed by crowds of people, and arranged themselves on a fine sandy beach, in front of one of the governor's houses, where they exhibited a native dance, called *hura araapapa*.

The five musicians first seated themselves in a line on the ground, and spread a piece of folded cloth on the sand before them. Their instrument was a large calabash, or rather two, one of an oval shape about three feet high, the other perfectly round, very neatly fastened to it, having also an aperture about three inches in diameter at the top. Each musician held his instrument before him with both hands, and produced his music by striking it on the ground, where he had laid the piece of cloth, and beating it with his fingers, or the palms of his hands. As soon as they began to sound their calabashes, the dancer, a young man, about the middle stature, advanced through the opening crowd. His jet-black hair hung in loose and flowing ringlets on his naked shoulders; his necklace was made of a vast number of strings of nicely braided human hair, tied together behind, while a *paraoa* (an ornament made of a whale's tooth) hung pendent from it on his breast; his wrists were ornamented with bracelets, formed of polished tusks of the hog, and his ankles with loose buskins, thickly set with dog's teeth, the rattle of which, during the dance, kept time with the music of the calabash drum. A beautiful yellow tapa was tastefully fastened round his loins, reaching to his knees. He began his dance in front of the musicians, and moved forwards and backwards, across the area, occasionally chanting the achievements of former kings of Hawaii. The governor sat at the end of the ring, opposite to the musicians, and appeared gratified with the performance, which continued until the evening.

Don Quixote's Plan

From *Don Quixote, 1605* | Miguel de Cervantes (1547–1616)

Translated by Tobias Smollett (1721–1771)

He was seized with the strangest whim that ever entered the brain
of a madman. This was no other, than a full persuasion, that it was
highly expedient and necessary, not only for his own honour, but also
for the good of the public, that he should profess knight-errantry,
and ride through the world in arms, to seek adventures, and conform
in all points to the practice of those itinerant heroes, whose exploits
he had read; redressing all manner of grievances, and courting all
occasions of exposing himself to such dangers, as in the event would
entitle him to everlasting renown. This poor lunatic looked upon
himself already as good as seated, by his own single valour, on the
throne of Trebisond; and intoxicated with these agreeable vapours
of his unaccountable folly, resolved to put his design in practice
forthwith.

Iceland First Seen

William Morris (1834–1896)

Lines 1–14

Lo from our loitering ship
a new land at last to be seen;
Toothed rocks down the side of the firth
on the east guard a weary wide lea,
And black slope the hillsides above,
striped adown with their desolate green:
And a peak rises up on the west
from the meeting of cloud and of sea.
Foursquare from base unto point
like the building of Gods that have been.
The last of that waste of the mountains
all cloud-wreathed and snow-flecked and grey,
And bright with the dawn that began
just now at the ending of day.

Market Etiquette

From *Perfume from Provence, 1935* | Winifred Fortescue (1888–1951)

To appear in the market without a *filet* (string bag) is deeply resented by the vendors. That I learned early. Packing-paper is rare and local newspapers are sparsely paged; string is almost unknown, and raffia costs money. I was regarded with a reproachful eye; I was marked down as a novice; and, as I was informed by Emilia on my return, the price of the vendor's time wasted in packing up my purchases was added to the bill for goods supplied. It is far cheaper to carry a string bag when shopping in Provence.

Notebooks

From *The Songlines, 1987* | Bruce Chatwin (1940–1989)

I started rearranging the caravan as a place to work in.

There was a plywood top which pulled out over the second bunk to make a desk. There was even a swivelling office chair. I put my pencils in a tumbler and my Swiss Army knife beside them. I unpacked some exercise pads and, with the excessive neatness that goes with the beginning of a project, I made three neat stacks of my 'Paris' notebooks.

In France, these notebooks are known as *carnets moleskins*: 'moleskine', in this case, being its black oilcloth binding. Each time I want to Paris, I would buy a fresh supply from a *papeterie* in the Rue de l'Ancienne Comédie. The pages were squared and the end-papers held in place with an elastic band. I had numbered them in series. I wrote my name and address on the front page, offering a reward to the finder. To lose a passport was the least of one's worries: to lose a notebook was a catastrophe.

In twenty odd years of travel, I lost only two. One vanished on an Afghan bus. The other was filched by the Brazilian secret police, who, with a certain clairvoyance, imagined that some lines I had written – about the wounds of a Baroque Christ – were a description, in code, of their own work on political prisoners.

Young Men

From *Essays: Of Travel, 1625* | Francis Bacon (1561–1626)

Travel, in the younger sort, is a part of education, in the elder, a part of experience. He that travelleth into a country, before he hath some entrance into the language, goeth to school, and not to travel. That young men travel under some tutor, or grave servant, I allow well; so that he be such a one that hath the language, and hath been in the country before; whereby he may be able to tell them what things are worthy to be seen, in the country where they go; what acquaintances they are to seek; what exercises, or discipline, the place yieldeth. For else, young men shall go hooded, and look abroad little.

The Road to the Emerald City

From *The Wonderful Wizard of Oz, 1900* | L. Frank Baum (1856–1919)

With Toto trotting along soberly behind her, she started on her journey.

There were several roads nearby, but it did not take her long to find the one paved with yellow bricks. Within a short time she was walking briskly toward the Emerald City, her silver shoes tinkling merrily on the hard, yellow road-bed. The sun shone bright and the birds sang sweetly, and Dorothy did not feel nearly so bad as you might think a little girl would who had been suddenly whisked away from her own country and set down in the midst of a strange land.

She was surprised, as she walked along, to see how pretty the country was about her. There were neat fences at the sides of the road, painted a dainty blue color, and beyond them were fields of grain and vegetables in abundance. Evidently the Munchkins were good farmers and able to raise large crops. Once in a while she would pass a house, and the people came out to look at her and bow low as she went by; for everyone knew she had been the means of destroying the Wicked Witch and setting them free from bondage. The houses of the Munchkins were odd-looking dwellings, for each was round, with a big dome for a roof. All were painted blue, for in this country of the East blue was the favorite color.

James Fenton's Refusal

From *In Trouble Again: A Journey Between the Orinoco and the Amazon*, *1988* | Redmond O'Hanlon (1947–)

I would persuade the civilized companion of my Borneo journey, the poet James Fenton, to visit the Venezuelan Amazons with me. He would be flattered to be asked. He would be delighted to come.

After supper at the long table in James' kitchen (a map of Borneo still hung on the wall), halfway through a bottle of Glenmorangie, I judged the time was ripe.

'James,' I said, 'you are looking ill. You are working far too hard writing all these reviews. You need a break. Why don't you come to the Amazon with me?'

'Are you listening seriously?'

'Yes.'

'Are you sitting comfortably?'

'Yes.'

'Then I want you to know,' said James, shutting his eyes and pressing his palms up over his face and the top of his bald head, *'that I would not come with you to High Wycombe.'*

Etna

From *Sea and Sardinia, 1921* | D. H. Lawrence (1885–1930)

Etna, that wicked witch, resting her thick white snow under heaven, and slowly, slowly rolling her orange-coloured smoke. They called her the Pillar of Heaven, the Greeks. It seems wrong at first, for she trails up in a long, magical, flexible line from the sea's edge to her blunt cone, and does not seem tall. She seems rather low, under heaven. But as one knows her better, oh awe and wizardy! Remote under heaven, aloof, so near, yet never with us. The painters try to paint her, and the photographers to photograph her, in vain. Because why? Because the near ridges, with their olives and white houses, these are with us. Because the river-bed, and Naxos under the lemon groves, Greek Naxos deep under dark-leaved, many-fruited lemon groves, Etna's skirts and skirt-bottoms, these still are our world, our own world. Even the high villages among the oaks, on Etna. But Etna herself, Etna of the snow and secret changing winds, she is beyond a crystal wall. When I look at her, low, white, witch-like under heaven, slowly rolling her orange smoke and giving sometimes a breath of rose-red flame, then I must look away from earth, into the ether, into the low empyrean. And there, in that remote region, Etna is alone. If you would see her, you must slowly take off your eyes from the world and go a naked seer to the strange chamber of the empyrean. Pedestal of heaven! The Greeks had a sense of the magic truth of things. Thank goodness one still knows enough about them to find one's kinship at last. There are so many photographs, there are so infinitely many water-colour drawings and oil paintings which purport to render Etna. But pedestal of heaven! You must cross the invisible border. Between the foreground, which is our own, and Etna, pivot of winds in lower heaven, there is a dividing line. You must change your state of mind. A metempsychosis. It is no use thinking you can see and behold Etna and the foreground both at once. Never. One or the other. Foreground and a transcribed Etna. Or Etna, pedestal of heaven.

Water-Front Streets

Langston Hughes (1901–1967)

The spring is not so beautiful there, —
 But dream ships sail away
To where the spring is wondrous rare
 And life is gay.

The spring is not so beautiful there, —
 But lads put out to sea
Who carry beauties in their hearts
 And dreams, like me.

Souks at Fez

From *In Morocco, 1920* | Edith Wharton (1862–1937)

Fez is sombre, and the bazaars clustered about its holiest sanctuaries form its most sombre quarter. Dusk falls there early, and oil-lanterns twinkle in the merchants' niches while the clear African daylight still lies on the gardens of upper Fez. This twilight adds to the mystery of the *souks*, making them, in spite of profane noise and crowding and filth, an impressive approach to the sacred places.

Until a year or two ago, the precincts around Moulay Idriss and El Kairouiyin were *horm*, that is, cut off from the unbeliever. Heavy beams of wood barred the end of each *souk*, shutting off the sanctuaries, and the Christian could only conjecture what lay beyond. Now he knows in part; for, though the beams have not been lowered, all comers may pass under them to the lanes about the mosques, and even pause a moment in their open doorways.

A Surprise in Bulgaria

From *Minarets in the Mountains: A Journey into Muslim Europe, 2021* | Tharik Hussain (1979–)

Pencil-thin, snow-white minarets topped by sharp pointed cones peered up at us as we wound our way down the sweeping plains of northern Bulgaria, close to the Romanian border. Each one stood beside the unmistakeable outline of a small mosque.

Some lay in ruins. Others were locked up. On or two, though, had tiny cemeteries, where the grass was neatly trimmed around historic turban-shaped tombstones. When we stopped to peer through the windows, colourful prayer rugs were piled up against walls where worn *tasbihs* (prayer beads) hung from small hooks. It began to dawn on me: these were living ancient Muslim villages. But what on earth were they doing here?

Bermudas

Andrew Marvell (1621–1678)

Lines 1–20

Where the remote *Bermudas* ride
In th' Ocean's bosome unespy'd,
From a small Boat, that row'd along,
The list'ning Winds receiv'd this Song.
　　What should we do but sing his Praise
That led us through the wat'ry Maze
Unto an Isle so long unknown,
And yet far kinder than our own?
Where he the huge Sea-Monsters wracks,
That lift the Deep upon their Backs,
He lands us on a grassy Stage,
Safe from the Storms and Prelat's rage.
He gave us this eternal Spring
Which here enamells every thing,
And sends the Fowls to us in care,
On daily Visits through the Air.
He hangs in shades the Orange bright,
Like golden Lamps in a green Night;
And does in the Pomegranates close
Jewels more rich than *Ormus* shows.

Unique to England

From *Rural Rides, 1830* | William Cobbett (1763–1835)

Chesham is a nice little town, lying in a deep and narrow valley, with a stream of water running through it. All along the country that I have come the labourers' dwellings are good. They are made of what they call *brick-nog* (that is to say, a frame of wood, and a single brick thick, filling up the vacancies between the timber). They are generally covered with tile. Not *pretty* by any means; but they are good; and you see here, as in Kent, Sussex, Surrey, and Hampshire, and, indeed, in almost every part of England, that most interesting of all objects, that which is such an honour to England, and that which distinguishes it from all the rest of the world, namely, those *neatly kept and productive little gardens round the labourers' houses*, which are seldom unornamented with more or less of flowers. We have only to look at these to know what sort of people English labourers are.

Not a Traveller's Tale

From *The Sudden View: A Mexican Journey, 1953*

Sybille Bedford (1911–2006)

On the train to Mexico City:

We felt like hot food that night and went to the dining car which
turned out to be an apartment decorated with machine-carved
Spanish Renaissance woodwork of astonishing gloom and ugliness.
Dinner, which you are supposed to order like a deaf-mute, by
scribbling your unattainable wishes on a pad of paper, was a
nondescript travesty of food served with the quite imaginative
disregard of what goes with what that seems to be the tradition of
the American table d'hôte. The one starch and vegetable of the day
is supposed to be eaten as an accompaniment to any of the main
dishes on the menu. So if it is cauliflower and French-fried potatoes,
cauliflower and French-fried potatoes will appear on your plate
whether you are having the Broiled Halibut Steak, the Corned-beef
Hash, the Omelette or the Lamb Chops. I have seen – not eaten –
such inspired misalliances as tinned asparagus tips and spaghetti
curled around a fried mackerel. This is not a traveller's tale.

The Plains of Nebraska

From *The Amateur Emigrant, 1895*

Robert Louis Stevenson (1850–1894)

It had thundered on the Friday night, but the sun rose on Saturday without a cloud. We were at sea – there is no other adequate expression – on the plains of Nebraska. I made my observatory on the top of a fruit-waggon, and sat by the hour upon that perch to spy about me, and to spy in vain for something new. It was a world almost without a feature; an empty sky, an empty earth; front and back, the line of railway stretched from horizon to horizon, like a cue across a billiard-board; on either hand, the green plain ran till it touched the skirts of heaven. Along the track innumerable wild sunflowers, no bigger than a crown-piece, bloomed in a continuous flower-bed; grazing beasts were seen upon the prairie at all degrees of distance and diminution; and now and again we might perceive a few dots beside the railroad which grew more and more distinct as we drew nearer, till they turned into wooden cabins, and then dwindled and dwindled in our wake until they melted into their surroundings, and we were once more alone upon the billiard-board. The train toiled over this infinity like a snail; and being the one thing moving, it was wonderful what huge proportions it began to assume in our regard. It seemed miles in length, and either end of it within but a step of the horizon.

Home-Thoughts, From the Sea

Robert Browning (1812–1889)

Nobly, nobly Cape Saint Vincent to the North-West died away;
Sunset ran, one glorious blood-red, reeking into Cadiz Bay;
Bluish mid the burning water, full in face Trafalgar lay;
In the dimmest North-East distance, dawned Gibraltar grand and gray;
'Here and here did England help me: how can I help England?' – say,
Whoso turns as I, this evening, turn to God to praise and pray,
While Jove's planet rises yonder, silent over Africa.

The Last Entry

From *Journals, 1912* | Robert Falcon Scott (1868–1912)

Thursday March 29:

Since the 21st we have had a continuous gale from W.S.W. and S.W. We had fuel to make two cups of tea apiece and bare food for two days on the 20th. Every day we have been ready to start for our depot *11 miles* away, but outside the door of the tent it remains a scene of whirling drift. I do not think we can hope for any better things now. We shall stick it out to the end, but we are getting weaker, of course, and the end cannot be far.

It seems a pity, but I do not think I can write more.
R. SCOTT.

[Last entry]
For God's sake look after our people.

Hospitality

From *The Valleys of the Assassins, 1934* | Freya Stark (1893–1993)

It is unlucky to reach a nomad's tent in the master's absence.

The laws of hospitality are based on the axiom that a stranger is an enemy until he has entered the sanctuary of somebody's tent: after that, his host is responsible, not only for his safety, but for his general acceptability with the tribe. He is treated at first with suspicion, and gradually with friendliness as he explains himself – very much as if he were trying to enter a county neighbourhood in England, for the undeveloped mind is much the same in Lincolnshire or Luristan. From the very first, however, once he is a guest, he is safe, in every district I have ever been in except the wilder regions of Lakistan. This is the only arrangement which makes travel possible in a tribal country: but it makes the adoption of a guest a responsibility, and the master of the house or some influential representative is alone willing to undertake it.

30 March

A Bodyguard

From *From Rome to San Marino: A Walk in the Steps of Garibaldi, 1982* | Oliver Knox (1923–2002)

'Is he your bodyguard?'

'Yes indeed. Very good idea to take one to Rome nowadays. Well, walking all over Italy actually.' There was too much of a queue behind me to add further information about the footsteps of Garibaldi.

'I said is he your bodyguard, sir?'

I was with my son at Heathrow. A brief conversation about bodyguards may have been a little over-solicitous coming from an airport official, yet did not seem particularly remarkable, the eleventh victim of kidnapping of the year having that morning been reported. Perhaps it was something asked nowadays of all passengers to Italy, when accompanied by younger, tougher men?

Or perhaps it was just a well-worn joke?

Those skyward glances of sons in which embarrassment, pity, impatience and contempt mingle, are probably familiar to most fathers, violent kicks on the shins rather less usual, and more painful.

'Oh God! Boarding-card, not bodyguard. Boarding-card. Really.'

APRIL

The Sea Lay Asleep

The Baths in Sofia

From *The Turkish Embassy Letters, 1717*

Lady Mary Wortley Montagu (1689–1762)

Adrianople,
1 April 1717

To Lady –

I went to the bagnio about ten o'clock. It was already full of women.
It is built of stone, in the shape of a dome, with no windows but in
the roof, which gives light enough. There were five of these domes
joined together, the outmost being less than the rest and serving
only as a hall, where the portress stood at the door. Ladies of quality
generally give this woman the value of a crown or ten shillings and
I did not forget that ceremony. The next room is a very large one
paved with marble, and all round it raised two sofas of marble one
above the other. There were four fountains of cold water in this room,
falling first into marble basins, and then running on the floor in little
channels made for that purpose, which carried the streams into the
next room, something less than this, with the same sort of marble
sofas, but so hot with steams of sulphur proceeding from the baths
joining to it, 'twas impossible to stay there with one's clothes on. The
two other domes were the hot baths, one of which had cocks
of cold water turning into it to temper it to what degree of warmth
the bathers have a mind to.

From Darkest Peru

From *A Bear Called Paddington*, 1958 | Michael Bond (1926–2017)

Mr and Mrs Brown meet a bear at Paddington Station:

'I'm a very rare sort of bear,' he replied importantly. 'There aren't many of us left where I come from.'

'And where is that?' asked Mrs Brown.

The bear looked around carefully before replying. 'Darkest Peru. I'm not really supposed to be here at all. I'm a stowaway!'

'A stowaway?' Mr Brown lowered his voice and look anxiously over his shoulder. He almost expected to see a policeman standing behind him with a notebook and pencil, taking everything down.

'Yes,' said the bear. 'I emigrated, you know.' A sad expression came into its eyes. 'I used to live with my Aunt Lucy in Peru, but she had to go into a home for retired bears.'

'You don't mean to say you've come all the way from South America by yourself?' exclaimed Mrs Brown.

The bear nodded. 'Aunt Lucy always said she wanted me to emigrate when I was old enough. That's why she taught me to speak English.'

Emigration

From *The Promised Land, 1912* | Mary Antin (1881–1949)

Had I been brought to America a few years earlier, I might have written that in such and such a year my father emigrated, just as I would state what he did for a living, as a matter of family history. Happening when it did, the emigration became of the most vital importance to me personally. All the processes of uprooting, transportation, replanting, acclimatization, and development took place in my own soul. I felt the pang, the fear, the wonder, and the joy of it. I can never forget, for I bear the scars. But I want to forget – sometimes I long to forget. I think I have thoroughly assimilated my past – I have done its bidding – I want now to be of to-day. It is painful to be consciously of two worlds. The Wandering Jew in me seeks forgetfulness. I am not afraid to live on and on, if only I do not have to remember too much. A long past vividly remembered is like a heavy garment that clings to your limbs when you would run. And I have thought of a charm that should release me from the folds of my clinging past. I take the hint from the Ancient Mariner, who told his tale in order to be rid of it. I, too, will tell my tale, for once, and never hark back any more. I will write a bold 'Finis' at the end, and shut the book with a bang!

Opening the Shutters on the First Morning in Italy

From *The Enchanted April, 1922* | Elizabeth von Arnim (1866–1941)

All the radiance of April in Italy lay gathered together at her feet. The sun poured in on her. The sea lay asleep in it, hardly stirring. Across the bay the lovely mountains, exquisitely different in colour, were asleep too in the light; and underneath her window, at the bottom of the flower-starred grass slope from which the wall of the castle rose up, was a great cypress, cutting through the delicate blues and violets and rose-colours of the mountains and the sea like a great black sword.

She stared. Such beauty; and she there to see it. Such beauty; and she alive to feel it. Her face was bathed in light. Lovely scents came up to the window and caressed her. A tiny breeze gently lifted her hair. Far out in the bay a cluster of almost motionless fishing boats hovered like a flock of white birds on the tranquil sea. How beautiful, how beautiful. Not to have died before this ... to have been allowed to see, breathe, feel this ... She stared, her lips parted. Happy? Poor, ordinary, everyday word. But what could one say, how could one describe it? It was as though she could hardly stay inside herself, it was as though she were too small to hold so much of joy, it was as though she were washed through with light.

Safe Harbour

From *The Aeneid, 29–19 BC* | Virgil (70–19 BC)

Translated by John Dryden (1631–1700)

Book I, lines 228–242

Within a long Recess there lies a Bay,
An Island shades it from the rolling Sea,
And forms a Port secure for Ships to ride.
Broke by the jutting Land on either side:
In double Streams the briny Waters glide.
Betwixt two rows of Rocks, a Sylvan Scene
Appears above, and Groves for ever green:
A Grott is form'd beneath, with Mossy Seats,
To rest the *Nereids*, and exclude the Heats.
Down thro' the Cranies of the living Walls
The Crystal Streams descend in murm'ring Falls.
No Haulsers need to bind the Vessels here,
Nor bearded Anchors, for no Storms they fear.
Sev'n Ships within this happy Harbour meet,
The thin Remainders of the scatter'd Fleet.

The High Land

From *O Pioneers!, 1913* | Willa Cather (1873–1947)

When the road began to climb the first long swells of the Divide, Alexandra hummed an old Swedish hymn, and Emil wondered why his sister looked so happy. Her face was so radiant that he felt shy about asking her. For the first time, perhaps, since that land emerged from the waters of geologic ages, a human face was set toward it with love and yearning. It seemed beautiful to her, rich and strong and glorious. Her eyes drank in the breadth of it, until her tears blinded her.

A Hotel in Paris

From *Travelling Abroad, All the Year Round, 1860*

Charles Dickens (1812–1870)

7 April

At Paris, I took an upper apartment for a few days in one of the
hotels of the Rue de Rivoli; my front windows looking into the
garden of the Tuileries (where the principal difference between
the nursemaids and the flowers seemed to be that the former were
locomotive and the latter not): my back windows looking at all the
other back windows in the hotel, and deep down into a paved yard,
where my German chariot had retired under a tight-fitting archway,
to all appearance for life, and where bells rang all day without
anybody's minding them but certain chamberlains with feather
brooms and green baize caps, who here and there leaned out of
some high window placidly looking down, and where neat waiters
with trays on their left shoulders passed and repassed from morning
to night.

The Sleeping Car

From *The Great Railway Bazaar, 1975* | Paul Theroux (1941–)

The romance associated with the sleeping car derives from its extreme privacy, combining the best features of a cupboard with forward movement. Whatever drama being enacted in this moving bedroom is heightened by the landscape passing the window: a swell of hills, the surprise of mountains, the loud metal bridge, or the melancholy sight of people standing under yellow lamps. And the notion of travel as a continuous vision, a grand tour's succession of memorable images across a curved earth – with none of the distorting emptiness of air or sea – is possible only on a train. A train is a vehicle that allows residence: dinner in the diner, nothing could be finer.

8 April

A Bedroom Away From Home

From *À La Recherche du Temps Perdu: À l'Ombre des Jeunes Filles en Fleurs, 1918* | Marcel Proust (1871–1922)

Translated as *Remembrance of Things Past: Within a Budding Grove* by K. C. Scott Moncrieff (1889–1930)

It is our noticing them that puts things in a room, our growing used to them that takes them away again and clears a space for us. Space there was none for me in my bedroom (mine in name only) at Balbec; it was full of things which did not know me, which flung back at me the distrustful look that I had cast at them, and, without taking any heed of my existence, shewed that I was interrupting the course of theirs. The clock – whereas at home I heard my clock tick only a few seconds in a week, when I was coming out of some profound meditation – continued without a moment's interruption to utter, in an unknown tongue, a series of observations which must have been most uncomplimentary to myself, for the violet curtains listened to them without replying, but in an attitude such as people adopt who shrug their shoulders to indicate that the sight of a third person irritates them. They gave to this room with its lofty ceiling a semi-historical character which might have made it a suitable place for the assassination of the Duc de Guise, and afterwards for parties of tourists personally conducted by one of Messrs. Thomas Cook and Son's guides, but for me to sleep in – no.

Home Thoughts, From Abroad

Robert Browning (1812–1889)

I

Oh, to be in England
Now that April's there,
And whoever wakes in England
Sees, some morning, unaware,
That the lowest boughs and brushwood sheaf
Round the elm-tree bole are in tiny leaf,
While the chaffinch sings on the orchard bough
In England – now!

II

And after April, when May follows,
And the whitethroat builds, and all the swallows!
Hark, where my blossomed pear-tree in the hedge
Leans to the field and scatters on the clover
Blossoms and dewdrops – at the bent spray's edge –
That's the wise thrush; he sings each song twice over,
Lest you should think he never could recapture
The first fine careless rapture!
And though the fields look rough with hoary dew
All will be gay when noontide wakes anew
The buttercups, the little children's dower
– Far brighter than this gaudy melon-flower!

Buying a Tarantass

From *On Sledge and Horseback to Outcast Siberian Lepers,
1891* | Kate Marsden (1859–1931)

I had to buy a tarantass before leaving, and created quite a stir by my efforts to come out on the right side of a bargain. Three specimens of this vehicle were brought for me to see, all rubbishing affairs. For one of them I was asked the modest sum of fifty roubles. I packed off men and vehicles, energetically shaking my head, and saying 'No.' In half an hour there were other arrivals, worse than the first; and the price demanded was seventy roubles each. To end matters, I said I should take a tarantass belonging to the Governor. By this time a crowd of villagers had collected to see a foreigner do business. There was a great deal of whispering and talking, and then, when the owners of different vehicles began quarrelling and fighting, the hubbub was immense. To see these men fight would have brought a look of contempt on the faces of English fighters. There were no double fists; it was simply an amiable encounter to see which could lay the other on the ground first. I thought whether it was possible to carry on wars after the same pattern, that is, without the shedding of blood and the infliction of pain. After a lot more chattering, a messenger was sent to me to say I might have a sound and safe tarantass for thirty roubles. I accepted the offer, and also gained valuable experience in doing business.

A Premonition?

From *The Lost Camels of Tartary, 1998* | John Hare (1934–2022)

The night of 12 April was perfect. It was utterly still and myriad stars twinkled overhead. To the north-west, comet Hale-Bopp displayed its vibrant tail with an astonishing brightness. We went to bed happy, well-fed and content.

But the Gobi should never be taken for granted. The line that divides success and disaster is finely tuned. The restless spirits of the desert lie constantly in wait, ever ready to pull the rug from under the feet of the complacent traveller. That night I had the most extraordinary dream. Dressed in a bright blue gown, I was guest of honour at a ceremony. I looked out at a sea of upturned and expectant faces that stretched, like the lake bed of Lop Nur, to the far, far horizon. At first I ignored the tug on my sleeve, I was too busy staring at the gigantic gathering. But the tugging continued and, somewhat annoyed, I glanced down. A courtier was kneeling beside me, a Cheshire cat-like smile on his face. He was holding up an open tin of dead, dry fish. What was I supposed to do with them? I turned to look back at the huge crowd. Their whole manner had changed. Their faces were no longer benign. They were angry, hostile. I hadn't done what they expected me to do. The fish! What was I supposed to do with the fish?

On 13 April my journal records that, 'A fresh wind got up on the night of the 12th. About 2.00 a.m. it developed into a powerful sand storm. The next morning, amidst a wreckage of flattened tentage and buckled tent poles, we emerged in a howling wind to discover that all but two of our camels had fled. Hyper-sensitive young Ben and an ailing elder remained, as for the rest, they had completely vanished. We are over 280 kilometres from our base camp.'

Encouraging Others

From *Journal Canton to Rangoon, 1882* | Charles Wahab (1837–1882)

Preface

Should the following pages ever be considered worthy to appear in print, it will be desirable that the reader should know the purpose for which they are written. They are not written to give information – either general or scientific – about the countries traversed. To do that is the special object of the head of the expedition; and – besides his better qualifications, it would be – in a manner poaching on his manor, to attempt to do the same thing. Further, they make no pretensions to giving accounts of the life of the peoples visited; indeed, there are no opportunities for investigating these, and any attempt to describe them would be altogether unsatisfactory and little more than a pretence. These pages then are written with the express object of encouraging others to follow the writer's track …

… The writer will, he hopes, lose no opportunity of first tempting some enterprising readers to follow him; and, secondly, of giving such details of his own experiences, and tendering advice to his successors as will make their journey in many particulars, more comfortable and efficient than his own.

The General Prologue

From *The Canterbury Tales* | Geoffrey Chaucer (c. 1343–1400)

Lines 1–18

Whan that Aprill with his shourés soote
The droghte of March hath perced to the roote,
And bathed every veyne in swich licour
Of which vertu engendred is the flour;
Whan Zephirus eek with his sweeté breeth
Inspired hath in every holt and heeth
The tendre croppés, and the yongé sonne
Hath in the Ram his halvé cours yronne,
And smalé fowelés maken melodye,
That slepen al the nyght with open ye
(So priketh hem nature in hir corages);
Thanne longen folk to goon on pilgrimages,
And palmerés for to seken straunge strondes,
To ferné halwes, kowthe in sondry londes;
And specially from every shires ende
Of Engelond to Caunterbury they wende,
The hooly blisful martir for to seke,
That hem hath holpen whan that they were seeke.

It's My Route

From *Forbidden Journey, 1937* | Ella Maillart (1903–1997)

My plan grew clear. I would go to Sian like Tannberg, then to Tsaidam. There, with the help of the Smigunovs, I would work out the best means of getting to Kashgar.

I told my news to Peter Fleming.

. . . .

Hearing me speak of the Tsaidam and the Smigunovs, he had said coldly: 'As a matter of fact, I'm going back to Europe by that route. You can come with me if you like ...'

'I beg your pardon,' I had answered. 'It's my route and it's I who'll take you, if I can think of some way in which you might be useful to me.'

The controversy still rages.

Two's Company?

From *News from Tartary, 1936* | Peter Fleming (1907–1971)

We got on well together, though we both paraded our conviction, which was perhaps not wholly justified, that we should have got on better by ourselves. I had no previous experience of a woman traveller, but Kini [Ella Maillart] was the antithesis of the popular conception of that alarming species. She had, it is true, and in a marked degree, the qualities which distinguish these creatures in the books they write about themselves. She had courage and enterprise and resource; in endurance she excelled most men. She was also what is known as 'good with the natives', and knew, when dealing with a proud but simple people whose language she did not speak, where to be formal and where to be mildly the buffoon. She could eat anything and sleep anywhere. The only chink in her armour was her very keen sense of smell; here alone I, who have none, could count myself the better equipped.

Differing widely in character and temperament, we had one thing in common, and that was our attitude to our profession (or vocation, or whatever you like to call it). We were united by an abhorrence of the false values placed – whether by its exponents or by the world at large – on what can most conveniently be referred to by its trade-name of Adventure. From an aesthetic rather than an ethical point of view, we were repelled by the modern tendency to exaggerate, romanticize, and at last cheapen out of recognition the ends of the earth and the deeds done in their vicinity. It was almost the only thing we ever agreed about.

A Novel Bed

From *Wonderful Adventures of Mrs Seacole in Many Lands,*
1857 | Mary Seacole (1805–1881)

I begged my brother to find me a bed somewhere. He failed to do
so completely, and in despair I took the matter in my own hands;
and stripping the green oilskin cloth from the rough table – it
would not be wanted again until to-morrow's breakfast – pinned up
some curtains round the table's legs, and turned in with my little
servant beneath it. It was some comfort to know that my brother,
his servants, and Mac brought their mattresses, and slept upon it
above us. It was a novel bed, and required some slight stretch of
the imagination to fancy it a four-poster; but I was too tired to be
particular, and slept soundly.

Equipment

From *A Short Walk in the Hindu Kush*, 1958

Eric Newby (1919–2006)

'We'd better not take all of it,' Hugh said. 'They might wonder why we've got so much stuff if we don't know how to use it.'

Over the last weeks the same thought had occurred to me constantly.

'What about the tent?'

The tent had arrived that morning. It had been described to me by the makers as being suitable for what they called 'the final assault'. With its sewn-in ground-sheet, special flaps so that it could be weighed down with boulders, it convinced me, more than any other single item of equipment, that we were going, as the books have it, 'high'. It had been specially constructed for the curious climatic conditions we were likely to encounter in the Hindu Kush.

'I shouldn't take *that*, if I were you,' said my wife with sinister emphasis. 'The children tried to put it up in the garden after lunch. Whoever made it forgot to make holes for the poles.'

'Are you sure?'

'Quite sure. You know it's got those poles shaped like a V, that you slip into a sort of pocket in the material. Well, they haven't made any pockets, so you can't put it up.'

'It's lucky you found out. We should have looked pretty silly on Mir Samir.'

You're going to look pretty silly at any rate. I shouldn't be surprised if they've done the same thing to your sleeping-bags.'

'Have you telephoned the makers?'

'That's no use. If you send it back to them, you'll never see it again. I've sent for the little woman who makes my dresses. She's coming tomorrow morning.'

Into Foreign Lands

From *The Progress of Error* | William Cowper (1731–1800)

Lines 369–378

From school to Cam or Isis, and thence home;
And thence, with all convenient speed, to Rome,
With rev'rend tutor, clad in habit lay,
To tease for cash, and quarrel with, all day;
With memorandum-book for ev'ry town,
And ev'ry post, and where the chaise broke down;
His stock, a few French phrases got by heart;
With much to learn, but nothing to impart,
The youth, obedient to his sire's commands,
Sets off a wand'rer into foreign lands.

The Bay of Biscay

From *The Female Soldier: The Surprising Life and Adventures of Hannah Snell, 1750* | Hannah Snell (1723–1792)

Disguised as James Gray, Hannah Snell enlists and joins Admiral Boscawen's fleet on board the *Swallow* sloop:

On their first setting sail, they enjoyed as fine weather, and as fair Winds as could possibly be wished for, to convey a Ship safely and expeditiously from one Harbour to another. But no sooner were they arrived in the Bay of *Biscay* than the Scene was altered; their favourable Weather converted into a dismal Hurricane, and their smooth placed Ocean, changed into Billows, which threaten'd them with immediate Death, by this Moment raising them to the Clouds, and in the next plunging them, as it were, to the Centre of the Earth. The Danger may be easily estimated, from the Circumstance, for the *Swallow* was as strong and well built a Vessel, as any belonging to his Majesty's Navy of her Burden: yet such was the Stress of Weather, that she sprung her Main-mast, and lost not only the Gib-Boom, but also two Top-masts. After they had for several Days been beat about in this imminent Danger, they with great Difficulty arrived in the Port of *Lisbon*, which was great Joy to them, after having suffered so much in the Bay of *Biscay*, where every Moment they had been in danger of being swallowed up in the vast Abyss. In this Port, which to them was like a safe Asylum, or Sanctuary, to a Man pursued by a hungry and enraged Lyon, they continued three Weeks; because the Vessel was so damaged, that the Number of Hands employed in refitting her could not do it sooner.

Abroad

From *A Taste for Travel, 1985* | John Julius Norwich (1929–2018)

I have travelled, in one way or another, all my life. I have loved every moment of it, and fully intend to go on until I drop. There are all too many parts of the world I have never seen; and although with increasing age I am bound to become less and less of a traveller and more and more of a tourist, I am determined to get to them somehow. But travel, as we all know, is not just a matter of sightseeing, of playing a vast, global game of Happy Families until every country, natural wonder and ancient monument can be ticked off the list; it carries its own excitement, and its own satisfaction. I have never left this country, by ship, car, train, or even by aeroplane, without experiencing that same thrill of expectancy that I felt when I first crossed the Channel at the age of six; nor have I ever set foot on foreign soil without being conscious of a moment's quickening of the heartbeat – the realization that I was, once again, *abroad*.

The Soldier

Rupert Brooke (1887–1915)

If I should die, think only this of me:
    That there's some corner of a foreign field
That is for ever England. There shall be
    In that rich earth a richer dust concealed;
A dust whom England bore, shaped, made aware,
    Gave, once, her flowers to love, her ways to roam,
A body of England's, breathing English air,
    Washed by the rivers, blest by the suns of home.

And think, this heart, all evil shed away,
    A pulse in the eternal mind, no less
        Gives somewhere back the thoughts by England given;
Her sights and sounds; dreams happy as her day;
    And laughter, learnt of friends; and gentleness,
        In hearts at peace, under an English heaven.

November–December 1914

Rupert Brooke's Grave

From *The Glorious Adventure, 1927*

Richard Halliburton (1900–1939: disappeared while attempting to sail a Chinese junk across the Pacific Ocean from Hong Kong to San Francisco)

April 23

It was not an easy journey. To visit the grave of Rupert Brooke one must endure as difficult a fifteen miles of jagged terrain as it is possible to imagine. From noon till darkness Achilles and Roderic and I picked our way on horseback along the trail: now beside the sea indented with marble grottoes, the home of the sea nymphs, where the water was immeasurably deep and incomparably emerald; now over the olive-dotted watershed across more miles of pale pink rocks where the dwarf holly made deep green patterns against the coral mountains. Colour, colour, in land and sea – a great rock-garden fragrant with sage and thyme, splashed with poppy red, canopied by the bluest sky on earth, gilded by eternal summer, set in the beryl Ægean that breaks upon these marble shores with a fringe of snowy foam. This is Skyros – this is the island where Rupert Brooke died on a French hospital ship that happened to be accompanying his Gallipoli-bound transport and had anchored in a bay just off the southern coast.

The sun had gone down behind the mountain we had crossed as we approached this bay. Our trail led along the white sand of the twilight beach. Achilles suddenly turned inland, following the dry bed of the creek, and for a mile led us struggling up through the undergrowth that blocked our way. Then, suddenly, a flat little plateau shaded by a circle of hoary olive trees; and there in the centre of these grey mourners was the grave.

In his most poetic fancy Brooke could have desired no lovelier spot. On three sides the marble mountains shield it; seaward there is a glorious vista of the island-dotted ocean, bluer than the sky itself which looks straight down through the wreath of olive trees upon the tomb. The flowering sage that perfumes all of Skyros grows thickest here. There is a sweetness in the air, a calmness in the ancient trees, a song in the breeze through the branches, a poem in the picture of the sea.

Setting Off to Circumnavigate the Globe

From *Sailing Alone Around the World*, 1900 |

Joshua Slocum (1844–1909: disappeared after heading south from Martha's Vineyard)

I spent a season in my new craft fishing on the coast, only to find that I had not the cunning properly to bait a hook. But at last the time arrived to weigh anchor and get to sea in earnest. I had resolved on a voyage around the world, and as the wind on the morning of April 24, 1895, was fair, at noon I weighed anchor, set sail, and filled away from Boston, where the *Spray* had been moored snugly all winter. The twelve-o'clock whistles were blowing just as the sloop shot ahead under full sail. A short board was made up the harbor on the port tack, then coming about she stood seaward, with her boom well off to port, and swung past the ferries with lively heels. A photographer on the outer pier at East Boston got a picture of her as she swept by, her flag at the peak throwing its folds clear. A thrilling pulse beat high in me. My step was light on deck in the crisp air. I felt that there could be no turning back, and that I was engaging in an adventure the meaning of which I thoroughly understood. I had taken little advice from any one, for I had a right to my own opinions in matters pertaining to the sea.

. . . .

Waves dancing joyously across Massachusetts Bay met her coming out of the harbor to dash them into myriads of sparkling gems that hung about her at every surge. The day was perfect, the sunlight clear and strong. Every particle of water thrown into the air became a gem, and the *Spray*, bounding ahead, snatched necklace after necklace from the sea, and as often threw them away. We have all seen miniature rainbows about a ship's prow, but the *Spray* flung out a bow of her own that day, such as I had never seen before. Her good angel had embarked on the voyage; I so read it in the sea.

The Merit of England

From *English Traits, 1856* | Ralph Waldo Emerson (1803–1882)

As soon as you enter England, which, with Wales, is no larger than the State of Georgia,* this little land stretches by an illusion to the dimensions of an empire.

The innumerable details, the crowded succession of towns, cities, cathedrals, castles, and great and decorated estates, the number and power of the trades and guilds, the military strength and splendour, the multitudes of rich and of remarkable people, the servants and equipages, all these catching the eye, and never allowing it to pause, hide all boundaries, by the impression of magnificence and endless wealth.

1 reply to all the urgencies that refer me to this and that object indispensably to be seen, – Yes, to see England well needs a hundred years; for, what they told me was the merit of Sir John Soane's Museum, in London, – that it was well packed and well saved, – is the merit of England; – it is stuffed full, in all corners and crevices, with towns, towers, churches, villas, palaces, hospitals, and charity-houses. In the history of art, it is a long way from a cromlech to York minster; yet all the intermediate steps may still be traced in this all-preserving island.

*Add South Carolina, and you have more than an equivalent for the area of Scotland.

Kioto

From *Tales of Travels, 1923* | George Curzon, 1st Marquess Curzon of
Kedleston (1859–1925)

The town is exquisitely situated in a cup between mountain ranges,
quaintly outlined, and clothed with an astonishing wealth of trees.
From the eastern range, where the visitor is probably lodged, he will
get a wonderful outlook, both at sunrise and at nightfall. In the early
dawn the entire city is drowned in a sea of white vapour, from which
only the huge hooded roofs of the temples emerge, black and solemn,
like the inverted hulls of gigantic ships. Suddenly, across the mist
booms the sonorous stroke of some vast temple-bell, and rolls away in
melancholy vibrations. At night the dusky mass of houses, stretching
for miles, twinkles with the light of a thousand lanterns that glimmer
from the lintels and dance along the streets. A swarm of fire-flies
would seem to be flitting in the aisles of some dim and sombre
forest, from whose recesses float upwards the indescribable hum of
congregated humanity, street cries and laughter, the sound of voices,
and the tinkling of guitars.

At festival time, and when the *matsuris*, or religious holidays,
are celebrated, Kioto is especially worthy of a visit. The whole town
turns out merry-making; the temple precincts are blocked from
morn till night by gaily-dressed crowds; the tea-houses overflow
with customers; the singing girls extract rich harvest; and copper
pieces rain into the tills of itinerant purveyors of entertainment and
theatrical shows. One street in particular is ablaze with a succession
of gaudily-decorated booths, containing acrobats, jugglers, storytellers, peep-shows, pantomimes, and plays. These are crowded from
daybreak to sunset.

Montmartre

From *The Autobiography of Alice B. Toklas, 1933*

Gertrude Stein (1874–1946)

1907

Gertrude Stein and I about ten days later went to Montmartre,
I for the first time. I have never ceased to love it. We go there every
now and then and I always have the same tender expectant feeling
that I had then. It is a place where you were always standing and
sometimes waiting, not for anything to happen, but just standing.
The inhabitants of Montmartre did not sit much, they mostly
stood which was just as well as the chairs, the dining room chairs
of France, did not tempt one to sit. So I went to Montmartre and
I began my apprenticeship of standing.

27 April

Paris in Spring

Sara Teasdale (1884–1933)

The city's all a-shining
   Beneath a fickle sun,
A gay young wind's a-blowing,
   The little shower is done.
But the rain-drops still are clinging
   And falling one by one –
Oh it's Paris, it's Paris,
   And spring-time has begun.

I know the Bois is twinkling
   In a sort of hazy sheen,
And down the Champs the gray old arch
   Stands cold and still between.
But the walk is flecked with sunlight
   Where the great acacias lean,
Oh it's Paris, it's Paris,
   And the leaves are growing green.

The sun's gone in, the sparkle's dead,
   There falls a dash of rain,
But who would care when such an air
   Comes blowing up the Seine?
And still Ninette sits sewing
   Beside her window-pane,
When it's Paris, it's Paris,
   And spring-time's come again.

Into Afghanistan

From *Danziger's Travels: Beyond Forbidden Frontiers*, 1987

Nick Danziger (1958–)

Crossing illegally from Iran:

We set off at a run, a crouching run to avoid being spotted. We were
approaching the site of the Pasdaran control post which we had to
pass and in the darkness we could see the lights of Iranian patrol cars
as they roved the desert. We rested here until it was pitch dark, and
then Abdul gave me one of two branches of shrub he had collected.
It was time to make the final dash across the frontier.

I soon discovered what the shrub was for. You held it in front
as you dashed at headlong pace through the black night over the
featureless terrain, and it gave you warnings of depressions and
hollows or rises in the land. However you were travelling so fast
that there was no time to respond to such warnings. It was a bit like
skiing at night. Our turbans wrapped across our faces for protection
from the sand, we would scamper a few hundred yards, then stop,
fixed to the ground like lizards, before scampering on, keeping an
ever watchful eye out for the patrol cars of the Pasdaran, which
were fortunately easy to detect because of their bright headlights
and red taillights.

Finally we came to a big ditch with steep banks on either side.
This was a manmade demarcation line – the physical frontier
between the two countries. No sooner had we climbed the opposite
bank and caught our breath than Abdul stood up fully, stretched
himself, and grinned.

'Welcome to Afghanistan,' he said with obvious relief, throwing
aside the branches. 'It's OK now – we have no worries!'

Travelling in Tibet

From *Trespassers on the Roof of the World, 1982*

Peter Hopkirk (1930–2014)

In the heart of Central Asia, buttressed by the highest mountains on earth, soars the immense natural fortress of Tibet. Its extraordinary altitude – nearly three miles up in the sky – caused Victorian travellers to christen it 'The Roof of the World'. Lhasa, its remote and mysterious capital, so long closed to foreigners, they named 'The Forbidden City'.

One celebrated explorer, Sven Hedin, described Tibet as 'the most stupendous upheaval to be found on the face of our planet', and a glance at a relief map will show this to be no exaggeration. Some of its passes teeter at 20,000 feet, while two-thirds of this vast, storm-swept tableland lies at 15,000 feet or more. Lhasa, standing at 12,000 feet, is the world's highest capital, and those with raised blood-pressure are well advised to stay away. Travelling in Tibet presents other peculiar problems. Water boils there at a lower temperature than at lower altitudes. To plunge one's hand into boiling water is bearable – just. Cooking thus becomes a laborious business, and Tibet has never been famous for its cuisine.

MAY

I Slipped the Bonds of Earth

Restoring the Romance

From *A Motor-Flight Through France, 1908*

Edith Wharton (1862–1937)

The motor-car has restored the romance of travel.

Freeing us from all the compulsions and contacts of the railway, the bondage to fixed hours and the beaten track, the approach to each town through the area of ugliness and desolation created by the railway itself, it has given us back the wonder, the adventure and the novelty which enlivened the way of our posting grand-parents. Above all these recovered pleasures must be ranked the delight of taking a town unawares, stealing on it by back ways and unchronicled paths, and surprising in it some intimate aspect of past time, some silhouette hidden for half a century or more by the ugly mask of railway embankments and the iron bulk of a huge station. Then the villages that we missed and yearned for from the windows of the train – the unseen villages have been given back to us! – and nowhere could the importance of the recovery have been more delightfully exemplified than on a May afternoon in the Pas-de-Calais, as we climbed the long ascent beyond Boulogne on the road to Arras.

Modes of Transport

From *Alarms and Discursions, 1910* | G. K. Chesterton (1874–1936)

To me personally, at least, it would never seem needful to own a motor, any more than to own an avalanche. An avalanche, if you have luck, I am told, is a very swift, successful, and thrilling way of coming down a hill. It is distinctly more stirring, say, than a glacier, which moves an inch in a hundred years. But I do not divide these pleasures either by excitement or convenience, but by the nature of the thing itself. It seems human to have a horse or bicycle, because it seems human to potter about; and men cannot work horses, nor can bicycles work men, enormously far afield of their ordinary haunts and affairs.

But about motoring there is something magical, like going to the moon; and I say the thing should be kept exceptional and felt as something breathless and bizarre. My ideal hero would own his horse, but would have the moral courage to hire his motor. Fairy tales are the only sound guidebooks to life; I like the Fairy Prince to ride on a white pony out of his father's stables, which are of ivory and gold. But if in the course of his adventures he finds it necessary to travel on a flaming dragon, I think he ought to give the dragon back to the witch at the end of the story. It is a mistake to have dragons about the place.

Questions From the Greatest Cyclop

From *Odyssey, 8–7th century* BC | Homer (8th century BC)

Translated by George Chapman (c. 1559–1634)

'Ho! guests! What are ye? Whence sail ye these seas?
Traffic, or rove ye, and like thieves oppress
Poor strange adventurers, exposing so
Your souls to danger, and your lives to woe?'
This utter'd he, when fear from our hearts took
    The very life, to be so thunder-strook
With such a voice, and such a monster see;
But thus I answer'd: 'Erring Grecians, we
From Troy were turning homewards; but by force
Of adverse winds, in far-diverted course.
Such unknown ways took, and on rude seas toss'd,
As Jove decreed, are cast upon this coast.'

Inland Cruising

From *The Cruise of the Snark, 1911* | Jack London (1876–1916)

We expect to do a lot of inland work. The smallness of the *Snark* makes this possible. When we enter the land, out go the masts and on goes the engine. There are the canals of China, and the Yang-tse River. We shall spend months on them if we can get permission from the government. That will be the one obstacle to our inland voyaging – governmental permission. But if we can get that permission, there is scarcely a limit to the inland voyaging we can do.

When we come to the Nile, why we can go up the Nile. We can go up the Danube to Vienna, up the Thames to London, and we can go up the Seine to Paris and moor opposite the Latin Quarter with a bow-line out to Notre Dame and a stern-line fast to the Morgue. We can leave the Mediterranean and go up the Rhône to Lyons, there enter the Saône, cross from the Saône to the Maine through the Canal de Bourgogne, and from the Marne enter the Seine and go out the Seine at Havre. When we cross the Atlantic to the United States, we can go up the Hudson, pass through the Erie Canal, cross the Great Lakes, leave Lake Michigan at Chicago, gain the Mississippi by way of the Illinois River and the connecting canal, and go down the Mississippi to the Gulf of Mexico. And then there are the great rivers of South America. We'll know something about geography when we get back to California.

Meccah

From *Personal Narrative of a Pilgrimage to El-Medinah and Meccah, 1855–1856* | Sir Richard Burton (1821–1890)

There at last it lay, the bourn of my long and weary pilgrimage, realising the plans and hopes of many and many a year. The mirage medium of Fancy invested the huge catafalque and its gloomy pall with peculiar charms. There were no giant fragments of hoar antiquity as in Egypt, no remains of graceful and harmonious beauty as in Greece and Italy, no barbaric gorgeousness as in the buildings of India; yet the view was strange, unique, and how few have looked upon the celebrated shrine! I may truly say that, of all the worshippers who clung weeping to the curtain, or who pressed their beating hearts to the stone, none felt for the moment a deeper emotion than did the Haji from the far north. It was as if the poetical legends of the Arab spoke truth, and that the waving wings of angels, not the sweet breeze of morning, were agitating and swelling the black covering of the shrine. But, to confess humbling truth, theirs was the high feeling of religious enthusiasm, mine was the ecstasy of gratified pride.

A Letter From Don Otavio

From *The Sudden View: A Mexican Journey, 1953*

Sybille Bedford (1911–2006)

The countryside grew wilder, weltering rays struck the lake and the water glistened in milky rainbow colours. Birds appeared. On we dragged and shook and rumbled with no end in view. Then a train of mules came into sight, broke into a gallop, raced towards us in a cloud of dust, reined in and effected a trembling standstill. A man leapt from the saddle. He bowed to E.* and handed her a large mauve envelope.

On crested paper, above a triple-barrelled signature, we read:

Villa El Dorado,

San Pedro Tlayacán

Your Madams,

Distinguished Esquire,

¡Your entire servant, being apprised to his profoundest confusion of Your unbecoming way to his undignified house, the disgraced rascals through obdurate tardiness having returned the insufficient boat without Your Unparalleled Favours to his eternal shame, is sending three unworthy mules, scant shelter and a humble sustenance for Your Facile progress and implores You to dispense him for the abomination of the travel!

Q. B. S. P

Otavio de … y … y …

'Your friend seems very civil, Anthony,' said E.

*E: Sybille's travelling companion, referred to as E. or E.M.A throughout. The book is dedicated to Esther Murphy Arthur. Anthony: E.'s second cousin.

155

The Caravans

From *The Caravaners, 1930* | Elizabeth von Arnim (1866–1941)

There were three; all alike, sober brown vehicles, easily distinguishable, as I was pleased to notice, from common gipsy carts. Clean curtains fluttered at the windows, the metal portions were bright, and the names painted prettily on them were the Elsa, the Ilsa, and the Ailsa.

It was an impressive moment, the moment of our first setting eyes upon them. Under those frail roofs were we for the next four weeks to be happy, as Edelgard said, and healthy and wise – 'Or,' I amended shrewdly on hearing her say this, '*vice versa.*'

The Gipsy Caravan

From *The Wind in the Willows, 1908* | Kenneth Grahame (1859–1932)

[Toad] 'I've discovered the real thing, the only genuine occupation for a lifetime. I propose to devote the remainder of mine to it, and can only regret the wasted years that lie behind me, squandered in trivialities. Come with me, dear Ratty, and your amiable friend also, if he will be so very good, just as far as the stable-yard, and you shall see what you shall see!'

He led the way to the stable-yard accordingly, the Rat following with a most mistrustful expression; and there, drawn out of the coach-house into the open, they saw a gipsy caravan, shining with newness, painted a canary-yellow picked out with green, and red wheels.

'There you are!' cried the Toad, straddling and expanding himself. 'There's real life for you, embodied in that little cart. The open road, the dusty highway, the heath, the common, the hedgerows, the rolling downs! Camps, villages, towns, cities! Here to-day, up and off to somewhere else to-morrow! Travel, change, interest, excitement! The whole world before you, and a horizon that's always changing!'

Diaries

From *Essays: Of Travel, 1625* | Francis Bacon (1561–1626)

It is a strange thing, that in sea voyages, where there is nothing to be seen, but sky and sea, men should make diaries; but in land-travel, wherein so much is to be observed, for the most part they omit it; as if chance were fitter to be registered, than observation. Let diaries, therefore, be brought in use.

9 May

High Flight

John Gillespie Magee (1922–1941)

Oh! I have slipped the surly bonds of earth
And danced the skies on laughter-silvered wings;
Sunward I've climbed, and joined the tumbling mirth
Of sun-split clouds, – and done a hundred things
You have not dreamed of – wheeled and soared and swung
High in the sunlit silence. Hov'ring there,
I've chased the shouting wind along, and flung
My eager craft through footless halls of air.
Up, up the long, delirious burning blue
I've topped the wind-swept heights with easy grace
Where never lark, or even eagle flew;
And, while with silent, lifting mind I've trod
The high untrespassed sanctity of space,
Put out my hand, and touched the face of God.

10 May

St Petersburg

From *Among the Russians, 1983* | Colin Thubron (1939–)

It was a pure creation of the emperor's will. Raised on stone and
wooden piles among the marshy islets of his newly conquered
bridgehead on the Baltic, this 'window on Europe' became a base for
Peter's infant navy and a self-consciously Western capital. Exposed
to sudden floods and sunk in a lacework of streams, its birth was a
nightmare. Peter drove on its builders like a flail. They were marched
here in tens of thousands under armed guard from all over the
empire. Shelterless and half-starved, thousands died of dysentery and
scurvy, or were swept away by flood. They deserted in hordes. But
thousands more were marched up to replace them; and the nobility,
who hated the site, were forced by imperial decree to live and build
stone houses there. 'On one side the sea,' moaned a court jester, 'on
the other sorrow, on the third moss, on the fourth a sigh.'

Escape to Canada

From *The Refugee: Narratives of Fugitive Slaves in Canada,*
1856 | Benjamin Drew (1812–1903); quotation from Mrs John Little (dates
unknown)

One Sunday morning, being on a prairie where we could see no
house – about fifty miles west of Springfield – we ventured to travel
by day. We encountered an animal, which at first we supposed to be
a dog; but when he came near, we concluded it to be a wolf. We went
on and crossed a stream, and then we saw three large wood-wolves,
sneaking around as if waiting for darkness. As we kept on, the three
wolves kept in sight, now on one hand, and now on the other. I felt
afraid, expecting they would attack us: but they left us. Afterward
we made a fire with elder-stalks, and I undertook to make some corn
bread. I got it mixed, and put it on the fire, – when I saw a party of
men and boys on horseback, apparently approaching us. I put out
the fire; they turned a little away, and did not appear to perceive us:
I rekindled the fire, and baked our bread. John managed to keep us
well supplied with pies and bread. We used to laugh to think how
people would puzzle over who drank the milk and left the pitchers,
and who hoked the dough.

I got to be quite hardy – quite used to water and bush-whacking;
so that by the time I got to Canada, I could handle an axe, or hoe, or
any thing. I felt proud to be able to do it.

The Evening Fire

From *Travels in Arabia Deserta, 1888* | C. M. Doughty (1843–1926)

Pleasant, as the fiery heat of the desert daylight is done, is our homely
evening fire. The sun gone down upon a highland steppe of Arabia,
whose common altitude is above three thousand feet, the thin dry
air is presently refreshed, the sand is soon cold; wherein yet at three
fingers' depth is left a sunny warmth of the past day's heat until the
new sunrise. After a half hour it is the blue night, the clear hoary
starlight in which there shines the girdle of the milky way, with a
marvellous clarity. As the sun is setting, the nomad housewife brings
in a truss of sticks and dry bushes, which she has pulled or hoed with
a mattock (a tool they have seldom) in the wilderness; she casts down
this provision by our hearthside, for the sweet-smelling evening fire.

13 May

Leaving London

From *The Modern Traveller* | Hilaire Belloc (1870–1953)

Chapter IV

The ship was dropping down the stream,
The Isle of Dogs was just abeam,
   And Sin and Blood and I
Saw Greenwich Hospital go past,
And gave a look – (for them the last) –
   Towards the London sky!
Ah! nowhere have I ever seen
A sky so pure and so serene!

Did we at length, perhaps, regret
   Our strange adventurous lot?
And were our eyes a trifle wet
With tears that we repressed, and yet
   Which started blinding hot?
Perhaps – and yet, I do not know,
For when we came to go below,
   We cheerfully admitted
That though there was a smell of paint
(And though a very just complaint
Had to be lodged against the food),
The cabin furniture was good
   And comfortably fitted.
And even out beyond the Nore
We did not ask to go ashore.

A Different Reception

From 'Historical Sketch of the Jubilee Singers', Part II, *Fisk University News: The Jubilee Singers*, October 1911 |

Ella Sheppard (1851–1914)

The Jubilee Singers plan a visit to England, 1873:
An evidence of civic and social prejudice was shown through the refusal of one after another of the ocean steamship lines to take us as cabin passenger. Finally the Cunard Line received us on the good ship 'Batavia.' The kindness of the captain and crew we shall never forget.

. . . .

Second Campaign Abroad, 1875:
On May 15th our reorganized company of eleven members, with Mr. White and Miss Gilbert, our loved chaperone, again sailed for England. It was gratifying to find that more than one steamship line which had before refused us passage, now offered it to us at reduced rates, but we turned to the Cunard ship 'Algeria'.

15 May

Ruled Off the Maps

From *Scoop, 1938* | Evelyn Waugh (1903–1966)

Ishmaelia, that hitherto happy commonwealth, cannot conveniently
be approached from any part of the world. It lies in the North-
Easterly quarter of Africa, giving colour by its position and shape to
the metaphor often used of it – 'the Heart of the Dark Continent',
Desert, forest and swamp, frequented by furious nomads, protect its
approaches from those more favoured regions which the statesmen of
Berlin and Geneva have put to school under European masters. An
inhospitable race of squireens cultivate the highlands and pass their
days in the perfect leisure which those peoples alone enjoy who are
untroubled by the speculative or artistic itch.

Various courageous Europeans in the seventies of the last century
came to Ishmaelia, or near it, furnished with suitable equipment
of cuckoo clocks, phonographs, opera hats, draft-treaties and flags
of the nations which they had been obliged to leave. They came
as missionaries, ambassadors, tradesmen, prospectors, natural
scientists. None returned. They were eaten, every one of them; some
raw, others stewed and seasoned – according to local usage and the
calendar (for the better sort of Ishmaelites have been Christian for
many centuries and will not publicly eat human flesh, uncooked,
in Lent, without special and costly dispensation from their bishop).
Punitive expeditions suffered more harm than they inflicted and
in the nineties humane counsels prevailed. The European powers
independently decided that they did not want that profitless
piece of territory; that the one thing less desirable than seeing a
neighbour established there, was the trouble of taking it themselves.
Accordingly, by general consent, it was ruled off the maps and its
immunity guaranteed.

Practicalities and Permission

From *A Ride Along the Great Wall, 1987*

Robin Hanbury-Tenison (1936–)

The first thing we found out was that it was impossible. While the door to China is opening wider than it ever has before, there are still large parts of the country that are closed to foreigners and these include most regions through which the Great Wall runs.

. . . .

[Months later]

I was told that our military permit had arrived and I could take it to Public Security. There more forms were required, and whilst filling them in I took pleasure from being able to put 'horse' under 'Method of Travel'. They had not had one of those before, but passed it and I was handed the first ever Aliens' Travel Permit starting at Shanhaiguan and ending at Jiayuguan. Although the permitted route was not what we had requested by a long way, it did take us from one end of the Wall to the other and for about half the way we were to be allowed to ride along it.

. . . .

It is very unlikely that anybody ever has or ever will travel the whole way along the Wall itself from one end to the other. Apart from the physical impossibility of anyone except a mountaineer doing so today because of the cliffs which intercept it and its broken condition, the steepness of the terrain through which it passes for the first few hundred miles makes it extremely difficult to stay close to the Wall. Often it runs along a ridge with a sheer drop on either side.

17 May

Poor Behaviour on a Train

From *Diary, 1870* | Francis Kilvert (1840–1879)

Wednesday 18 May

Went down to the Bath Flower Show in Sydney College Gardens. Found the first train going down was an Excursion train and took a ticket for it. The carriage was nearly full. In the Box tunnel as there was no lamp, the people began to strike foul brimstone matches and hand them to each other all down the carriage. All the time we were in the tunnel these lighted matches were travelling from hand to hand in the darkness. Each match lasted the length of the carriage and the red ember was thrown out of the opposite window, by which time another lighted match was seen travelling down the carriage. The carriage was chock full of brimstone fumes, the windows both nearly shut, and by the time we got out of the tunnel I was almost suffocated. Then a gentleman tore a lady's pocket handkerchief in two, seized one fragment, blew his nose with it, and put the rag in his pocket. She then seized his hat from his head, while another lady said that the dogs of Wootton Bassett were much more sociable than the people.

Elopement

From *Their Eyes Were Watching God, 1937*

Zora Neale Hurston (1891–1960)

19 May

Jacksonville. Tea Cake's letter had said Jacksonville. He had worked in the railroad shops up there before and his old boss had promised him a job come next pay day. No need for Janie to wait any longer. Wear the new blue dress because he meant to marry her right from the train. Hurry up and come because he was about to turn into pure sugar thinking about her. Come on, baby, papa Tea Cake never could be mad with you!

Janie's train left too early in the day for the town to witness much, but the few who saw her leave bore plenty witness. They had to give it to her, she looked good, but she had no business to do it. It was hard to love a woman that always made you feel so wishful.

The train beat on itself and danced on the shiny steel rails mile after mile. Every now and then the engineer would play on his whistle for the people in the towns he passed by. And the train shuffled on to Jacksonville, and to a whole lot of things she wanted to see and to know.

A Mixed Reception

From *South, 1919* | Ernest Shackleton (1874–1922)

Reaching the Whaling Station on South Georgia:

In memories we were rich. We had pierced the veneer of outside things. We had 'suffered, starved, and triumphed, grovelled down yet grasped at glory, grown bigger in the bigness of the whole.' We had seen God in His splendours, heard the text that Nature renders. We had reached the naked soul of man.

Shivering with cold, yet with hearts light and happy, we set off towards the whaling-station, now not more than a mile and a half distant. The difficulties of the journey lay behind us. We tried to straighten ourselves up a bit, for the thought that there might be women at the station made us painfully conscious of our uncivilized appearance. Our beards were long and our hair was matted. We were unwashed and the garments that we had worn for nearly a year without a change were tattered and stained. Three more unpleasant-looking ruffians could hardly have been imagined. Worsley produced several safety-pins from some corner of his garments and effected some temporary repairs that really emphasized his general disrepair. Down we hurried, and when quite close to the station we met two small boys ten or twelve years of age. I asked these lads where the manager's house was situated. They did not answer. They gave us one look – a comprehensive look that did not need to be repeated. Then they ran from us as fast as their legs would carry them. We reached the outskirts of the station and passed through the 'digesting-house,' which was dark inside. Emerging at the other end, we met an old man, who started as if he had seen the Devil himself and gave us no time to ask any question. He hurried away. This greeting was not friendly. Then we came to the wharf, where the man in charge stuck to his station. I asked him if Mr. Sorlle (the manager) was in the house.

'Yes,' he said as he stared at us.

'We would like to see him,' said I.

'Who are you?' he asked.

'We have lost our ship and come over the island,' I replied.

'You have come over the island?' he said in a tone of entire disbelief.

The man went towards the manager's house and we followed him. I learned afterwards that he said to Mr. Sorlle: 'There are three funny-looking men outside, who say they have come over the island and they know you. I have left them outside.' A very necessary precaution from his point of view.

Mr. Sorlle came out to the door and said, 'Well?'

'Don't you know me?' I said.

'I know your voice,' he replied doubtfully. 'You're the mate of the *Daisy*.'

'My name is Shackleton,' I said.

Immediately he put out his hand and said, 'Come in. Come in.'

Ships That Pass in the Night

Paul Laurence Dunbar (1872–1906)

Out in the sky the great dark clouds are massing;
    I look far out into the pregnant night,
Where I can hear a solemn booming gun
    And catch the gleaming of a random light,
That tells me that the ship I seek is passing, passing.

My tearful eyes my soul's deep hurt are glassing;
    For I would hail and check that ship of ships.
I stretch my hands imploring, cry aloud,
    My voice falls dead a foot from mine own lips,
And but its ghost doth reach that vessel, passing, passing.

O Earth, O Sky, O Ocean, both surpassing,
    O heart of mine, O soul that dreads the dark!
Is there no hope for me? Is there no way
    That I may sight and check that speeding bark
Which out of sight and sound is passing, passing?

Ladies Island

From 'Life on the Sea Islands', *Atlantic Monthly*, Part I,
May 1864 | Charlotte Forten Grimké (1837–1914)

We rowed across to Ladies Island, which adjoins St. Helena,
through the splendors of a grand Southern sunset. The gorgeous
clouds of crimson and gold were reflected as in a mirror in the
smooth, clear waters below. As we glided along, the rich tones
of the negro boatmen broke upon the evening stillness, –
sweet, strange, and solemn.

22 May

The Necessity of Nightshirts

From *The Glorious Adventure, 1927* | Richard Halliburton (1900–1939: disappeared while attempting to sail a Chinese junk across the Pacific Ocean from Hong Kong to San Francisco)

At the summit of Mount Olympus Richard Halliburton and his companion Roderic Crane carve their names in the rock:

The final E and N were completed. We pocketed our knives and harkened at last to Lazarus' wails of distress – too late. One sweep of the wind, and the fog, with startling suddenness, from all directions at once, had thrown its impenetrable blanket over us. We drew back from the brink, in alarm.

'Oh, it will soon pass by,' I said encouragingly to Rod. 'It's still two hours before darkness. Things will clear up in time.'

'I hope so,' he replied, shivering a bit from the damp clinging mist. 'We really can't spend the night up here, – we haven't our nightshirts.'

A Good Place to Hide

From *The Thirty-Nine Steps, 1915* | John Buchan (1875–1940)

Then I got out an atlas and looked at a big map of the British Isles.
My notion was to get off to some wild district, where my veldcraft
would be of some use to me, for I would be like a trapped rat in a
city. I considered that Scotland would be best, for my people were
Scotch and I could pass anywhere as an ordinary Scotsman. I had
half an idea at first to be a German tourist, for my father had had
German partners, and I had been brought up to speak the tongue
pretty fluently, not to mention having put in three years prospecting
for copper in German Damaraland. But I calculated that it would be
less conspicuous to be a Scot, and less in a line with what the police
might know of my past. I fixed on Galloway as the best place to go.
It was the nearest wild part of Scotland, so far as I could figure it out,
and from the look of the map was not over thick with population.

A search in Bradshaw informed me that a train left St Pancras
at 7.10, which would land me at any Galloway station in the late
afternoon.

The Late Evening Call to Prayer

From *Minarets in the Mountains: A Journey into Muslim Europe,* 2021 | Tharik Hussain (1979–)

It was the melodious cry of the *muezzin* that hastened me towards my first destination in Sarajevo. The sacred words inviting Muslims to prayer cascaded through the valley where Bosnia and Herzegovina's capital city nestles. Squeezed along a narrow east–west corridor on the banks of the Miljacka River as it emerges serpentine from the surrounding mountains, old Sarajevo still resembles a bustling medieval city.

All around me were narrow alleyways leading to historic quarters once the exclusive domain of metalworkers, leather markets, gold dealers and coffee sellers. Some were still home to their modern incarnations, jostling for room with the new al fresco restaurants, cafés and boutique tourist shops.

The late evening *adhan* (call to prayer) is always quite enchanting. An inky darkness enveloped the green hills as the serene Arabic words rippled through the valley; one by one the mosques came alive. Every time a new one joined the growing chorus, I turned my head to notice another tall, historic minaret I hasn't seen before. They seemed to be everywhere, each an ancient testimony that Sarajevo has always been a Muslim city.

Waving at Trains

From *The Railway Children, 1906* | E. Nesbit (1858–1924)

'I say,' Phyllis suggested, 'let's all wave to the Green Dragon as it goes by. If it's a magic dragon, it'll understand and take our loves to Father. And if it isn't, three waves aren't much. We shall never miss them.'

So when the Green Dragon tore shrieking out of the mouth of its dark lair, which was the tunnel, all three children stood on the railing and waved their pocket-handkerchiefs without stopping to think whether they were clean handkerchiefs or the reverse. They were, as a matter of fact, very much the reverse.

And out of a first-class carriage a hand waved back. A quite clean hand. It held a newspaper. It was the old gentleman's hand.

After this it became the custom for waves to be exchanged between the children and the 9.15.

And the children, especially the girls, liked to think that perhaps the old gentleman knew Father, and would meet him 'in business,' wherever that shady retreat might be, and tell him how his three children stood on a rail far away in the green country and waved their love to him every morning, wet or fine.

Youth and Maturity

From *Canadian Occasions, 1940* | John Buchan (1875–1940)

Canada Club Dinner, London, 27th May 1935

If Canada has the vigour of youth, she also has the balance and the just perspective of maturity. She is an integrated nation, united long ago by her own act, and with her unity riveted and compacted by partnership in the enterprises of peace and the sacrifices of war. And from Britain and France she draws the same tradition – that great Mediterranean tradition of Greece and Rome, which I believe to be the basis of civilisation. She is no rootless people, deriving a fickle inspiration from transient fashions, but a nation broad-based upon the central culture of mankind. She has her own proud heritage and she is loyal to it, for the first virtues in a people or an individual is loyalty to what they know and love.

Chance Benefits

From *Letters written during a short residence in Sweden, Norway and Denmark, 1796* | Mary Wollstonecraft (1759–1797)

Tonsberg, Norway:

By chance I found a fine rivulet filtered through the rocks, and confined in a basin for the cattle. It tasted to me like a chalybeate; at any rate, it was pure; and the good effect of the various waters which invalids are sent to drink depends, I believe, more on the air, exercise, and change of scene, than on their medicinal qualities. I therefore determined to turn my morning walks towards it, and seek for health from the nymph of the fountain, partaking of the beverage offered to the tenants of the shade.

Chance likewise led me to discover a new pleasure equally beneficial to my health. I wished to avail myself of my vicinity to the sea and bathe; but it was not possible near the town; there was no convenience. The young woman whom I mentioned to you proposed rowing me across the water amongst the rocks; but as she was pregnant, I insisted on taking one of the oars, and learning to row. It was not difficult, and I do not know a pleasanter exercise. I soon became expert, and my train of thinking kept time, as it were, with the oars, or I suffered the boat to be carried along by the current, indulging a pleasing forgetfulness or fallacious hopes.

The Enormity and Power of Nature

From *The Last Secrets of the Silk Road*, 2000

Alexandra Tolstoy (1973–)

Kyrgyzstan was even more spectacular than we had expected. I have always regarded borders as fairly intangible concepts, but crossing the one between Uzbekistan and Kyrgyzstan dissolved all my preconceptions. As soon as we entered Kyrgyzstan, faces, climate and terrain changed instantly. Green fields, thickly covered with wild flowers, stretched out in front of us to the mountains running across the distant horizon, with their jagged edges silhouetted against the clear blue sky. Out of these mountains which were several layers deep, rose a snow-capped chain that seemed almost removed from the rest. This crest glittered in the sun like a crown on those sternly majestic peaks. Even at such a great distance their immensity overwhelmed us. Suddenly I felt the enormity and power of nature. Everything was bright and vibrant and we seemed to be viewing the world with a new vision that gave each object more definition and depth than before: the icily clear river that gushed through its banks with such vigour and the little droplets of sparkling water that appeared to dance on the surface; the luxuriant grass and the sea of vivid flowers; the people themselves, so fresh and healthy looking, with their rosy cheeks and dark hair. Here was a beauty more infinite than anything I had seen before in my life.

29 May

Eternal London Haunts Us Still

From *Rhymes on the Road: Extracted From the Journal of a Travelling Member of the Pococurante Society, 1819*

Thomas Moore (1779–1852)

Extract IX, lines 1–18

And is there then no earthly place
   Where we can rest, in dream Elysian
Without some cursed, round English face,
   Popping up near, to break the vision?

'Mid northern lakes, 'mid southern vines,
   Unholy cits we're doomed to meet;
Nor highest Alps nor Apennines
   Are sacred from Threadneedle-street!

If up the Simplon's path we wind,
Fancying we leave this world behind,
Such pleasant sounds salute one's ear
As – 'Baddish news from 'Change, my dear –

The Funds – (phew, curse this ugly hill!)
Are lowering fast – (what! higher still?) –
And – (zooks, we're mounting up to Heaven!) –
Will soon be down to sixty-seven.'

Go where we may – rest where we will,
Eternal London haunts us still.

The Promenade

From *Old Calabria, 1915*

Norman Douglas (1868–1952)

The Belvedere is not my promenade:

My promenade lies yonder, on the other side of the valley, where the grave old Suabian castle sits on its emerald slope. It does not frown; it reposes firmly, with an air of tranquil and assured domination; 'it has found its place,' as an Italian observed to me. Long before Frederick Barbarossa made it the centre of his southern dominions, long before the Romans had their fortress on the site, this eminence must have been regarded as the key of Apulia. All round the outside of those turreted walls (they are nearly a mile in circumference; the enclosure, they say, held sixty thousand people) there runs a level space. This is my promenade, at all hours of the day. Falcons are fluttering with wild cries overhead; down below, a long unimpeded vista of velvety green, flecked by a few trees and sullen streamlets and white farmhouses – the whole vision framed in a ring of distant Apennines. The volcanic cone of Mount Vulture, land of Horace, can be detected on clear days; it tempts me to explore those regions. But eastward rises up the promontory of Mount Gargano, and on the summit of its nearest hill one perceives a cheerful building, some village or convent, that beckons imperiously across the intervening lowlands.

31 May

JUNE

The Great Wall Was Visible

Setting Out

From *As I Walked Out One Midsummer Morning, 1969*

Laurie Lee (1914–1997)

It was a bright Sunday morning in early June, the right time to be leaving home. My three sisters and a brother had already gone before me; two other brothers had yet to make up their minds. They were still sleeping that morning, but my mother had got up early and cooked me a heavy breakfast, had stood wordlessly while I ate it, her hand on my chair, and had then helped me pack up my few belongings. There had been no fuss, no appeals, no attempt at advice or persuasion, only a long and searching look. Then, with my bags on my back, I'd gone out into the early sunshine and climbed through the long wet grass to the road.

It was 1934. I was nineteen years old, still soft at the edges, but with a confident belief in good fortune. I carried a small rolled-up tent, a violin in a blanket, a change of clothes, a tin of treacle biscuits, and some cheese. I was excited, vain-glorious, knowing I had far to go; but not, as yet, how far. As I left home that morning and walked away from the sleeping village, it never occurred to me that others had done this before me.

Oases

From *On Central Asian Tracks, 1933* | Sir Marc Aurel Stein (1862–1943)

The cultivated ground within the Tarim basin could never have borne
more than an extremely slight proportion to the extent of absolute
desert it comprises. As the map shows, the green oases of the basin
appear like mere specks and splashes on the big canvas of yellow
and light brown which marks the desert. The aridity of the climate
accounts for the striking uniformity in physical conditions which
prevails throughout these oases. Whatever their position or size,
the traveller sees everywhere the same fields of wheat, maize
or cotton slightly terraced for irrigation; the same winding lanes lined
with white poplars and willows; the same little arbours or orchards
inviting him with their shade and their plentiful produce
of European fruits.

2 June

Dream-Land

Edgar Allan Poe (1809–1849)

Verses 1, 2

By a route obscure and lonely,
Haunted by ill angels only,
Where an Eidolon, named NIGHT,
On a black throne reigns upright,
I have reached these lands but newly
From an ultimate dim Thule –
From a wild weird clime that lieth, sublime,
Out of SPACE – Out of TIME.

Bottomless vales and boundless floods,
And chasms, and caves, and Titan woods,
With forms that no man can discover
For the tears that drip all over;
Mountains toppling evermore
Into seas without a shore;
Seas that restlessly aspire,
Surging, unto skies of fire;
Lakes that endlessly outspread
Their lone waters – lone and dead, –
Their still waters – still and chilly
With the snows of the lolling lily.

Returning to Nigeria

From *Looking for Transwonderland: Travels in Nigeria, 2012*

Noo Saro-Wiwa (1976–)

Once upon a time, Lagos was a placid cluster of islands and creeks
separated from the Atlantic by lagoons, where local men caught fish,
the cry of white ibis could be heard and snakes shimmied among
the bushes. By the fifteenth century, the area had become a busy
slave port. Under British colonial rule it became Nigeria's economic
and political capital. The grasses, wild birds and trees were quickly
devoured by urbanization, its wild metastasis cluttering the cityscape
so densely that it seems to have made a crater that has sent the rest
of the country tumbling into it. Nobody knows how many people
live in Lagos; it could be 10 million, it could be 17 million – no
one is counting the teams of street urchins and shanty dwellers, or
the illegal buildings erected under the distracted eyes of previous
governments.

Although populated by every Nigerian ethnicity, Lagos is a city
of the Yoruba, the dominant ethnic group in the south-west. Their
melodic lingua franca sounded in the streets around me, as foreign to
my ears as any language from Cameroon or Ghana. I had arrived in
a country I'd never lived in, and a city I'd visited only briefly twice
before, among a thoroughly foreign-sounding people. It was the
most alienating of homecomings. I might as well have arrived
in the Congo.

Driving to Minsk

From *Among the Russians, 1983* | Colin Thubron (1939–)

I was conscious above all of the stunned desolation which seems to permeate these plains. It has to do, I think, less with their actual poverty – sandy soil, poor drainage – than with the inarticulate vastness of which they form a part. Without the nearness of towns or the presence of hills, the sky takes on a terrible passive force. Stand anywhere here, and three-quarters of your field of vision is engulfed by it, adding a pitiless immensity to the size of the land. The sun and clouds hang permanent and immobile in its blue. They curve above you like a Tiepolo ceiling. Everything beneath is exposed. The weather itself assumes a threatening, total quality, so that the earth can momentarily wither under a flagellating sun, and rain burst like a cataclysm.

Above all, people – their houses, traffic, cattle – grow pitifully incidental. The villages I passed generally stood far off the road – wooden cottages with asbestos or tin roofs pitched steep against the snow. They were small, abstract – a civilization stretched puny in the fields, like a language I didn't know. Its people, it seemed, were not enclosed and nurtured, made private or different by the folds of valleys or mountains. They were figures in a landscape, living under the naked sky in the glare of infinity.

Approaching Manhattan

From *The Great Gatsby, 1925* | F. Scott Fitzgerald (1896–1940)

Over the great bridge, with the sunlight through the girders making
a constant flicker upon the moving cars, with the city rising up across
the river in white heaps and sugar lumps all built with a wish out of
non-olfactory money. The city seen from the Queensboro Bridge is
always the city seen for the first time, in its first wild promise of all
the mystery and the beauty in the world.

6 June

The Coast

From *The Modern Traveller* | Hilaire Belloc (1870–1953)

Chapter IV

On June the 7th after dark
A young and very hungry shark
    Came climbing up the side.
It ate the Chaplain and the Mate –
But why these incidents relate?
    The public must decide,
That nothing in the voyage out
Was worth their bothering about,
Until we saw the coast, which looks
Exactly as it does in books.

7 June

The Parting of the Red Sea

Exodus, 14:15–22 | The King James Bible, 1611

15: And the Lord said unto Moses, Wherefore criest thou unto me?
Speak unto the children of Israel, that they go forward.

16: But lift thou up thy rod, and stretch out thine hand over the
sea, and divide it: and the children of Israel shall go on dry ground
through the midst of the sea.

17: And I, behold, I will harden the hearts of the Egyptians, and they
shall follow them: and I will get me honour upon Pharaoh, and upon
all his host, upon his chariots, and upon his horsemen.

18: And the Egyptians shall know that I am the Lord, when I have
gotten me honour upon Pharaoh, upon his chariots, and upon his
horsemen.

19: And the angel of God, which went before the camp of Israel,
removed and went behind them; and the pillar of the cloud went
from before their face, and stood behind them.

20: And it came between the camp of the Egyptians and the camp
of Israel, and it was a cloud and darkness to them, but it gave light by
night to these: so that the one came not near the other all the night.

21: And Moses stretched out his hand over the sea; and the
Lord caused the sea to go back by a strong east wind all that night,
and made the sea dry land, and the waters were divided.

22: And the children of Israel went into the midst of the sea upon
the dry ground: and the waters were a wall unto them on their right
hand, and on their left.

A Tramp's Summer Vacation

From *The Autobiography of a Super-Tramp, 1908*

W. H. Davies (1871–1940)

We were determined to be in the fashion, and to visit the various delightful watering places on Long Island Sound. Of course it would be necessary to combine business with pleasure, and pursue our calling as beggars. With the exception of begging our food, which would not be difficult, seeing that the boarding houses were full, and that large quantities of good stuff were being made, there was no reason why we should not get as much enjoyment out of life as the summer visitors. We would share with them the same sun and breeze; we could dip in the surf at our own pleasure, and during the heat of the day we could stretch our limbs in the green shade, or in the shadow of some large rock that overlooked the Sound.

The Wall

From A Ride Along the Great Wall, 1987

Robin Hanbury-Tenison (1936–)

Now the Great Wall was visible most of the time on our right, sometimes only a mile or two away. It was exciting to see how much of it was still there. Although totally unrestored and neglected since the end of the Ming dynasty in the sixteenth century it seemed to be virtually intact. Grass and weeds grew between the building blocks and the watch towers and crenellations had crumbled, but it was still a massive and awe-inspiring place. Once we were able to count twenty-seven watch towers on the horizon where a great line of mountains stretched away into the distance. At other times they seemed to ring the plains around. There the Wall came right down to our level before rising up into the hills again and disappearing.

10 June

A Baroness in Search of a Fortune

From *The Europeans, 1878* | Henry James (1843–1916)

The sunset was superb; they stopped to look at it; Felix declared that
he had never seen such a gorgeous mixture of colors. The Baroness
also thought it splendid; and she was perhaps the more easily pleased
from the fact that while she stood there she was conscious of much
admiring observation on the part of various nice-looking people who
passed that way, and to whom a distinguished, strikingly-dressed
woman with a foreign air, exclaiming upon the beauties of nature on
a Boston street corner in the French tongue, could not be an object
of indifference. Eugenia's spirits rose. She surrendered herself to a
certain tranquil gaiety. If she had come to seek her fortune, it seemed
to her that her fortune would be easy to find. There was a promise of
it in the gorgeous purity of the western sky; there was an intimation
in the mild, unimpertinent gaze of the passers of a certain natural
facility in things.

A Fairy Scene

From *The Heart of a Continent, 1896*

Francis Younghusband (1863–1942)

At last, just as the sun set, we reached the glacier at the foot of the
pass. We were in safety once more. The tension was over, and the
last and greatest obstacle in my journey had been surmounted.
Those moments when I stood at the foot of the pass are long to be
remembered by me – moments of intense relief, and of deep gratitude
for the success that had been granted. Such feelings as mine were
now cannot be described in words, but they are known to every one
who has had his heart set on one great object and has accomplished
it. I took one last look at the pass, never before or since seen by a
European, and then we started away down the glacier to find some
bare spot on which to lay our rugs and rest.

The sun had now set, but, fortunately for us, there was an
abundance of light, and the night was marvellously beautiful, so
that, tired as I was, I could not but be impressed by it. The moon
was nearly full, the sky without a cloud, and in the amphitheatre
of snowy mountains and among the icy seracs of the glacier, not
one speck of anything but the purest white was visible. The air at
these altitudes, away from dust and with no misty vapour in it, was
absolutely clear, and the soft silvery rays of the moon struck down
upon the glistening mountains in unsullied radiance. The whole
effect was of some enchanting fairy scene; and the sternness of the
mountains was slowly softened down till lost, and their beauty in its
purest form alone remained.

12 June

If Once You Have Slept on an Island

Rachel Field (1894–1942)

If once you have slept on an island
    You'll never be quite the same;
You may look as you looked the day before
    And go by the same old name,

You may bustle about in street and shop
    You may sit at home and sew,
But you'll see blue water and wheeling gulls
    Wherever your feet may go.

You may chat with the neighbors of this and that
    And close to your fire keep,
But you'll hear ship whistle and lighthouse bell
    And tides beat through your sleep.

Oh! you won't know why and you can't say how
    Such a change upon you came,
But once you have slept on an island,
    You'll never be quite the same!

The Journey Home

From *A House of Gentlefolk, 1859* | Ivan Turgenev (1818–1883)

Translated by Constance Garnett (1861–1946)

Four days later, he set off for home. His coach rolled quickly along the soft cross-road. There had been no rain for a fortnight; a fine milky mist was diffused in the air and hung over the distant woods; a smell of burning came from it. A multitude of darkish clouds with blurred edges were creeping across the pale blue sky; a fairly strong breeze blew a dry and steady gale, without dispelling the heat. Leaning back with his head on the cushion and his arms crossed on his breast, Lavretsky watched the furrowed fields unfolding like a fan before him, the willow bushes as they slowly came into sight, and the dull ravens and rooks, who looked sidelong with stupid suspicion at the approaching carriage, the long ditches, overgrown with mugwort, wormwood, and mountain ash; and as he watched the fresh fertile wilderness and solitude of this steppe country, the greenness, the long slopes, and valleys with stunted oak bushes, the grey villages, and scant birch trees, – the whole Russian landscape, so long unseen by him, stirred emotion at once pleasant, sweet and almost painful in his heart, and he felt weighed down by a kind of pleasant oppression. Slowly his thoughts wandered; their outlines were as vague and indistinct as the outlines of the clouds which seemed to be wandering at random overhead.

Preparations and Escape

From *The Adventures of Huckleberry Finn, 1884*

Mark Twain (1835–1910)

I took the sack of corn meal and took it to where the canoe was hid,
and shoved the vines and branches apart and put it in; then I done
the same with the side of bacon; then the whisky-jug. I took all
the coffee and sugar there was, and all the ammunition; I took the
wadding; I took the bucket and gourd; I took a dipper and a tin cup,
and my old saw and two blankets, and the skillet and the coffee-pot.
I took fish-lines and matches and other things – everything that was
worth a cent. I cleaned out the place.

. . . .

I didn't lose no time. The next minute I was a-spinning down stream
soft but quick in the shade of the bank. I made two mile and a half,
and then struck out a quarter of a mile or more towards the middle
of the river, because pretty soon I would be passing the ferry
landing, and people might see me and hail me. I got out amongst
the driftwood, and then laid down in the bottom of the canoe and
let her float.

Travel by the Loire

From *Castles and Chateaux of Old Touraine and the Loire Country, 1906* | Francis Miltoun (1871–1943) and Blanche McManus (1869–1935)

From Blois to Angers, on the right bank, extends a long dike which carries the roadway beside the river for a couple of hundred kilometres. This is one of the charms of travel by the Loire. The only thing usually seen on the bosom of the river, save an occasional fishing punt, is one of those great flat-bottomed ferry-boats, with a square sail hung on a yard amidships, such as Turner always made an accompaniment to his Loire pictures, for conditions of traffic on the river have not greatly changed.

Whenever one sees a barge or a boat worthy of classification with those one finds on the rivers of the east or north, or on the great canals, it is only about a quarter of the usual size; so, in spite of its great navigable length, the waterway of the Loire is to be considered more as a picturesque and healthful element of the landscape than as a commercial proposition.

Tents

From *Travels with a Tangerine: A Journey in the Footnotes of Ibn Battutah*, 2001 | Tim Mackintosh-Smith (1961–)

When IB [Ibn Battutah] arrived in Birgi, 'the Sultan was passing the summer on a mountain thereabouts on account of the great heat. We climbed up to the mountain by a road that had been hewn in its side, and reached his camp just before noon. There we alighted, by a stream of water shaded by walnut trees.

'There is IB's road,' Yalçin said, pointing to a track terraced into the flank of the mountain. It was the following morning, and we were looking up at the massif of Bozdağ squatting over the town on its great sunburnt hunkers.

IB was not a happy camper; he soon grew restless in Sultan Muhammad's summer retreat. Still, he carefully described his accommodation, 'a tent which is called by them a kharquh, made of wooden laths put together in the form of a cupola and covered with pieces of felt; the upper part can be opened to admit light and air'. The design is old enough to appear in Aeschylus, whose Scythians 'dwell in latticed huts high-poised on easy wheels' – a reference to the mobile version of the yurt that IB saw later in the land of the Golden Horde. Formerly this mini geodesic dome was found from Anatolia to Manchuria. Now, although the Turks themselves have abandoned these round tents, they still survive elsewhere in Asia (and have recently crossed the Bering Strait to Oregon where, as New Age housing, the teepee is passé.

. . . .

I was surprised to find Bozdağ a substantial settlement of concrete houses and tea-gardens. 'The rich people in Birgi and Ödemiş come here for the summer,' Yalçin explained, 'just like the Sultan. Only they have villas now, not tents.' IB, the unhappy camper, would have approved.

A Sixteenth-century Anthology

From *The Principal Navigations, Voyages, Traffiques and Discoveries of the English Nation, 1598–1600*

Richard Hakluyt (1552/3–1616)

Preface to the second edition, 1598

Into what dangers and difficulties they plunged themselves, I tremble to recount. For first they were to expose themselves unto the rigour of the stern and uncouth northern seas, then they were to sail by the ragged and perilous coast of Norway, to frequent the uncharted shores of Finmark, to double the dreadful and misty North Cape, and as it were to open an unlock the sevenfold mouth of Dvina. Unto what drifts of snow and mountains of ice even in June, July, and August, unto what hideous over-falls, uncertain currents, dark mists and fogs, and divers other fearful inconveniences they were subject and in danger of, I wish you rather learn out of the voyages of Sir Hugh Willoughby, Stephen Burrough, Arthur Pet and the rest.

. . . .

But no man should imagine that our foreign trades of merchandise have been comprised within some few years, there he may plainly see in an ancient testimony translated out of the Saxon Tongue, how our merchants were often wont for traffic's sake to cross the wide seas.

Spanish Scenery

From *Tales of the Alhambra, 1832* | Washington Irving (1783–1859)

Many are apt to picture Spain to their imaginations as a soft southern region, decked out with the luxuriant charms of voluptuous Italy. On the contrary, though there are exceptions in some of the maritime provinces, yet, for the greater part, it is a stern, melancholy country, with rugged mountains, and long sweeping plains, destitute of trees, and indescribably silent and lonesome, partaking of the savage and solitary character of Africa. What adds to this silence and loneliness, is the absence of singing-birds, a natural consequence of the want of groves and hedges. The vulture and the eagle are seen wheeling about the mountain-cliffs, and soaring over the plains, and groups of shy bustards stalk about the heaths; but the myriads of smaller birds, which animate the whole face of other countries, are met with in but few provinces in Spain, and in those chiefly among the orchards and gardens which surround the habitations of man.

. . . .

But though a great part of Spain is deficient in the garniture of groves and forests, and the softer charms of ornamental cultivation, yet its scenery is noble in its severity and in unison with the attributes of its people; and I think that I better understand the proud, hardy, frugal, and abstemious Spaniard, his manly defiance of hardships, and contempt of effeminate indulgences, since I have seen the country he inhabits.

An Irresistible Challenge

From *Danziger's Travels: Beyond Forbidden Frontiers, 1987*

Nick Danziger (1958–)

As dawn filtered into the Spartan bus station hall, so the two mouse-hole sized kiosks opened to sell tickets underneath an enormous map of the province, showing the bus-routes crossing it. Xinjiang, the size of Iran, represents a sixth of the total area of China, and yet it contains only one per cent of the total population. At its centre lies the TaklaMakan, one of the world's largest deserts, 900 kilometres in length and nearly 500 kilometres wide. Surrounded to the north, west and south by high mountains, and to the east by the marshy salt wastes of Lop Nur, China's nuclear testing ground, the TaklaMakan is still one of the remotest areas on earth. Xinjiang boasts some of the world's tallest mountains, including K2, and the world's second lowest basin – the Turfan Depression 154 metres below sea level. Similar to the extremes of height and depth in topography are the extremes of temperature. Winter lows can descend to -30 degrees Celsius, and summer highs can reach 50 degrees. As if this wasn't forbidding enough, the desert is swept by the *boran* sand and pebble storm which has been known to bury whole caravans, and which can reach speeds of 180 kph. The TaklaMakan presented the kind of challenge I simply can't resist.

My Midsummer Reading

Most lists of recommended reading come at the end of books. This list comes in the middle, although there is, confusingly, another list at the end of the book. This list, I hope, comes in time for summer holidays and long days with time for reading. Readers working their way through this anthology chronologically, or probably even those dipping in at random, will have quickly realized that I am drawn to certain destinations, in literature if not reality. Also that I am not in search of absolute truths; to a greater or lesser extent, most people who write about places add a little or a lot of themselves to their descriptions. I am perfectly happy with this.

As a child I spent hours lying on the lawn or in the attic, with my nose in a book. As I grew older I continued the habit, mostly from an arm- or deck-chair, indulging my travel fantasies in the pages of a book. According to my mood, my two most frequent fantasies involved moving abroad, specifically to Venice or somewhere in Italy, Paris or rural France, or travelling in search of adventure, specifically taking to the high seas in a galleon or crossing the wilds of Central Asia in a vintage car. Neither was ever going to happen; I loved my home too much, but the following books were the ones which fuelled these fantasies. A mix of old and new, I have reread some so often that I am almost word perfect.

Paris
T. E. Carhart, *The Piano Shop on the Left Bank*, 2000
Edmund White, *The Flâneur: A Stroll through the Paradoxes of Paris*, 2001

Rural France

Monty Don, *The Road to Le Tholonet*, 2013

Richard Goodman, *French Dirt: The Story of a Garden in the South of France*, 1991

Dirk Bogarde, *An Orderly Man*, 1983

Venice

Italo Calvino, *Invisible Cities*, 1972

J. G. Links, *Venice for Pleasure*, 1966, 1973, 1979, 1984

Donna Leon, *Death at La Fenice* (and following stories in the Commissario Brunetti series), 1992 onwards

Cees Nooteboom, *Venice*, 2019

Elsewhere in Italy

Elizabeth Bowen, *A Time in Rome*, 1959

Hisham Matar, *A Month in Siena*, 2019

Eric Newby, *Love and War in the Apennines*, 1971 and *A Small Place in Italy*, 1994

The High Seas

Patrick O'Brian, *Master and Commander* (and following novels in the Aubrey–Maturin series), 1971–2004

Peking to Paris Car Rally

Luigi Barzini, *Peking to Paris*, 1907

Cassia St Clair, *Race to the Future*, 2023

Occasionally, I think of travelling, by bicycle, car, train, ship, aeroplane or foot. As well as the books in this anthology, the following allow me to roam far and wide around the world while remaining firmly at home.

Josie Dew, *The Wind in my Wheels*, 1992

Jason Elliot, *An Unexpected Light*, 1999

Erika Fatland, *High*, 2022

Ben Fogle, *Up*, 2018

Pico Iyer, *The Global Soul*, 2000

Nicholas Jubber, *Epic Continent*, 2019

Ryszard Kapuściński, *Travels with Herodotus*, 2007

Fitzroy MacLean, *Eastern Approaches*, 1949

Rory MacLean, *Magic Bus*, 2006

Matthew Parris, *Inca-Kola*, 1990

Jonathan Raban, *Coasting*, 1986

Monisha Rajesh, *Around the World in 80 Trains*, 2019

Edward Ayearst Reeves, *Royal Geographic Society: Hints to Travellers*, 2 volumes, 1935

Lisa St Aubin de Terán, *The Slow Train to Milan*, 1983

Tiziano Terzani, *A Fortune-teller Told Me*, 1997

Sara Wheeler, *Mud and Stars*, 2019

The View From a Train in China

From *Maiden Voyage, 1943* | Denton Welch (1915–1948)

I sat looking out of the window at the eternal hills and plains and cities of dried mud. Everything was the same, tawny, earth-brown. Even the city walls were of baked-gold mud which made them look imitation, like the scenery at a searchlight tattoo.

Fields of poppies raged against the universal mud colour. They were not only the scarlet that we see in English cornfields, but pink, white, mauve, crimson and deep, dried-blood purple. They were as large as garden flowers.

'What are those flowers for?' I asked Mr Butler.

'For opium, of course,' he answered.

'But they're not allowed to sell opium now, I'm told. How can they still grow it openly like this?'

'The art of turning a blind eye is practiced with even greater virtuosity in the East than in the West.' He smiled as if he had said something very neat and witty.

The Road to Dover

From *Travels Through France and Italy, 1766*

Tobias Smollett (1721–1771)

Letter I

Boulogne sur mer, June 23, 1763

A man who travels with a family of five persons, must lay his account with a number of mortifications; and some of these I have already happily overcome. Though I was well acquainted with the road to Dover, and made allowances accordingly, I could not help being chagrined at the bad accommodation and impudent imposition to which I was exposed. These I found the more disagreeable, as we were detained a day extraordinary on the road, in consequence of my wife's being indisposed.

I need not tell you this is the worst road in England with respect to the conveniences of travelling, and must certainly impress foreigners with an unfavourable opinion of the nation in general. The chambers are in general cold and comfortless, the beds paultry, the cookery execrable, the wine poison, the attendance bad, the publicans insolent, and the bills extortion; there is not a drop of tolerable malt liquor to be had from London to Dover.

A Yearly Holiday

From *Siren Land, 1911* | Norman Douglas (1868–1952)

The advice of a Flemish gentleman whom I met, in bygone years,
at Casamicciola:

Like most of his countrymen, mynheer had little *chiaro-scuro* in his
composition; he was prone to call a spade, a spade; but his 'rational
view of life,' as he preferred to define it, was transfigured and
irradiated by a childlike love of nature. 'Where there is no landscape,'
he used to say, 'there I sit (i.e. drink) without pleasure. Only beasts
sit indoors.' Every morning he went in search of new farm-houses
in which to *sit* during the afternoon and evening. And every night,
with tremendous din, he was carried to bed. He never apologised
for this disturbance; it was his yearly holiday, he explained. He must
have possessed an enviable digestion, for he was up with the lark and
I used to hear him at his toilette, singing strange ditties of Meuse
or Scheldt. Breakfast over, he would sally forth on his daily quest,
thirsty and sentimental as ever. One day, I remember, he discovered
a cottage more seductive than all the rest – 'with a view over Vesuvius
and the coastline – a view, I assure you, of entrancing loveliness!'
That evening he never came home at all.

Adlestrop

Edward Thomas (1878–1917)

Yes. I remember Adlestrop –
The name, because one afternoon
Of heat the express-train drew up there
Unwontedly. It was late June.

The steam hissed. Someone cleared his throat.
No one left and no one came
On the bare platform. What I saw
Was Adlestrop – only the name

And willows, willow-herb, and grass,
And meadowsweet, and haycocks dry,
No whit less still and lonely fair
Than the high cloudlets in the sky.

And for that minute a blackbird sang
Close by, and round him, mistier,
Farther and farther, all the birds
Of Oxfordshire and Gloucestershire.

Old Cities

From *Exploration Fawcett, 1953*

Col. P. H. Fawcett (1867–1925: disappeared, probably on the Culiseú river in Mato Grosso, western Brazil)

The existence of the old cities I do not for a moment doubt. How could I? I myself have seen a portion of one of them – and that is why I observed that it was imperative for me to go again. The remains seemed to be those of an outpost of one of the bigger cities, which I am convinced is to be found, together with others, if a properly organized search is carried out. Unfortunately I cannot induce scientific men to accept even the supposition that there are traces of an old civilization in Brazil. I have travelled much in places not familiar to other explorers, and the wild Indians have told me again and again of the buildings, the character of the people, and the strange things beyond.

One thing is certain. Between the outer world and the secrets of ancient South America a veil has descended, and the explorer who seeks to penetrate this veil must be prepared to face hardships and dangers that will tax his endurance to the utmost. The chances are that he will not get through, but if he should – if he is lucky enough to run the gauntlet of savages and come out alive – he will be in a position to further our historical knowledge immeasurably.

26 June

The Brazilian Jungle

From *Brazilian Adventure, 1933* | Peter Fleming (1907–1971)

We came into Rio at sunset. This must surely be the best time to do it.

For some hours Brazil had been in sight, a dark-green formidable outline, a coast (as far as we could see) almost unscathed by man. The huge cliffs slanted a little backwards, as if the land had been reined in sharply on the brink of salt perdition. The charging jungle stopped short only at the sea. I get the impression of a sub-continent with imperfect self-control.

Farewell

From *Dover to Munich* | C. S. Calverley (1831–1884)

Farewell, farewell! Before our prow
   Leaps in white foam the noisy channel,
A tourist's cap is on my brow,
   My legs are cased in tourists' flannel:

Around me gasp the invalids –
   The quantity to-night is fearful –
I take a brace or so of weeds,
   And feel (as yet) extremely cheerful.

The night wears on: – my thirst I quench
   With one imperial pint of porter;
Then drop upon a casual bench –
   (The bench is short, but I am shorter) –

Place 'neath my head the *harve-sac*
   Which I have stowed my little all in,
And sleep, though moist about the back,
   Serenely in an old tarpaulin.

In Praise of the *Endeavour*

From *A Voyage to the South Pole and Round the World*, 1777

James Cook (1728–1779)

Upon the whole, I am firmly of opinion, that no ships are so proper for discoveries in distant unknown parts, those constructed as was the *Endeavour*, in which I performed my former voyage. For no ships of any other kind can contain stores and provisions sufficient (in proportion to the necessary number of men), considering the length of time it will be necessary they should last. And, even if another kind of ships could stow a sufficiency, yet, on arriving at the parts for discovery, they would still, from the nature of their construction and be *less fit* for the purpose.

Hence it may be concluded, so little progress had been hitherto made in discoveries in the Southern Hemisphere. For all ships which attempted it before the *Endeavour*, were unfit for it; although the officers employed in them had done the utmost in their power.

It was upon these considerations that the *Endeavour* was chosen for that voyage. It was to these properties in her, that those on board owed their preservation; and hence we enabled to prosecute discoveries in these seas so much longer than any other ship ever did; or could do. And, although discovery was not the first object of that voyage, I could venture to traverse a far greater space of sea, till then unnavigated, to discover tracks of country in high and low South latitudes, and to persevere longer in exploring and surveying more correctly the extensive coasts of those new-discovered countries, than any former Navigator, perhaps, had done during one voyage.

Deceived

From *A Narrative of the Life and Travels of Mrs. Nancy Prince, 1850* | Nancy Prince (1799–after 1856)

After leaving Jamaica, the vessel was tacked to a south–west course. I asked the Captain what this meant. He said he must take the current, as there was no wind. Without any ceremony, I told him it was not the case, and told the passengers that he had deceived us. There were two English men that were born on the island, that had never been on the water; before the third day passed, they asked the Captain why they had not seen Hayti. He told them they passed when they were asleep. I told them it was not true, he was steering south south–west. The passengers in the steerage got alarmed, and every one was asking the Captain what this meant. The ninth day we made land. 'By –,' said the Captain, 'this is Key West; come, passengers, let us have a vote to run over the neck, and I will go ashore and bring aboard fruit and turtle.' They all agreed but myself. He soon dropped anchor. The officers from the shore came on board and congratulated him on keeping his appointment, thus proving that my suspicions were well founded. The Captain went ashore with these men, and soon came back, called for the passengers, and asked for their vote for him to remain until the next day, saying that he could, by this delay, make five or six hundred dollars, as there had been a vessel wrecked there lately. They all agreed but myself. The vessel was soon at the side of the wharf. In one hour there were twenty slaves at work to unload her; every inducement was made to persuade me to go ashore, or set my feet on the wharf. A law had just been passed there that every free colored person coming there, should be put in custody on their going ashore; there were five colored persons on board; none dared to go ashore, however uncomfortable we might be in the vessel, or however we might desire to refresh ourselves by a change of scene. We remained at Key West four days.

JULY

There, From the Summit, I Saw the City

Bears

From *On Sledge and Horseback to Outcast Siberian Lepers,*
1891 | Kate Marsden (1859–1931)

We mounted again and went on. The usual chattering this time was
exchanged for a dead silence, this being our first bear experience; but
we grew wiser as we proceeded, and substituted noise for silence. We
hurried on, as fast as possible, to get through the miles of forests and
bogs. I found it best not to look about me, because, when
I did so, every large stump of a fallen tree took the shape of a bear.
When my horse stumbled over the roots of a tree, or shied at some
object unseen by me, my heart began to gallop. However, all our
preparations were wasted, for the bear remained conspicuous by his
absence; and, when the danger was passed, we all became very brave
and talkative. We had a few simple devices for scaring away bears as
we rode through the forest later on. The men used to sing and shout
their hardest; bells were placed on some of the horses, and we had
tin boxes half filled with stones in one hand, which we continually
shook, thus making a great clattering noise.

I can just imagine how some brave bear-hunter will laugh in
his sleeve, as he reads this simple mode of keeping off the ferocious
creatures, which had just woke up ravenous from their winter's sleep.
But, you see, we were not hunting for bears, but searching for lepers,
which makes all the difference in the world.

Over the Great Windy Waters

From *Amours de Voyage* | Arthur Hugh Clough (1819–1961)

Canto I

Over the great windy waters, and over the clear-crested summits,
　　Unto the sun and the sky, and unto the perfecter earth,
Come, let us go, – to a land wherein gods of the old time wandered,
　　Where every breath even now changes to ether divine.
Come, let us go; though withal a voice whisper, 'The world that we
live in,
　　Whithersoever we turn, still is the same narrow crib;
'Tis but to prove limitation, and measure a cord, that we travel;
　　Let who would 'scape and be free go to his chamber and think;
'Tis but to change idle fancies for memories wilfully falser;
　　'Tis but to go and have been.' – Come, little bark! let us go.

Fosso di Valle Inversa

From *From Rome to San Marino, 1982* | Oliver Knox (1923–2002)

The valley down into which we now zigzagged is called by the curious name 'Fosso di valle inversa', and it did indeed give us the impression that we were walking uphill through that sultry pre-noon, rather than slowly, very slowly, descending towards the Aniene, tributary of the Tiber. The optical illusion may have been due to the valley narrowing, and its wooded sides becoming steeper as we approached the turreted Castello del Passerano – just as though we were indeed climbing upstream, towards a strongpoint. Perfect ambush country! Easy to imagine the French cavalry reining in at the top of the defile, and the long column trapped. That may well have been Garibaldi's fear as he hastened towards the mountains, even though he was still under cover of darkness as he pressed his army along, riding up and down, in hushed tones exhorting his officers.

What an extraordinary speed he made! It was something his enemies could never get used to. To have left the gates of Rome at eight o'clock and arrived at Tivoli, nearly fifty kilometres distant by this route, by seven the next morning! And this was the main body, for an advance guard of the cavalry road ahead. Our respect for the infantry, our understanding of the need for copious requisitions of boots at every stopping-place, grew as we trudged on, train-cheaters though we had been. Two hours of walking had taken us exactly ten kilometres on, and midday was approaching.

The 4th of July

From *Domestic Manners of the Americans, 1832*

Fanny Trollope (1779–1863)

And now arrived the 4th of July, that greatest of all American
festivals. On the 4th of July, 1776, the declaration of their
independence was signed, at the State-house in Philadelphia.
To me, the dreary coldness and want of enthusiasm in American
manners is one of their greatest defects, and I therefore hailed the
demonstrations of general feeling which this day elicits with real
pleasure. On the 4th of July the hearts of the people seem to awaken
from a three hundred and sixty-four days' sleep; they appear high-
spirited, gay, animated, social, generous, or at least liberal in expense;
and would they but refrain from spitting on that hallowed day,
I should say, that on the 4th of July, at least, they appeared to be an
amiable people. It is true that the women have but little to do with
the pageantry, the splendour, or the gaiety of the day; but, setting
this defect aside, it was indeed a glorious sight to behold a jubilee so
heartfelt as this; and had they not the bad taste and bad feeling to
utter an annual oration, with unvarying abuse of the mother country,
to say nothing of the warlike manifesto called Declaration of
Independence, our gracious king himself might look upon the scene
and say that it was good; nay, even rejoice, that twelve millions of
bustling bodies, at four thousand miles distance from his throne and
his altars, should make their own laws, and drink their own tea, after
the fashion that pleased them best.

The Shift From Traveller to Tourist

From *A Taste for Travel, 1985* | John Julius Norwich (1929–2018)

There's no doubt about it: the easier it becomes to travel, the harder
it is to be a traveller. Half a century ago, any young Englishman
prepared to venture beyond the shores of Western Europe could
lay claim to the title; patience, resourcefulness and a robustness of
digestion were the only qualities he needed. A year or two later he
could return, the pride of his family, the envy of his friends: a trail-
blazer, a hero. Alas, those days are over. Everybody goes everywhere
– or nearly everywhere – buying their air tickets with their credit
cards and being met by airport buses, secure in the knowledge that
their hotel reservations have been confirmed, that the rent-a-car
firm is expecting them, and that it will be perfectly safe to drink the
Coca-cola.

The man who started the rot, I fear, was that disagreeable old
abstainer Thomas Cook, who, already by the middle of the century,
had developed the idea of insulating his clients as far as possible from
the uncouth conditions all too frequently prevailing in foreign parts
by swathing them in a protective cocoon of block bookings, meal
vouchers and – most dangerous of all – temperance. He began indeed
by offering them even more: on the very first excursion that he ever
organized, which took place on Monday, 5 July 1841, the 570 people
intrepid enough to venture – at the cost of one shilling – the ten
miles from Leicester to Loughborough and back enjoyed the services
of a full brass band, to say nothing of tea and buns at Mr Paget's
Park. The age of the tourist had arrived.

Recuerdo

Edna St Vincent Millay (1892–1950)

We were very tired, we were very merry –
We had gone back and forth all night on the ferry.
It was bare and bright, and smelled like a stable –
But we looked into a fire, we leaned across a table,
We lay on a hill-top underneath the moon;
And the whistles kept blowing, and the dawn came soon.

We were very tired, we were very merry –
We had gone back and forth all night on the ferry;
And you ate an apple, and I ate a pear,
From a dozen of each we had bought somewhere;
And the sky went wan, and the wind came cold,
And the sun rose dripping, a bucketful of gold.

We were very tired, we were very merry,
We had gone back and forth all night on the ferry.
We hailed, 'Good morrow, mother!' to a shawl-covered head,
And bought a morning paper, which neither of us read;
And she wept, 'God bless you!' for the apples and pears,
And we gave her all our money but our subway fares.

At Sea Not School

From *A Voyage to the South Pole and Round the World*, 1777

James Cook (1728–1779)

I shall therefore conclude this introductory discourse with desiring
the reader to excuse the inaccuracies of style, which doubtless he will
frequently meet with in the following narrative; and that, when such
occur, he will recollect that it is the production of a man, who has
not had the advantage of much school education, but who has been
constantly at sea from his youth; and though, with the assistance of
a few good friends, he has passed through all the stations belonging
to a seaman, from an apprentice boy in the coal trade, to a Post
Captain in the Royal Navy, he has had no opportunity of cultivating
letters. After this account of myself, the public must not expect from
me the elegance of a fine writer, or the plausibility of a professed
book-maker; but will, I hope, consider me as a plain man, zealously
exerting himself in the service of his Country, and determined to
give the best account he is able of his proceedings.

Plymouth Sound

July 7 1776

All Islanders Love Travelling

From *The Happy Traveller: A Book for Poor Men, 1923*

Rev. Frank Tatchell, Vicar of Midhurst (1906–1935)

Dedicated to young adventurers of the future in the hope that they may have as much FUN out of travelling as I have had.

. . . .

We are often held back from satisfying this inborn craving by thinking it too difficult or too costly a thing for us to attempt – misconceptions which I will try to dispel.

In one of his essays, Cowley says that the getting out of doors is the hardest part of the journey, and it is a man's own fault if he dies without seeing anything of the wonderful world in which he lives. Laziness and a tame surrender to the tyranny of circumstances hold back many of us who would be ideal travellers could we but take the first step. But if your lot does not please you, you can, with determination, change it. Once aware of your bonds, you are on the highroad to freedom, and need not be dissuaded by those who tell you that you must know your own country before venturing abroad. You will have time enough for that when you settle down.

Impressions de Voyage

Oscar Wilde (1854–1900)

The sea was sapphire coloured, and the sky
   Burned like a heated opal through air,
   We hoisted sail; the wind was blowing fair
For the blue lands that to the Eastward lie.
From the steep prow I marked with quickening eye
   Zakynthos, every olive grove and creek,
   Ithaca's cliff, Lycaon's snowy peak,
And all the flower-strewn hills of Arcady.
The flapping of the sail against the mast,
   The ripple of the water on the side,
   The ripple of girls' laughter at the stern,
The only sounds: – when 'gan the West to burn,
   And a red sun upon the seas to ride,
   I stood upon the soil of Greece at last!

A Runaway

From *Michel the Giant: An African in Greenland, 1981*

Tété-Michel Kpomassie (1941–)

Translated by James Kirkup (1918–2009)

It was not enough just to get the idea of going to Greenland. It was important to find out how to get there, to find the country on the map and see its position in relation to Togo, my starting point. Next morning, I returned to the bookshop and asked for a map of the world. The one they showed me was in colours ranging from darkest green to brightest yellow, indicating the characteristic vegetation of each country: equatorial forest, temperate forest, monsoon forest, Mediterranean vegetation, steppe, prairie, wooded savanna. In the midst of this fine, warm range of shades, Greenland appeared with not a touch of inviting colour: only a greyish border, indicating the tundra, traced a grudging line round three-quarters of the country's area; the whole interior was a uniform white. Another book told me its size: 2,175,600 square kilometres, the biggest island in the world. Lying to the north of America, Greenland extended in one enormous mass of ice to the Pole.

It seemed further away from Togo and Africa than I could ever have imagined. Never in all my life would I have enough money to travel there directly! And even supposing my father spared me from returning to the sacred forest, his modest salary as foreman at UNELCO (Union Électrique Coloniale), the Overseas Electric Union, could never pay for the journey. Anyway, he would never let me leave for Greenland at the age of sixteen. So, to carry out my plan, I could only act in secret: I would have to run away from home.

The City

From *The Path to Rome, 1902* | Hilaire Belloc (1870–1953)

As I slept, Rome, Rome still beckoned me, and I woke in a struggling light as though at a voice calling, and slipping out I could not but go on to the end.

The small square paving of the Via Cassia, all even like a palace floor, rang under my steps. The parched banks and strips of dry fields showed through the fog (for its dampness did not cure the arid soil of the Campagna). The sun rose and the vapour lifted. Then, indeed, I peered through the thick air – but still I could see nothing of my goal, only confused folds of brown earth and burnt-up grasses, and farther off rare and un-northern trees.

I passed an old tower of the Middle Ages that was eaten away at its base by time or the quarrying of men; I passed a divergent way on the right where a wooden sign said 'The Triumphal Way,' and I wondered whether it could be the road where ritual had once ordained that triumphs should go. It seemed lonely and lost, and divorced from any approach to sacred hills.

The road fell into a hollow where soldiers were manoeuvring. Even these could not arrest an attention that was fixed upon the approaching revelation. The road climbed a little slope where a branch went off to the left, and where there was a house and an arbour under vines. It was now warm day; trees of great height stood shading the sun; the place had taken on an appearance of wealth and care. The mist had gone before I reached the summit of the rise.

There, from the summit, between the high villa walls on either side – at my very feet I saw the City.

The Prison Ship

From *For the Term of His Natural Life, 1874*

Marcus Clarke (1846–1881)

Save for the man at the wheel and the guard at the quarter-railing, he was alone on the deck. A few birds flew round about the vessel, and seemed to pass under her stern windows only to appear again at her bows. A lazy albatross, with the white water flashing from his wings, rose with a dabbling sound to leeward, and in the place where he had been glided the hideous fin of a silently-swimming shark. The seams of the well-scrubbed deck were sticky with melted pitch, and the brass plate of the compass-case sparkled in the sun like a jewel. There was no breeze, and as the clumsy ship rolled and lurched on the heaving sea, her idle sails flapped against her masts with a regularly recurring noise, and her bowsprit would seem to rise higher with the water's swell, to dip again with a jerk that made each rope tremble and tauten. On the forecastle, some half-dozen soldiers, in all varieties of undress, were playing at cards, smoking, or watching the fishing-lines hanging over the catheads.

So far the appearance of the vessel differed in nowise from that of an ordinary transport. But in the waist a curious sight presented itself. It was as though one had built a cattle-pen there. At the foot of the foremast, and at the quarter-deck, a strong barricade, loop-holed and furnished with doors for ingress and egress, ran across the deck from bulwark to bulwark. Outside this cattle-pen an armed sentry stood on guard; inside, standing, sitting, or walking monotonously, within range of the shining barrels in the arm chest on the poop, were some sixty men and boys, dressed in uniform grey. The men and boys were prisoners of the Crown, and the cattle-pen was their exercise ground. Their prison was down the main hatchway, on the 'tween decks, and the barricade, continued down, made its side walls.

Exultation is the Going

Emily Dickinson (1830–1886)

Exultation is the going
Of an inland soul to sea,
Past the houses – past the headlands –
Into deep Eternity –

Bred as we, among the mountains,
Can the sailor understand
The divine intoxication
Of the first league out from land?

13 July

Newport in Summer

From *The Age of Innocence, 1920* | Edith Wharton (1862–1937)

Archer had tried to persuade May to spend the summer on a remote
island off the coast of Maine (called, appropriately enough,
Mount Desert), where a few hardy Bostonians and Philadelphians
were camping in 'native' cottages, and whence came reports of
enchanting scenery and a wild, almost trapper-like existence amid
woods and waters.

But the Wellands always went to Newport, where they owned one
of the square boxes on the cliffs, and their son-in-law could adduce
no good reason why he and May should not join them there. As Mrs.
Welland rather tartly pointed out, it was hardly worth while for May
to have worn herself out trying on summer clothes in Paris if she was
not to be allowed to wear them; and this argument was of a kind to
which Archer had as yet found no answer.

I Survey the Island

From *Robinson Crusoe, 1719* | Daniel Defoe (1660–1731)

It was on the 15th of July that I began to take a more particular survey of the island itself. I went up the creek first, where, as I hinted, I brought my rafts on shore. I found after I came about two miles up, that the tide did not flow any higher, and that it was no more than a little brook of running water, very fresh and good; but this being the dry season, there was hardly any water in some parts of it – at least not enough to run in any stream, so as it could be perceived. On the banks of this brook I found many pleasant savannahs or meadows, plain, smooth, and covered with grass; and on the rising parts of them, next to the higher grounds, where the water, as might be supposed, never overflowed, I found a great deal of tobacco, green, and growing to a great and very strong stalk. There were divers other plants, which I had no notion of or understanding about, that might, perhaps, have virtues of their own, which I could not find out. I searched for the cassava root, which the Indians, in all that climate, make their bread of, but I could find none. I saw large plants of aloes, but did not understand them. I saw several sugar-canes, but wild, and, for want of cultivation, imperfect. I contented myself with these discoveries for this time, and came back, musing with myself what course I might take to know the virtue and goodness of any of the fruits or plants which I should discover, but could bring it to no conclusion; for, in short, I had made so little observation while I was in the Brazils, that I knew little of the plants in the field; at least, very little that might serve to any purpose now in my distress.

The Port of Algeciras

From *As I Walked Out One Midsummer Morning, 1969*

Laurie Lee (1914–1997)

The Port of Algeciras had a potency and charm which I'd found
nowhere else till then. It was a scruffy little town built round an
open drain and smelling of fruit skins and rotten fish. There were
a few brawling bars and modest brothels; otherwise the chief activity
was smuggling. At most street-corners one would be offered exotic
items of merchandise unavailable anywhere else in Spain – mouldy
chocolate, laddered stockings, damp American cigarettes, leaky
Parkers, and fake Swiss watches.

But for all its disreputable purposes and confidence-trickery,
it seemed a town entirely free of malice, and even the worst of its
crooks were so untrained in malevolence that no one was expected
to take them seriously. In its position as a bridge between Europe
and Morocco, the port could have equalled Marseilles in evil, but its
heart wasn't in it, in spite of the opportunities, and it preferred small
transgressions with lesser rewards.

Algeciras was a clearing-house for odds and ends, and I stayed
there about two weeks.

. . . .

I was half in love with Algeciras and its miniature villainies, and felt
I could have stayed on there indefinitely. But part of my plan at that
time was still to follow the coast round Spain, so I had to leave it and
get on to Málaga.

Umbrellas and Fans

From *A New Voyage Round the World, 1697*

William Dampier (1651–1715)

The *Chinese* have no Hats, Caps, or Turbans; but when they walk abroad, they carry a small Umbrello in their Hands, wherewith they fence their Head from the Sun or the Rain, by holding it over their Heads. If they walk but a little way, they carry only a large Fan made of Paper, or Silk, of the same fashion as those our Ladies have, and many of them are brought over hither; one of these every Man carries in his Hand if he do but cross the Street, skreening his Head with it, if he hath not an Umbrello with him.

Poop-poop

From *The Wind in the Willows, 1908* | Kenneth Grahame (1859–1932)

In an instant (as it seemed) the peaceful scene was changed, and with a blast of wind and a whirl of sound that made them jump for the nearest ditch, it was on them! The 'Poop-poop' rang with a brazen shout in their ears, they had a moment's glimpse of an interior of glittering plate-glass and rich morocco, and the magnificent motor-car, immense, breath-snatching, passionate, with its pilot tense and hugging his wheel, possessed all earth and air for the fraction of a second, flung an enveloping cloud of dust that blinded and enwrapped them utterly, and then dwindled to a speck in the far distance, changed back into a droning bee once more.

. . . .

Toad sat straight down in the middle of the dusty road, his legs stretched out before him, and stared fixedly in the direction of the disappearing motor-car. He breathed short, his face wore a placid, satisfied expression, and at intervals he faintly murmured 'Poop-poop!'

. . . .

'Glorious, stirring sight!' murmured Toad, never offering to move. 'The poetry of motion! The *real* way to travel! The *only* way to travel! Here to-day – in next week to-morrow! Villages skipped, towns and cities jumped - always somebody else's horizon! O bliss! O poop-poop! O my! O my!'

Hatchards Bookshop

From *The Books that Bind, 2018* | Mark Staples (1980–)

Miles of books, a marathon of the mind. If we took all the books and
piled them up vertically you could stand on the top one and spin a
planet. Or you could wrap them horizontally round the world like
train tracks and alight wherever you like.

The First Man on the Moon

20 July, 1969 | Neil Armstrong (1930–), Buzz Aldrin (1930–)

At 10:56 p.m. Eastern Daylight Time. Armstrong is ready to plant the first human foot on another world. With more than half a billion people watching on television, he climbs down the ladder and proclaims: 'That's one small step for a man, one giant leap for mankind.'

Aldrin joins him shortly, and offers a simple but powerful description of the lunar surface: 'magnificent desolation.' They explore the surface for two and a half hours, collecting samples and taking photographs.

They leave behind an American flag, a patch honoring the fallen Apollo 1 crew, and a plaque on one of *Eagle*'s legs. It reads, 'Here men from the planet Earth first set foot upon the moon. July 1969 A.D. We came in peace for all mankind.'

The River Niger

From *Travels in the Interior Districts of Africa, 1799*

Mungo Park (1771–1806)

July 20–21

Just before it was dark we took up our lodging for the night at a small
village, where I procured some victuals for myself and some corn
for my horse, at the moderate price of a button; and was told that
I should see the Niger (which the negroes call Joliba, or the Great
Water) early the next day. The lions are here very numerous; the
gates are shut a little after sunset, and nobody allowed to go out. The
thoughts of seeing the Niger in the morning, and the troublesome
buzzing of mosquitoes, prevented me from shutting my eyes during
the night; and I had saddled my horse, and was in readiness before
daylight, but, on account of the wild beasts, we were obliged to wait
until the people were stirring and the gates opened. This happened
to be a market day at Sego, and the roads were everywhere filled with
people carrying different articles to sell. We passed four large villages,
and at eight o'clock saw the smoke over Sego.

As we approached the town I was fortunate enough to overtake
the fugitive Kaartans, to whose kindness I had been so much
indebted in my journey through Bambarra. They readily agreed
to introduce me to the king; and we rode together through some
marshy ground, where, as I was anxiously looking around for the
river, one of them called out, *Geo affili!* ('See the water!') and, looking
forwards, I saw with infinite pleasure the great object of my mission
– the long-sought-for majestic Niger, glittering in the morning sun,
as broad as the Thames at Westminster, and flowing slowly *to the
eastward*. I hastened to the brink, and having drunk of the water,
lifted up my fervent thanks in prayer to the Great Ruler of all things
for having thus far crowned my endeavours with success.

21 July

A Dream of Fair Women

Alfred, Lord Tennyson (1809–1892)

I

As when a man, that sails in a balloon,
    Downlooking sees the solid shining ground
Stream from beneath him in the broad blue noon,
    Tilth, hamlet, mead and mound:

II

And takes his flags and waves them to the mob,
    That shout below, all faces turned to where
Glows rubylike the far-up crimson globe,
    Filled with a finer air:

III

So, lifted high, the Poet at his will
    Lets the great world flit from him, seeing all,
Higher thro' secret splendours mounting still,
    Self-poised, nor fears to fall,

IV

Hearing apart the echoes of his fame.
    While I spoke thus, the seedsman, memory,
Sowed my deep furrowed thought with many a name,
    Whose glory will not die.

The Route-Finder

From *Ascent of Rum Doodle, 1956* | W. E. Bowman (1911–1985)

Humphrey Jungle: radio expert and route-finder.

After three hectic months of preparation we met in London, on the eve of our departure, for a final review of our plans. Only Jungle, who was to have spoken on the use of the radio gear and his own methods of route-finding, was absent. He rang up to say he had taken the wrong bus and was not quite certain of his whereabouts; but he had just caught sight of the North Star and expected to join us shortly.

. . . .

The telephone bell rang. It was Jungle, who seemed in the best of spirits. He had, he said, definitely identified his whereabouts as Cockfosters. We congratulated him and said we would expect him shortly.

. . . .

At this point Jungle rang again. It was not Cockfosters, he said, but Richmond. He had seen Cockfosters on a bus, but it turned out that the bus was *going* to Cockfosters. Owing to this he had, of course, set off in the wrong direction, but would be with us shortly.

. . . .

At this point a knock was heard on the door. It was a sergeant from the local police station. A policeman in Lewisham had discovered a furtive stranger loitering near the gas works. He had been found in possession of maps and navigating instruments and had been arrested as a spy. He had given his name as Forest and this address as a reference. We gave the necessary assurances and asked the sergeant to transmit a message to the effect that we expected to see Jungle shortly.

The Contrast

From American National Baptist Convention, *Journals and Lectures*, 45–46, 1887 | Mary V. Cook (1863–1945)

How pleasant it is to wander over, and enjoy this beautiful world God has made. Its green meadows, its beautiful fields, its dense forests with wild flowers and rippling streams, its wide expanse of water and lofty mountains all delight us. But while charmed with its beauty, our joy is greater if we can comprehend that it was 'without form and void' and contrast its present beauty with the roughness of its former state.

24 July

An Italian Dream

From *Pictures from Italy, 1846* | Charles Dickens (1812–1870)

I had been travelling, for some days; resting very little in the night, and never in the day. The rapid and unbroken succession of novelties that had passed before me, came back like half-formed dreams; and a crowd of objects wandered in the greatest confusion through my mind, as I travelled on, by a solitary road. At intervals, some one among them would stop, as it were, in its restless flitting to and fro, and enable me to look at it, quite steadily, and behold it in full distinctness. After a few moments, it would dissolve, like a view in a magic-lantern; and while I saw some part of it quite plainly, and some faintly, and some not at all, would show me another of the many places I had lately seen, lingering behind it, and coming through it. This was no sooner visible than, in its turn, it melted into something else.

. . . .

In short, I had that incoherent but delightful jumble in my brain, which travellers are apt to have, and are indolently willing to encourage. Every shake of the coach in which I sat, half dozing in the dark, appeared to jerk some new recollection out of its place, and to jerk some other new recollection into it; and in this state I fell asleep.

Venetian Regattas

From *Venice, 1960* | Jan Morris (1926–2020)

Now and then they have regattas, partly impelled by the power of tradition, partly by the Tourist Office. In many a smoky *trattoria* you will see, carefully preserved behind glass, the trophies and banners of a regatta champion, or even his portrait in oils – it is customary to commission one: and there is still a lingering trace of popular enthusiasm to these races, a faint anthropological echo of folk rivalries and ancestral feuds. Fiercely and intently the competitors, sweat-bands to match their colourful oars, pound down the Grand Canal, or swing around the marker buoy beside the Public Gardens. A raggle-taggle fleet of small craft follows their progress, speedboats and rowing-boats and tumble-down skiffs, half-naked boys in canoes, big market barges, elegant launches, yachts, all tumbling hilariously along beside the gondolas, with their ferry steamers swerving precariously towards the quay, and a fine surge of foam and clatter of engines, as in some nightmare University Boat Race, half-way to a lunatic Putney.

But the best bit of the regatta comes later, in the evening. Then the new champions, pocketing their prize money or grappling with their suckling pig (the traditional fourth prize) are fêted by their fellow-gondoliers: and you will see them, gaily-hatted and singing jovially, parading down the Grand Canal in a large grey barge, with a row of bottles on a neatly spread table, a cheerful impresario playing an accordion, a string of fluttering pennants, and a radiation of fun, *bonhomie* and satisfaction.

26 July

Monasteries in Ladak

From *The Heart of a Continent, 1896*

Francis Younghusband (1863–1942)

Crossing the Zoji-la, the last of the passes on my way from Peking, we left behind us all the wooded beauties of Kashmir, its shady pine forest and bright flowery meadows, and entered that desolate region of barren mountains and unshaded valleys, where the sun beat down upon the unprotected rocks and produced a degree of heat which would never have been expected at altitudes of nine thousand feet and over, and which made still more trying the cold blasts which, when the sun had set, came down from the snow above. We were entering Ladak, an offshoot of Tibet, and the only redeeming feature in the country was the picturesqueness of its monasteries, perched high upon every prominent rock. As regards its natural scenery, it would be difficult to find any more dreary-looking country than Ladak. Its mountains, though lofty, are not grand or rugged, but resemble a monotonous succession of gigantic cinder-heaps. But the Buddhist monasteries, the fluttering prayer-flags, the chortens, and the many other signs of a religion almost totally unrepresented in India, gave the country a charm which just relieved it from utter condemnation.

A House at Florence

From *Aurora Leigh* | Elizabeth Barrett Browning (1806–1861)

Seventh Book, lines 515–541

I found a house, at Florence, on the hill
Of Bellosguardo. 'Tis a tower that keeps
A post of double-observation o'er
The valley of Arno (holding as a hand
The outspread city) straight toward Fiesole
And Mount Morello and the setting sun, –
The Vallombrosan mountains to the right,
Which sunrise fills as full as crystal cups
Wine-filled, and red to the brim because it's red.
No sun could die, nor yet be born, unseen
By dwellers at my villa: morn and eve
Were magnified before us in the pure
Illimitable space and pause of sky,
Intense as angels' garments blanched with God,
Less blue than radiant. From the outer wall
Of the garden, dropped the mystic floating grey
Of olive-trees, (with interruptions green
From maize and vine) until 'twas caught and torn
On that abrupt black line of cypresses
Which signed the way to Florence. Beautiful
The city lay along the ample vale,
Cathedral, tower and palace, piazza and street;
The river trailing like a silver cord
Through all, and curling loosely, both before
And after, over the whole stretch of land
Sown whitely up and down its opposite slopes,
With farms and villas.

William Wordsworth: Guide to the Lakes

From *A Literary Pilgrim in England, 1917*

Edward Thomas (1878–1917)

It is more natural and legitimate to associate Wordsworth with certain parts of England than any other great writer. And for three reasons: he spent the greater portion of his life in one district; he drew much of his scenery and human character from that district and used its place-names very freely in his poems; and both he and his sister left considerable records of his times and places of composition. Moreover, he wrote a guide to the Lakes and a poem that is not quite so useful as a guide-book, but much better.

29 July

A Disposition to be Pleased

From *Guide to the Lakes, 1835* | William Wordsworth (1770–1850)

After all, it is upon the *mind* which a traveller brings along with him that his acquisitions, whether of pleasure or profit, must principally depend. – May I be allowed a few words on this subject?

Nothing is more injurious to genuine feeling than the practice of hastily and ungraciously depreciating the face of one country by comparing it with that of another. True it is 'Qui *bene* distinguit bene *docet*'; yet fastidiousness is a wretched travelling companion; and the best guide to which, in matters of taste we can entrust ourselves, is a disposition to be pleased. For example, if a traveller be among the Alps, let him surrender up his mind to the fury of the gigantic torrents, and take delight in the contemplation of their almost irresistible violence, without complaining of the monotony of their foaming course, or being disgusted with the muddiness of the water – apparent even where it is violently agitated. In Cumberland and Westmorland, let not the comparative weakness of the streams prevent him from sympathising with such impetuosity as they possess; and, making the most of the present objects, let him, as he justly may do, observe with admiration the unrivalled brilliancy of the water, and that variety of motion, mood, and character, that arises out of the want of those resources by which the power of the streams in the Alps is supported.

Rafts and Interpreters

From *A Tramp Abroad, 1880* | Mark Twain (1835–1910)

While I was looking down upon the rafts that morning in
Heilbronn, the dare-devil spirit of adventure came suddenly upon
me, and I said to my comrades, –

'*I* am going to Heidelberg on a raft. Will you venture with me?'

Their faces paled a little, but they assented with as good a grace
as they could. Harris wanted to cable his mother, – thought it his
duty to do that, as he was all she had in this world, – so, while he
attended to this, I went down to the longest and finest raft and
hailed the captain with a hearty 'Ahoy, shipmate!' which put us upon
pleasant terms at once, and we entered upon business. I said we were
on a pedestrian tour to Heidelberg, and would like to take passage
with him. I said this partly through young Z, who spoke German
very well, and partly through Mr. X, who spoke it peculiarly. I can
understand German as well as the maniac that invented it, but I *talk*
it best through an interpreter.

The captain hitched up his trowsers, then shifted his quid
thoughtfully. Presently he said just what I was expecting he would
say, – that he had no license to carry passengers, and therefore was
afraid the law would be after him in case the matter got noised about
or any accident happened. So I *chartered* the raft and the crew and
took all the responsibilities on myself.

With a rattling song the starboard watch bent to their work and
hove the cable short, then got the anchor home, and our bark moved
off with a stately stride, and soon was bowling along at about two
knots an hour.

AUGUST

Turbid Turquoise Skies

The Pull of the Desert

From *Arabian Sands, 1959* | Wilfred Thesiger (1910–2003)

1 August

I first realized the hold the desert had upon me when travelling in the Hajaz mountains in the summer of 1946. A few months earlier I had been down on the edge of the Empty Quarter. For a while I had lived with the Bedu a hard and merciless life, during which I was always hungry and usually thirsty. My companions had been accustomed to this life since birth, but I had been racked by the weariness of long marches through wind-whipped dunes, or across plains where monotony was emphasized by the mirages shimmering through the heat. There was always the fear of raiding parties to keep us alert and tense, even when we were dazed by lack of sleep. Always our rifles were in our hands and our eyes searching the horizon. Hunger, thirst, heat, and cold: I had tasted them in full during those six months, and had endured the strain of living among an alien people who made no allowance for weakness. Often, in weariness of body and spirit, I had longed to get away.

. . . .

But I knew instinctively that it was the very hardness of life in the desert which drew me back there – it was the same pull that takes men back to the polar ice, to high mountains, and to the sea.

Where to Go?

From *The Phoenix and the Carpet, 1904* | E. Nesbit (1858–1924)

'I vote we let the Phoenix decide,' said Robert, at last. So they stroked it till it woke.

'We want to go somewhere abroad,' they said, 'and we can't make up our minds where.'

'Let the carpet make up *its* mind, if it has one,' said the Phoenix. 'Just say you wish to go abroad.'

So they did; and the next moment the world seemed to spin upside down, and when it was right way up again and they were ungiddy enough to look about them, they were out of doors.

Out of doors – this is a feeble way to express where they were. They were out of – out of the earth, or off it. In fact, they were floating steadily, safely, splendidly, in the crisp clear air, with the pale bright blue of the sky above them, and far down below the pale bright sun-diamonded waves of the sea. The carpet had stiffened itself somehow, so that it was square and firm like a raft, and it steered itself so beautifully and kept on its way so flat and fearless that no one was at all afraid of tumbling off. In front of them lay land.

XXVIII

From *The Black Riders* | Stephen Crane (1871–1900)

'Truth,' said a traveller,
'Is a rock, a mighty fortress;
Often have I been to it,
Even to its highest tower,
From whence the world looks black.'

'Truth,' said a traveller,
'Is a breath, a wind,
A shadow, a phantom;
Long have I pursued it,
But never have I touched
The hem of its garment.'

And I believed the second traveller;
For truth was to me
A breath, a wind,
A shadow, a phantom,
And never had I touched
The hem of its garment.

Okadas

From *Looking for Transwonderland: Travels in Nigeria, 2012*

Noo Saro-Wiwa (1976–)

Okadas are the scourge of Nigeria's roads. These Chinese-made, 100CC motorcycles buzz around the streets in their thousands like giant flies. They're popular because they're cheap and fast and can weave through the traffic go-slows that consume such a huge proportion of people's days. They barely existed as a form of transport in the 1980s, but when public transport fails, and the increasingly teeming roads aren't expanded, two wheels become the best option.

. . . .

I never intended to ride one of these things, but time was running out. Just one day in Lagos had taught me to blend into my surroundings by wearing a streetwise frown and barking my request. The okada man initially refused to take me to the bus stop I wanted ('It's too far'), but when I offered to double the fare he ordered me to 'Sit down'. The two of us sped off, and now I was an okada passenger rather than a pedestrian, my disdain for these bikes disappeared.

As we rode away from the museum, I privately applauded my driver's aggression when he mounted the pavement and beeped two terrified pedestrians out of the way. Back on the main ring road, he swerved violently through traffic, cussing any car driver who tried to run us off the road. My mood changed slightly when he slid close enough past the cars to endanger my kneecaps, and the wind yanked my headscarf from my head, tossing it far behind me. When my driver suddenly applied the brakes, I slammed jaw-first into his back, then clawed his torso as he lurched forward. At that moment, I could see why Nigerians are so religious: an okada ride will have the staunchest atheist praying for Christ's protection.

St. Mark's

From *The Stones of Venice, Introductory Chapters and Local Indices (Printed separately) for the Use of Travellers While Staying in Venice and Verona, 1879* | John Ruskin (1819–1900)

The pillars at the end of the 'Bocca di Piazza':
Between those pillars there opens a great light, and, in the midst of it, as we advance slowly, the vast tower of St. Mark seems to lift itself visibly forth from the level field of chequered stones; and, on each side, the countless arches prolong themselves into ranged symmetry, as if the rugged and irregular houses that pressed together above us in the dark alley had been struck back into sudden obedience and lovely order, and all their rude casements and broken walls had been transformed into arches charged with goodly sculpture, and fluted shafts of delicate stone.

And well may they fall back, for beyond those troops of ordered arches there rises a vision out of the earth, and all the great square seems to have opened from it in a kind of awe, that we may see it far away; – a multitude of pillars and white domes, clustered into a long low pyramid of coloured light; a treasure-heap, it seems, partly of gold, and partly of opal and mother-of-pearl, hollowed beneath into five great vaulted porches, ceiled with fair mosaic, and beset with sculpture of alabaster, clear as amber and delicate as ivory, – sculpture fantastic and involved, of palm leaves and lilies, and grapes and pomegranates, and birds clinging and fluttering among the branches, all twined together into an endless network of buds and plumes; and, in the midst of it, the solemn forms of angels, sceptred, and robed to the feet, and leaning to each other across the gates, their figures indistinct among the gleaming of the golden ground through the leaves beside them, interrupted and dim, like the morning light as it faded back among the branches of Eden, when first its gates were angel-guarded long ago.

Life on the Lagoon

From *The Quest for Corvo: An Experiment in Biography, 1934*

A. J. A. Symons (1900–1941)

Frederick Rolfe / Baron Corvo (1860–1913)

I came to Venice in August for a six week's holiday; and lived and worked and slept in my *barcheta* almost always. It seemed that, by staying on, I could most virtuously and most righteously cheat autumn and winter.

. . . .

I went swimming half a dozen times a day, beginning at white dawn, and ending after sunsets which set the whole lagoon ablaze with amethyst and topaz. Between friends, I will confess that I am not guiltless of often getting up in the night and popping silently overboard to swim for an hour in the clear of a great gold moon – plenilunio – or among the waving reflections of the stars. (O my goodness me, how heavenly a spot that is!) When I wanted a change of scene and anchorage, I rowed with my two gondogliere; and there is nothing known to physiculturalists (for giving you 'poise' and the organs and figure of a slim young Diadymenos) like rowing standing in the Mode Venetian. It is jolly hard work; but no other exercise bucks you up as does springing forward from your toe-tips and stretching forward to the full in pushing the oar, or produces such exquisite lassitude at night when your work is done. And I wrote quite easily for a good seven hours each day. Could anything be more felicitous?

Walking into Wales

From *Wild Wales, 1862* | George Borrow (1803–1881)

On the afternoon of Monday I sent my family off by the train to Llangollen, which place we had determined to make our headquarters during our stay in Wales. I intended to follow them next day, not in train, but on foot, as by walking I should be better able to see the country, between Chester and Llangollen, than by making the journey by the flying vehicle.

. . . .

Early the next morning I departed from Chester for Llangollen, distant about twenty miles; I passed over the noble bridge and proceeded along a broad and excellent road, leading in a direction almost due south through pleasant meadows. I felt very happy – and no wonder; the morning was beautiful, the birds sang merrily, and a sweet smell proceeded from the new-cut hay in the fields, and I was bound for Wales. I passed over the river Allan and through two villages called, as I was told, Pulford and Marford, and ascended a hill; from the top of this hill the view is very fine. To the east are the high lands of Cheshire, to the west the bold hills of Wales, and below, on all sides a fair variety of wood and water, green meads and arable fields.

7 August

Fantaisies Décoratives: Les Balloons

Oscar Wilde (1854–1900)

Against these turbid turquoise skies
    The light and luminous balloons
    Dip and drift like satin moons,
Drift like silken butterflies;

Reel with every windy gust,
    Rise and reel like dancing girls,
    Float like strange transparent pearls,
Fall and float like silver dust.

Now to the low leaves they cling,
    Each with coy fantastic pose,
    Each a petal of a rose
Straining at a gossamer string.

Then to the tall trees they climb,
    Like thin globes of amethyst,
    Wandering opals keeping tryst
With the rubies of the lime.

France is France

From *La Vie, 2023* | John Lewis-Stempel (1967–)

I was brought up to believe that the British are the nation of
gardeners but, traitorously, I think that the French may have the edge
these days with their commitments to good food, seasonal food. *Mon
potager*: satisfier of stomach. And soul.

But the French devotion to the *potager* is about French identity
too. To cut spinach from the *potager* for lunch is to continue in the
eternal, rural ways – a sort of French resistance to the modernization
of life, in the same way that L'Académie français contends Anglo-
Saxon incursions into the language of the Hexagon. France may be
home to some of the world's leading luxury brands (Louis Vuitton,
Chanel and Hermès), and may be a member of the European
Union, but it is resolutely nationalistic. In their hearts the French
do not consider France part of the EU, but the EU as an extension
of France. Free trade in France is a chimera; effectively the country
operates a cultural tariff system. Above the meat counter of Leclerc
supermarket, the biggest chain in France, hangs a sign: 'All our meat
is French.' Pick up *anything* in France, from dog food to pencils,
and it will say loud and clear, 'Fabriqué en France' or, occasionally,
issue the horror warning 'Contains non-French ingredients'. Go to
a French car park: 60 per cent of the cars will be Peugeot, Renault
or Citroën. Where do the French go on holiday? France. On the
national holiday of Bastille Day, every French *mairie* and every
French memorial is hung with the tricolore, often several times over.
On Remembrance Day we stand in the cemetery of La Roche beside
the war memorial, where Maire Alice Gaitier – wearing a *tricolore*
sash – intones the names of the dead, and we respond 'Mort pour
la France.' Not the apolitical, 'We remember them,' but, 'Died for
France.'

All this is fine by me. France is France.

Opera at Brunswick

From *Journal of a Tour through the Courts of Germany, 1764*

James Boswell (1740–1795)

Friday 10 August, 1764

The little gloom which I now feel of a morning seems a mere trifle.
Instead of those thick heavy clouds which pressed me down at
Utrecht, I find only thin dusky vapours, and they are soon dispersed.
After dining at Court, De Pless and I walked in the piazzas of
the Palace, and in the garden. He asked me what could occasion
melancholy, and with easy composure I gave him a lecture on
that distemper. Then he talked of religion, and carried me to see a
Catholic church.

   I then went to the opera, which at Brunswick is very noble.
The house is large, and the decorations much finer than in London.
The performers were very good. The piece was *Enea in Lazona* –
Æneas in Latium. He who played Turnus was no eunuch, and had
a bold manly voice, with which he did wonders. One air in which
occurred *rivale*, and another in which occurred la *traditore*, struck
me prodigiously. I had no notion of being so much affected by music.
My hypochondriac deadness is almost forgot. How happy am I now!
I dined at Court, and after this noble opera I returned to Court and
supped elegant and grand.

The Meeting of Light and Dark

From *Twilight in Italy, 1916* | D. H. Lawrence (1885–1930)

It is all so strange and varied: the dark-skinned Italians ecstatic in the night and the moon, the blue-eyed old woman ecstatic in the busy sunshine, the monks in the garden below, who are supposed to unite both, passing only in the neutrality of the average. Where, then, is the meeting-point: where in mankind is the ecstasy of light and dark together, the supreme transcendence of the afterglow, day hovering in the embrace of the coming night like two angels embracing in the heavens, like Eurydice in the arms of Orpheus, or Persephone embraced by Pluto?

Where is the supreme ecstasy in mankind, which makes day a delight and night a delight, purpose an ecstasy and a concourse in ecstasy, and single abandon of the single body and soul also an ecstasy under the moon? Where is the transcendent knowledge in our hearts, uniting sun and darkness, day and night, spirit and senses? Why do we not know that the two in consummation are one; that each is only part; partial and alone for ever; but that the two in consummation are perfect, beyond the range of loneliness or solitude?

Heidelberg

From *An Itinerary Containing His Ten Yeeres Travell, 1617*

Fynes Moryson (1566–1630)

1592

The third day in the morning wee went five miles to Heidelberg, through sandy fields, but fruitfull in corne, all lying in a plaine, as the rest of the way from Strassburg Heidelberg, hither, and neere Heidelberg we passed a great wood of Oakes, full of great heards of red Deare, which lay still by the way, and would not stirre for our cries, or feare of our Coach wheeles, but seemed to know their priviledge, all hunting being forbidden upon high penalties. Heidelberg is compassed with high Mountaines, on the South, East, and North sides; but towards the West, beyond the City and a long Suburbe, (being the sole Suburb in the Towne,) the Mountaines lie open. This Suburbe is longer then the City, and they both lie in great length from the East to the West, and they both consist almost of one streete, and are built in the plaine, though compassed with Mountains. On the South-east side there is a faire and pleasant market place, and not farre thence a very high Mountaine called Konigstull, that is, Kingly seat, upon the middle ascent whereof, is the Castle, in which the Phaltz-grave of the Rheine holds his Court, and upon the top of this Mountaine are the mines of an old Tower, blowen up with gun-powder. From this Mountaine on the South side runne caves under the Earth, to the Westeme part of the Mountaine of Goates, upon which Mountaine is a Tower called Trotz-keyser, as if it were a Tower built in despight of Cæsar, and it is worth the seeing, for the antiquity and building, having no gate, but being entered by the cave under the earth, and being built with lime tempered, not with water, but wine, incredibly durable, at the time when the Emperour making warre against the Phaltz-grave, besieged this City.

Freedom to Sail

From *Narrative of the Life of Frederick Douglass, 1845*

Frederick Douglass (1818–1895)

Our house stood within a few rods of the Chesapeake Bay, whose broad bosom was ever white with sails from every quarter of the habitable globe. Those beautiful vessels, robed in purest white, so delightful to the eye of freemen, were to me so many shrouded ghosts, to terrify and torment me with thoughts of my wretched condition. I have often, in the deep stillness of a summer's Sabbath, stood all alone upon the lofty banks of that noble bay, and traced, with saddened heart and tearful eye, the countless number of sails moving off to the mighty ocean. The sight of these always affected me powerfully. My thoughts would compel utterance; and there, with no audience but the Almighty, I would pour out my soul's complaint, in my rude way, with an apostrophe to the moving multitude of ships: –

'You are loosed from your moorings, and are free; I am fast in my chains, and am a slave! You move merrily before the gentle gale, and I sadly before the bloody whip! You are freedom's swift-winged angels, that fly round the world; I am confined in bands of iron! O that I were free! O, that I were on one of your gallant decks, and under your protecting wing! Alas! betwixt me and you, the turbid waters roll. Go on, go on. O that I could also go!'

Midnight on the Great Western

Thomas Hardy (1840–1928)

In the third-class seat sat the journeying boy,
    And the roof-lamp's oily flame
Played down on his listless form and face,
Bewrapt past knowing to what he was going,
      Or whence he came.

In the band of his hat the journeying boy
    Had a ticket stuck; and a string
Around his neck bore the key of his box,
That twinkled gleams of the lamp's sad beams
      Like a living thing.

What past can be yours, O journeying boy
    Towards a world unknown,
Who calmly, as if incurious quite
On all at stake, can undertake
      This plunge alone?

Knows your soul a sphere, O journeying boy,
    Our rude realms far above,
Whence with spacious vision you mark and mete
This region of sin that you find you in,
      But are not of?

The Border

From *On the Road, 1958* | Jack Kerouac (1922–1969)

And now we were ready for the last hundred and fifty miles to the magic border. We leaped into the car and off. I was so exhausted by now I slept all the way through Dilley and Encinal to Laredo and didn't wake up till they were parking the car in front of a lunchroom at two o'clock in the morning. 'Ah,' sighed Dean, 'the end of Texas, the end of America, we don't know no more.' It was tremendously hot: we were all sweating buckets. There was no night dew, not a breath of air, nothing except billions of moths smashing at bulbs everywhere and the low, rank smell of a hot river in the night nearby – the Rio Grande, that begins in cool Rocky Mountain dales and ends up fashioning world-valleys to mingle its heats with the Mississippi muds in the great Gulf.

· · · · · · · · · ·

We had no idea what Mexico would really be like. We were at sea level again, and when we tried to eat a snack we could hardly swallow it. I wrapped it up in napkins for the trip anyway. We felt awful and sad. But everything changed when we crossed the mysterious bridge over the river and our wheels rolled on official Mexican soil, though it wasn't anything but a carway for border inspection. Just across the street Mexico began. We looked with wonder. To our amazement, it looked exactly like Mexico. It was three in the morning, and fellows in straw hats and white pants were lounging by the dozen against battered pocky storefronts.

A Warning

From *Coryats Crudities, 1611* | Thomas Coryate (c. 1577–1617)

Turin

I am sory I can speake so little of so flourishing and beautifull a Citie.
For during that little time that I was in the citie, I found so great a
distemperature in my body, by drinking the sweete wines of Piemont,
that caused a grievous inflammation in my face and handes; so that
I had but a smal desire to walke much abroad in the streets. Therefore
I would advise all English-men that intend to travell into Italy, to
mingle their wine with water as soone as they come into the country,
for feare of ensuing inconveniences.

16 August

A Fine View

From *The Country of the Pointed Firs, 1896*

Sarah Orne Jewett (1849–1909)

We were standing where there was a fine view of the harbor and its long stretches of shore all covered by the great army of the pointed firs, darkly cloaked and standing as if they waited to embark. As we looked far seaward among the outer islands, the trees seemed to march seaward still, going steadily over the heights and down to the water's edge.

It had been growing gray and cloudy, like the first evening of autumn, and a shadow had fallen on the darkening shore. Suddenly, as we looked, a gleam of golden sunshine struck the outer islands, and one of them shone out clear in the light, and revealed itself in a compelling way to our eyes.

Into My Heart an Air That Kills

From *A Shropshire Lad, 1896* | A. E. Housman (1859–1936)

XL

Into my heart an air that kills
   From yon far country blows:
What are those blue remembered hills,
   What spires, what farms are those?

That is the land of lost content,
   I see it shining plain,
The happy highways where I went
   And cannot come again.

Driving Along the Corniche d'Or

From *Tender is the Night, 1934* | F. Scott Fitzgerald (1896–1940)

It was pleasant to drive back to the hotel in the late afternoon, above a sea as mysteriously colored as the agates and cornelians of childhood, green as green milk, blue as laundry water, wine dark. It was pleasant to pass people eating outside their doors, and to hear the fierce mechanical pianos behind the vines of country estaminets. When they turned off the Corniche d'Or and down to Gausse's Hôtel through the darkening banks of trees, set one behind another in many greens, the moon already hovered over the ruins of the aqueducts …

Fun

From *The Valleys of the Assassins, 1934* | Freya Stark (1893–1993)

Preface

An imaginative aunt who, for my ninth birthday, sent a copy of the *Arabian Nights*, was, I suppose, the original cause of trouble.

Unfostered and unnoticed, the little flame so kindled fed secretly on dreams. Chance, such as the existence of a Syrian missionary near my home, nourished it; and Fate, with long months of illness and leisure, blew it to a blaze bright enough to light my way through labyrinths of Arabic, and eventually to land me on the coast of Syria at the end of 1927.

Here, I thought, all difficulty was over: I had now but to look around me, to learn, and to enjoy.

And so it would have been had not those twin Virtues so fatal to the *joie de vivre* of our civilized West, the sense of responsibility and the illusion, dear to well-regulated minds, that every action must have a purpose – had not these virtues of Responsibility and Purpose met me at every step with the embarrassing enquiry: '*Why* are you here alone;' and: '*What* do you intend to *do?*'

· · · · · · · · · ·

I must admit that for my own part I travelled single-mindedly for fun. I learned my scanty Arabic for fun, and a little Persian – and then went for the same reason to look for the Assassin castles and the Luristan bronzes in the manner here related. And here I would like to thank the much-tried, frequently accused, and not unreasonably perplexed officials who came across me, for much indulgence, not always unmixed with disapproval, but invariably kind.

An Old Rule

From *South Wind, 1917* | Norman Douglas (1868–1952)

It was a pleasant rule. It ran to the effect that in the course of the forenoon all the inhabitants of Nepenthe, of whatever age, sex, or condition, should endeavour to find themselves in the market-place or piazza – a charming square, surrounded on three sides by the principal buildings of the town and open, on the fourth, to a lovely prospect over land and sea. They were to meet on this spot; here to exchange gossip, make appointments for the evening, and watch the arrival of newcomers to their island. An admirable rule! For it effectively prevented everybody from doing any kind of work in the morning; and after luncheon, of course, you went to sleep. It was delightful to be obliged, by iron convention, to stroll about in the bright sunshine, greeting your friends, imbibing iced drinks, and letting your eye stray down to the lower level of the island with its farmhouses embowered in vineyards; or across the glittering water towards the distant coastline and its volcano; or upwards, into those pinnacles of the higher region against whose craggy ramparts, nearly always, a fleet of snowy sirocco clouds was anchored. For Nepenthe was famous not only for its girls and lobsters, but also for its south wind.

Approaching Etna

From *In Sicily, 2000* | Norman Lewis (1909–1979)

While in Italy during the Second World War:

Everyone living under a volcano is affected by it whether they know or not. Land is cheap and the work hard. They farm the fertile land lying at the bottom of crevices and ravines, where, over three centuries, the lava has turned into good soil. Those who work this land look like Andean peones, with short legs, wide shoulders, high cheekbones, sleek black hair, and hands twice the normal size.

A cluster of roads led north from Catania and for the first few miles, until the lava came into sight, the going was easy. The lava fields, spreading over thirty-five miles, took my breath away. Many of those who had settled within fifteen miles of the city had bought land on the cheap, turning themselves into respected landowners. They had the famous Catanian sense of humour and they all laughed at nothing most of the time. 'If you're rich' – at least so they said – 'you have to plant palms around your house' – this being the local status symbol. They liked to point out that they were unlikely to live long enough to enjoy the fruit.

A few miles further north, with the volcano now in permanent view, the going became less easy, with narrower roads and sometimes diversions to avoid a recent lava flow. A cloud resembling in shape a Tudor flat hat hung above the cone of Etna and you could pick out fresh lava trails by the smoking vegetation. It was a landscape that demolished assumptions. You expected a white wilderness whereas what you saw were narrow ravines crowded with wildflowers of every conceivable colour, which scented the surroundings with a perfume penetrating even the sulphurous fumes of the lava.

22 August

Dwellers in Tents

From *Persian Pictures: From the Mountains to the Sea, 1894*

Gertrude Bell (1868–1926)

23 August

Beautiful as it is in its majestic loneliness, this country is not one
where men are tempted to seek an abiding dwelling. In the spring,
when the fresh grass clothes the bottom of the valleys, in the
summer, when the cool winds sweep the plain, they are content to
pitch their tents here, but with the first nip of autumn cold they
strike camp, and are off to warmer levels, leaving the high snow-
carpeted regions empty of all inhabitants but the wild goats and
the eagles. To-day, perhaps, the gloomiest depth of a narrow gorge,
which looks as though from the time of its creation no living thing
had disturbed its solitude, is strewn with black tents, flocks of horses
and camels crop the grass by the edge of the stream, the air is full
of the barking of dogs and the cries of women and children; but to-
morrow no sign of life remains – the nomads have moved onward,
silence has spread itself like a mantle from mountain to mountain,
and who can tell what sound will next strike against their walls?

Walking Under a Knapsack

From *Rambles Beyond Railways, 1851*

Wilkie Collins (1824–1889)

They had, by this time, accomplished their initiation into the process of walking under a knapsack, with the most complete and encouraging success. You, who in these days of vehement bustle, business, and competition, can still find time to travel for pleasure alone – you, who have yet to become emancipated from the thraldom of railways, carriages, and saddle-horses – patronize, I exhort you, that first and oldest-established of all conveyances, your own legs! Think on your tender partings nipped in the bud by the railway bell; think of crabbed cross-roads, and broken carriage-springs; think of luggage confided to extortionate porters, of horses casting shoes and catching colds, of cramped legs and numbed feet, of vain longings to get down for a moment here, and to delay for a pleasant half hour there – think of all these manifold hardships of riding at your ease; and the next time you leave home, strap your luggage on your shoulders, take your stick in your hand, set forth delivered from a perfect paraphernalia of incumbrances, to go where you will, how you will – the free citizen of the whole travelling world! Thus independent, what may you not accomplish? – what pleasure is there that you cannot enjoy?

The Style of a Seaman

From *A New Voyage Round the World, 1697*

William Dampier (1651–1715)

As to my Stile it cannot be expected, that a Seaman should affect
Politeness, for were I able to do it, yet I think I should be little
solicitous about it, in a work of this Nature. I have frequently indeed,
divested my self of Sea Phrases, to gratify the Land Reader; for which
the Seamen will hardly forgive me: And yet, possibly I shall not seem
Complaisant enough to the other; because I still retain the use of so
many Sea terms. I confess I have not been at all scrupulous in this
matter, either as to the one or the other of these; for I am persuaded,
that if what I say be intelligible, it matters not greatly in what words
it is expressed.

Neptune

From *The Aeneid, 29–19 BC* | Virgil (70–19 BC)

Translated by John Dryden (1631–1700)

Book I, lines 176–204

Meantime imperial *Neptune* heard the Sound
Of raging Billows breaking on the Ground;
Displeas'd, and fearing for his Wat'ry Reign,
He reard his awful Head above the Main:
Serene in Majesty, then rowl'd his Eyes
Around the Space of Earth, and Seas, and Skies.
He saw the *Trojan* Fleet dispers'd, distress'd
By stormy Winds and wintry Heav'n oppress'd.
Full well the God his Sister's envy knew,
And what her Aims, and what her Arts pursue:
He summon'd *Eurus* and the Western blast,
And first an angry glance on both he cast:
Then thus rebuk'd; Audacious Winds! from whence
This bold Attempt, this Rebel Insolence?
Is it for you to ravage Seas and Land,
Unauthoriz'd by my supreme Command?
To raise such Mountains on the troubl'd Main?
Whom I – But first 'tis fit, the Billows to restrain,
And then you shall be taught obedience to my Reign.
Hence, to your Lord my Royal Mandate bear,
The Realms of Ocean and the Fields of Air
Are mine, not his; by fatal Lot to me
The liquid Empire fell, and Trident of the Sea.
His pow'r to hollow Caverns is confin'd.
There let him reign, the Jailor of the Wind;
With hoarse Commands his breathing Subjects call,
And boast and bluster in his empty Hall.
He spoke: And while he spoke he smooth'd the Sea,
Dispell'd the Darkness and restor'd the Day.

The Destination

From *The Story of My Boyhood and Youth, 1913*

John Muir (1938–1914)

1849

There were quite a large number of emigrants aboard, many of them newly married couples, and the advantages of the different parts of the New World they expected to settle in were often discussed. My father started with the intention of going to the backwoods of Upper Canada. Before the end of the voyage, however, he was persuaded that the States offered superior advantages, especially Wisconsin and Michigan, where the land was said to be as good as in Canada and far more easily brought under cultivation; for in Canada the woods were so close and heavy that a man might wear out his life in getting a few acres cleared of trees and stumps. So he changed his mind and concluded to go to one of the Western States.

On our wavering westward way a grain-dealer in Buffalo told father that most of the wheat he handled came from Wisconsin; and this influential information finally determined my father's choice.

The Silhouette of a Broken Dome

From *The Road to Oxiana, 1937* | Robert Byron (1905–1941)

On approaching Herat, the road from Persia keeps close under the
mountains till it meets the road from Kushk, when it turns downhill
towards the town. We arrived in a dark but starlit night. This kind
of night is always mysterious; in an unknown country, after a sight
of the wild frontier guards, it produced an excitement such as I have
seldom felt. Suddenly the road entered a grove of giant chimneys,
whose black outlines regrouped themselves against the stars as we
passed. For a second, I was dumbfounded – expecting anything on
earth, but not a factory; until, dwarfed by these vast trunks, appeared
the silhouette of a broken dome, curiously ribbed, like a melon.
There is only one dome in the world like that, I thought, that anyone
knows of: the Tomb of Tamerlane at Samarcand. The chimneys
therefore must be minarets. I went to bed like a child on Christmas
Eve, scarcely able to wait for the morning.

Morning comes. Stepping out onto a roof adjoining the hotel,
I see seven sky-blue pillars rise out of the bare fields against the
delicate heather-coloured mountains. Down each the dawn casts
a highlight of pale gold. In their midst shines a blue melon-dome
with the top bitten off. Their beauty is more than scenic, depending
on light or landscape. On closer view, every tile, every flower, every
petal of mosaic contributes its genius to the whole. Even in ruin, such
architecture tells of a golden age.

The Vilest Spot

From 'George Walker at Suez', *Public Opinion, 1861; Tales of All Countries, Second Series, 1863* | Anthony Trollope (1815–1882)

Of all the spots on the world's surface that I, George Walker, of Friday Street, London, have ever visited, Suez in Egypt, at the head of the Red Sea, is by far the vilest, the most unpleasant, and the least interesting. There are no women there, no water, and no vegetation. It is surrounded, and indeed often filled, by a world of sand. A scorching sun is always overhead; and one is domiciled in a huge cavernous hotel, which seems to have been made purposely destitute of all the comforts of civilised life.

Loch Ness

From *The Journal of a Tour to the Hebrides, 1785*

James Boswell (1740–1795)

Monday 30th August

It was a delightful day. Loch Ness, and the road upon the side of it, shaded with birch trees, and the hills above it, pleased us much. The scene was as sequestered and agreeably wild as could be desired, and for a time engrossed all our attention.

To see Dr. Johnson in any new situation is always an interesting object to me; and, as I saw him now for the first time on horseback, jaunting about at his ease in quest of pleasure and novelty, the very different occupations of his former laborious life, his admirable productions, his *London*, his *Rambler*, &c. &c. immediately presented themselves to my mind, and the contrast made a strong impression on my imagination.

Songs

From *Don Juan, 1819–1824* | George Gordon, Lord Byron (1788–1824)

Canto the Third, LXXXV–LXXVI

Thus, usually, when he was ask'd to sing,
  He gave the different nations something national;
'Twas all the same to him – 'God save the king,'
  Or '*Ça ira*,' according to the fashion all:
His muse made increment of anything,
  From the high lyric down to the low rational:
If Pindar sang horse-races, what should hinder
Himself from being as pliable as Pindar?

In France, for instance, he would write a chanson;
  In England a six canto quarto tale;
In Spain, he'd make a ballad or romance on
  The last war – much the same in Portugal;
In Germany, the Pegasus he'd prance on
  Would be old Goethe's (see what says De Stael);
In Italy he'd ape the 'Trecentisti;'
In Greece, he'd sing some sort of hymn like this t' ye:

The isles of Greece, the Isles of Greece!
  Where burning Sappho loved and sung,
Where grew the arts of war and peace,
  Where Delos rose, and Phoebus sprung!
Eternal summer gilds them yet,
But all, except their sun, is set.

SEPTEMBER

Through Moor and Dale

A Western Voyage

James Elroy Flecker (1884–1915)

My friend the Sun – like all my friends
    Inconstant, lovely, far away –
Is out, and bright, and condescends
    To glory in our holiday.

A furious march with him I'll go
    And race him in the Western train,
And wake the hills of long ago
    And swim the Devon sea again.

I have done foolishly to head
    The footway of the false moonbeams,
To light my lamp and call the dead
    And read their long black printed dreams.

I have done foolishly to dwell
    With Fear upon her desert isle,
To take my shadowgraph to Hell,
    And then to hope the shades would smile.

And since the light must fail me soon
    (But faster, faster, Western train!)
Proud meadows of the afternoon,
    I have remembered you again.

And I'll go seek through moor and dale
    A flower that wastrel winds caress;
The bud is red and the leaves pale,
    The name of it Forgetfulness.

Then like the old and happy hills
    With frozen veins and fires outrun,
I'll wait the day when darkness kills
    My brother and good friend, the Sun.

Lake Tahoe

From A Lady's Life in the Rocky Mountains, 1879

Isabella Bird (1831–1904)

September 2.

I have found a dream of beauty at which one might look all one's life and sigh. Not lovable, like the Sandwich Islands, but beautiful in its own way! A strictly North American beauty: snow-splotched mountains, huge pines, red-woods, sugar pines, silver spruce; a crystalline atmosphere, waves of the richest color; and a pine-hung lake which mirrors all beauty on its surface. Lake Tahoe is before me, a sheet of water twenty-two miles long by ten broad, and in some places 1,700 feet deep. It lies at a height of 6,000 feet, and the snow-crowned summits which wall it in are from 8,000 to 11,000 feet in altitude. The air is keen and elastic. There is no sound but the distant and slightly musical ring of the lumberer's axe.

Composed Upon Westminster Bridge

William Wordsworth (1770–1850)

September 3, 1802
Written on the roof of a coach, on my way to France.

Earth has not anything to show more fair:
Dull would he be of soul who could pass by
A sight so touching in its majesty:
This City now doth, like a garment, wear
The beauty of the morning; silent, bare,
Ships, towers, domes, theatres, and temples lie
Open unto the fields, and to the sky;
All bright and glittering in the smokeless air.
Never did sun more beautifully steep
In his first splendour, valley, rock, or hill;
Ne'er saw I, never felt, a calm so deep!
The river glideth at his own sweet will:
Dear God! the very houses seem asleep;
And all that mighty heart is lying still!

'I too in Arcadia'

From Travels in Italy, 1786–1788, published 1816, 1817

Johann Wolfgang von Goethe (1749–1832)

Translated by A. J. W. Morrison (1806–1865)

Ratisbon, September 4, 1786

As early as 3 o'clock in the morning I stole out of Carlsbad, for otherwise I should not have been allowed to depart quietly. The band of friends who, on the 28th of August, rejoiced to celebrate my birthday, had in some degree acquired a right to detain me. However, it was impossible to stay here any longer. Having packed a portmanteau merely, and a knap-sack, I jumped alone into a post-chaise, and by half past 8, on a beautifully calm but foggy morning, I arrived at Zevoda. The upper clouds were streaky and fleecy, the lower ones heavy. This appeared to me a good sign. I hoped that, after so wretched a summer, we should enjoy a fine autumn. About 12, 1 got to Egra, under a warm and shining sun, and now, it occurred to me, that this place had the same latitude as my own native town, and it was a real pleasure to me once more to take my midday meal beneath a bright sky, at the fiftieth degree.

A Journey of False Hopes

The History of Mary Prince: A West Indian Slave, 1831

Mary Prince (1788–1833)

My master and mistress were going to England to put their son to
school, and bring their daughters home; and they took me with them
to take care of the child. I was willing to come to England: I thought
that by going there I should probably get cured of my rheumatism
and should return with my master and mistress, quite well, to my
husband. My husband was willing for me to come away, for he had
heard that my master would free me, – and I also hoped this might
prove true; but it was all a false report.

The steward of the ship was very kind to me. He and my husband
were in the same class in the Moravian Church. I was thankful
that he was so friendly, for my mistress was not kind to me on the
passage; and she told me, when she was angry, that she did not intend
to treat me any better in England than in the West Indies – that
I need not expect it. And she was as good as her word.

The Ruins of Copan

From *Incidents of Travel in Central America, Chiapas and Yucatan, 1841* | John L. Stephens (1805–1852)

We followed our guide, who, sometimes missing his way, with a constant and vigorous use of his machete, conducted us through the thick forest, among half-buried fragments, to fourteen monuments of the same character and appearance, some with more elegant designs, and some in workmanship equal to the finest monuments of the Egyptians; one displaced from its pedestal by enormous roots; another locked in the close embrace of branches of trees, and almost lifted out of the earth; another hurled to the ground, and bound down by huge vines and creepers; and one standing, with its altar before it, in a grove of trees which grew around it, seemingly to shade and shroud it as a sacred thing; in the solemn stillness of the woods, it seemed a divinity mourning over a fallen people. The only sounds that disturbed the quiet of this buried city were the noise of monkeys moving among the tops of the trees, and the cracking of dry branches broken by their weight.

On the Amazon

From *Jake's Escape, 1996* | Robin Hanbury-Tenison (1936–)

In a case of mistaken identity, Jake is kidnapped by terrorists.
He manages to escape:

He [Jake] had not done much boating before but he had read
all the Swallows and Amazons books as well as *Treasure Island* and
Robinson Crusoe and he had often imagined what it would be like.
Now he was going to find out.

. . . .

There were no disturbances in the night, but he took the precaution
of mooring the boat out in the lagoon and away from the shore so
that nothing could creep on board. And he was awake before dawn,
poling out into the river, starting up the engine and steaming away
straight into the sunrise.

Jake now travelled for several days without having a lot of time to
think about where he was going or what lay ahead. Navigating the
boat, feeding himself, fishing over the side, checking the engine and
that everything was shipshape above and below decks; that took up
nearly all his time. He found that the routine he made for himself
stopped him worrying, although the nagging fear that he would
never see his family again was always with him.

Swallows

Robert Louis Stevenson (1850–1894)

Swallows travel to and fro,
And the great winds come and go,
And the steady breezes blow,
    Bearing perfume, bearing love.
Breezes hasten, swallows fly,
Towered clouds forever ply,
And at noonday, you and I
    See the same sunshine above.

Dew and rain fall everywhere,
Harvests ripen, flowers are fair,
And the whole round earth is bare
    To the moonshine and the sun;
And the live air, fanned with wings,
Bright with breeze and sunshine, brings
Into contact distant things,
    And makes all the countries one.

Let us wander where we will,
Something kindred greets us still;
Something seen on vale or hill
    Falls familiar on the heart;
So, at scent or sound or sight,
Severed souls by day and night
Tremble with the same delight –
    Tremble, half the world apart.

The Ocean

From *The Skeleton Coast, 1997* | Benedict Allen (1960–)

Crossing the Skeleton Coast, where the Namib Dessert meets the Atlantic Ocean, Benedict Allen has three camels: Nelson, Jan and Andries.

9 September
To the beach. The camels hadn't been up close to water before – not more than a sheep trough-ful. We led them on foot. It was an important moment, a clue to how they will handle the Lange Wand.

Jan soon forgot about his sore pad. Surf was roaring towards us up the sand, foam boiling off the waves. Nelson wanted nothing to do with all this violence. He allowed us to walk him along the storm beach, but not a step nearer. I decided not to push him too hard, and after a while the camels did start to adjust to the screaming winds and detonating waves. Andries even paused to pick up some mussels to examine. We turned inland from North Rock along a road that has long since been wiped out by sand and repaved with shells.

Night-time: this is a restless place of high energy. The air moves by violently, slashing you with mists. Waves kick at the shore, tussling with the land.

The Dangers in Corsica

From *An Account of Corsica, 1768*

James Boswell (1740–1795)

10 September

1765

I was however under no apprehension in going to Corsica. Count
Rivarola the Sardinian consul, who is himself a Corsican, assuring
me that the island was then in a very civilized state; and besides,
that in the rudest times no Corsican would ever attack a stranger.
The Count was so good as to give me most obliging letters to many
people in the island. I had now been in several foreign countries.
I had found that I was able to accommodate myself to my fellow-
creatures of different languages and sentiments. I did not fear that it
would be a difficult task for me to make myself easy with the plain
and generous Corsicans.

The only danger I saw was, that I might be taken by some
of the Barbary Corsairs, and have a tryal of slavery among the
Turks at Algiers.

. . . .

The worthy Corsicans thought it was proper to give a moral lesson
to a young traveller just come from Italy. They told me that in their
country I should be treated with the greatest hospitality; but if
I attempted to debauch any of their women, I might lay my account
with instant death.

Sea-sickness

From *Three Men in a Boat (To Say Nothing of the Dog!)* 1889

Jerome K. Jerome (1859–1927)

It is a curious fact, but nobody ever is sea-sick – on land. At sea, you come across plenty of people very bad indeed, whole boat-loads of them; but I never met a man yet, on land, who had ever known at all what it was to be sea-sick. Where the thousands upon thousands of bad sailors that swarm in every ship hide themselves when they are on land is a mystery. If most men were like a fellow I saw on the Yarmouth boat one day, I could account for the seeming enigma easily enough. It was just off Southend Pier, I recollect, and he was leaning out through one of the port-holes in a very dangerous position. I went up to him to try and save him.

'Hi! come further in,' I said, shaking him by the shoulder. 'You'll be overboard.'

'Oh my! I wish I was,' was the only answer I could get; and there I had to leave him.

Three weeks afterwards, I met him in the coffee-room of a Bath hotel, talking about his voyages, and explaining, with enthusiasm, how he loved the sea.

'Good sailor!' he replied in answer to a mild young man's envious query; 'well, I did feel a little queer *once*, I confess. It was off Cape Horn. The vessel was wrecked the next morning.'

I said:

'Weren't you a little shaky by Southend Pier one day, and wanted to be thrown overboard?'

'Southend Pier!' he replied, with a puzzled expression.

'Yes; going down to Yarmouth, last Friday three weeks.'

'Oh, ah – yes,' he answered, brightening up; 'I remember now. I did have a headache that afternoon. It was the pickles, you know. They were the most disgraceful pickles I ever tasted in a respectable boat. Did *you* have any?'

For myself, I have discovered an excellent preventive against sea-sickness, in balancing myself. You stand in the centre of the deck, and, as the ship heaves and pitches, you move your body about, so as to keep it always straight. When the front of the ship rises, you lean forward, till the deck almost touches your nose; and when its back end gets up, you lean backwards. This is all very well for an hour or two; but you can't balance yourself for a week.

The Benefits of Canals

From *Travels in America, 1848* | Theodore Dwight (1796–1866)

The boat, though rough and offering no accommodations, in the
mean time had been sliding smoothly over the shining surface of
the canal, and had brought me into a beautiful grove of forest trees,
whose numberless stems, like the innumerable columns of some
extensive temple, were faithfully reflected below, while their thick
canopy of foliage also appeared repeated apparently from an
immense depth, so true was the mirror over which they hung.
Why, I asked myself, is travelling on our canals considered so
wearisome and destitute of interest? Here are noble productions of
nature multiplied around, silence and solitude undisturbed by the
rattling of wheels, and perfumed air unmingled with carriage dust.
Our canals often introduce us to the hearts of the forests; the retreats
of wild animals are almost exposed to our view, and the nests of rare
birds even hang over our heads. How can the public, how can some
of my friends most distinguished for taste, prefer the crowded stage
coach, the dusty and thickly inhabited road, with the heat of the sun
during a mid-day ride?

Motoring by Night

From *A Motor-Flight Through France, 1908*

Edith Wharton (1862–1937)

Though it was near sunset we pressed on for Vichy:
On good French roads, however, a motor-journey by night is not
without its compensations; and our dark flight through mysterious
fields and woods terminated, effectively enough, with the long
descent down a lamp-garlanded boulevard into the inanimate
white watering-place.

13 September

The Owl and the Pussy-cat

Edward Lear (1812–1888)

The Owl and the Pussycat went to sea
   In a beautiful pea-green boat,
They took some honey, and plenty of money,
   Wrapped up in a five-pound note.
The Owl looked up to the stars above,
   And sang to a small guitar,
'O lovely Pussy! O Pussy, my love,
   What a beautiful Pussy you are,
     You are,
     You are!
   What a beautiful Pussy you are!'

Pussy said to the Owl, 'You elegant fowl!
   How charmingly sweet you sing!
O let us be married! too long we have tarried:
   But what shall we do for a ring?'
They sailed away, for a year and a day,
   To the land where the Bong-tree grows,
And there in a wood a Piggy-wig stood,
   With a ring at the end of his nose,
     His nose,
     His nose.
   With a ring at the end of his nose.

'Dear Pig, are you willing to sell for one shilling
    Your ring?' Said the Piggy, 'I will.'
So they took it away and were married next day
    By the Turkey who lives on the hill.
They dined on mince, and slices of quince,
    Which they ate with a runcible spoon;
And hand in hand, on the edge of the sand
They danced by the light of the moon,
    The moon,
    The moon,
They danced by the light of the moon.

An Occasion

From *News from Tartary, 1936* | Peter Fleming (1907–1971)

The Mintaka Pass or the Pass of a Thousand Ibex, crossing from China to India:

About half-way up the track was inexplicably decorated with a fragment of *The Times* newspaper, and I took this for a good omen. Now I could see that the head of the pass was marked by four or five little pillars of close-piled stones. I was suddenly aware that this was an Occasion. In less than an hour our ambitions would be realized; the forlorn hope would have come off. In less than an hour we should be in India.

. . . .

Half an hour later, heralded by the raucous objurgations of the Turkis, the caravan came plunging into sight over the lip of the pass; Kini [Ella Maillart] reported a gruelling climb, and most of the ponies were in a bad way. It was getting late and we pushed on without delay – over the screes, into an awkward wilderness of boulders, across a patch of soggy ground, and out onto a little rocky platform whence we looked, for the first time, into India.

The snow had drawn off. Below us a glacier sprawled, grey and white, in the shadowed bottom of a gigantic pit. Opposite, wearing their wisps of cloud superbly, two towering snow-peaks were refulgent in the last of the sunlight. It was a sight to take your breath away.

'So far I like India,' said Kini.

15 September

So Far, I Liked India

From *Forbidden Journey, 1937* | Ella Maillart (1903–1997)

We departed from the last inhabited place on Chinese soil.
At last we came to three heaps of stones. They marked the summit of
the Mintaka, 15,600 feet above sea-level, an enormous maze of black
shining rocks. We had climbed nearly 3,000 feet in two hours.

I felt it was going to clear, for now the fine blue snow seemed to
be falling from a transparent mist, and I waited, letting the others
go on. To the east, on my left, I could just make out the summit we
saw in the early afternoon. From this high altitude I should soon be
able to see the Himalayas, the 'Dwelling-place of the Snows.' And at
last, straight in front of me, beyond the black curve of the rocky pass,
appeared one of the faces of the Mintaka, a triangular wall of snow,
glittering in the last rays of the sun. A proud mountain, with its head
turbaned in cloud, its lower slopes were deep in shadows through
which wound a river of ice. So far, I liked India.

Escaping War

From *Naples '44: An Intelligence Officer in the Italian Labyrinth, 1978* | Norman Lewis (1909–1979)

September 17

Attempts by the remaining section members to reach Salerno
having been abandoned, I could find nothing to prevent my taking
a sight-seeing trip. I therefore motor-cycled up to the hill village
of Capaccio, which had always been in sight from the beach-head,
presiding with cool if distant charm over the raucous confusion
below and representing for me all that was most romantic in the
landscape of Southern Italy.

At close quarters the charm was even more pungent; a place of
delicately interlocking white masses, and sparkling light. I rode with
some caution into a street which could have been almost English,
with narrow, picket-fenced front gardens in which grew recognizable
favourites as zinnias and sweet peas. The peace of this place after four
days of the racket of warfare was stunning.

Beyond Inverness

From *A Journey to the Western Isles of Scotland, 1775*

Samuel Johnson (1709–1784)

We were now to bid farewel to the luxury of travelling, and to enter a country upon which perhaps no wheel has ever rolled. We could indeed have used our post-chaise one day longer, along the military road to Fort *Augustus*, but we could have hired no horses beyond Inverness, and we were not so sparing of ourselves, as to lead them, merely that we might have one day longer the indulgence of a carriage.

At Inverness therefore we procured three horses for ourselves and a servant, and one more for our baggage, which was no very heavy load. We found in the course of our journey the convenience of having disencumbered ourselves, by laying aside whatever we could spare; for it is not to be imagined without experience, how in climbing crags, and treading bogs, and winding through narrow and obstructed passages, a little bulk will hinder, and a little weight will burthen; or how often a man that has pleased himself at home with his own resolution, will, in the hour of darkness and fatigue, be content to leave behind him every thing but himself.

Introductory

*From Rhymes on the Road: Extracted From the Journal of a
Travelling Member of the Pococurante Society, 1819* |

Thomas Moore (1779–1852)

The Gentleman from whose Journal the following extracts are taken,
tells the reader in his Introduction that the greater part of these
poems were written or composed in an old *calèche*, for the purpose
of beguiling the ennui of solitary travelling; and as verses made
by a gentleman in his sleep have lately been called 'a *psychological*
curiosity,' it is to be hoped that verses made by a gentleman
to keep himself awake may be honoured with some appellation
equally Greek.

. . . .

What various attitudes, and ways,
　　And tricks, we authors have in writing!
While some write sitting, some, like Bayes,
　　Usually stand while they're inditing.
Poets there are, who wear the floor out,
　　Measuring a line at every stride;
While some, like Henry Stephens, pour out
　　Rhymes by the dozen, while they ride.

Ravenna

From *Italian Hours, 1909* | Henry James (1843–1916)

20 September

For Ravenna, however, I had nothing but smiles – grave, reflective, philosophic smiles, I hasten to add, such as accord with the historic dignity, not to say the mortal sunny sadness, of the place. I arrived there in the evening, before, even at drowsy Ravenna, the festa of the Statuto had altogether put itself to bed. I immediately strolled forth from the inn, and found it sitting up a while longer on the piazza, chiefly at the café door, listening to the band of the garrison by the light of a dozen or so of feeble tapers, fastened along the front of the palace of the Government. Before long, however, it had dispersed and departed, and I was left alone with the grey illumination and with an affable citizen whose testimony as to the manners and customs of Ravenna I had aspired to obtain. I had, borrowing confidence from prompt observation, suggested deferentially that it wasn't the liveliest place in the world, and my friend admitted that it was in fact not a seat of ardent life. But had I seen the Corso? Without seeing the Corso one didn't exhaust the possibilities. The Corso of Ravenna, of a hot summer night, had an air of surprising seclusion and repose. Here and there in an upper closed window glimmered a light; my companion's footsteps and my own were the only sounds; not a creature was within sight. The suffocating air helped me to believe for a moment that I walked in the Italy of Boccaccio, hand-in-hand with the plague, through a city which had lost half its population by pestilence and the other half by flight. I turned back into my inn profoundly satisfied. This at last was the old-world dulness of a prime distillation; this at last was antiquity, history, repose.

The Sources of the Nile

From *The Histories, 426–415 BC* | Herodotus (484BC–c. 425 BC)

Translated by George Rawlinson (1812–1902)

Book II, chapters 28–29

28. I have found no one among all those with whom I have conversed, whether Egyptians, Libyans, or Greeks, Who professed to have any knowledge, except a single person. He was the scribe who kept the register of the sacred treasures of Athena in the city of Saïs, and he did not seem to me to be in earnest when he said that he knew them perfectly well. His story was as follows:– 'Between Syênê, a city of the Thabaïs, and Elephantiné, there are' (he said) 'two hills with sharp conical tops; the name of the one is Crophi, of the other, Mophi. Midway between them are the fountains of the Nile, fountains which it is impossible to fathom. Half the water runs northward into Egypt, half to the south towards Ethiopia.'
The fountains were known to be unfathomable, he declared, because Psammetichus, an Egyptian king, had made trial of them. He had caused a rope to be made, many thousand fathoms in length, and had sounded the fountain with it, but could find no bottom. By this the scribe gave me to understand, if there was any truth at all in what he said, that in this fountain there are certain strong eddies, and a regurgitation, owing to the force wherewith the water dashes against the mountains, and hence a sounding-line cannot be got to reach the bottom of the spring.

29. No other information on this head could I obtain from any quarter.

The Lost Trunk

From *The Virginian, 1902* | Owen Wister (1860–1938)

Medicine Bow was my station. I bade my fellow-travellers good-by, and descended, a stranger, into the great cattle land. And here in less than ten minutes I learned news which made me feel a stranger indeed.

My baggage was lost; it had not come on my train; it was adrift somewhere back in the two thousand miles that lay behind me. And by way of comfort, the baggage-man remarked that passengers often got astray from their trunks, but the trunks mostly found them after a while. Having offered me this encouragement, he turned whistling to his affairs and left me planted in the baggage-room at Medicine Bow. I stood deserted among crates and boxes, blankly holding my check, hungry and forlorn. I stared out through the door at the sky and the plains; but I did not see the antelope shining among the sage-brush, nor the great sunset light of Wyoming. Annoyance blinded my eyes to all things save my grievance: I saw only a lost trunk.

Travelling

William Wordsworth (1770–1850)

This is the spot: – how mildly does the sun
Shine in between the fading leaves! the air
In the habitual silence of this wood
Is more than silent: and this bed of heath,
Where shall we find so sweet a resting-place?
Come! – let me see thee sink into a dream
Of quiet thoughts, – protracted till thine eye
Be calm as water when the winds are gone
And no one can tell whither. – my sweet friend!
We two have had such happy hours together
That my heart melts in me to think of it.

A New Day

From *The Gobi Desert, 1942* | Mildred Cable (1878–1952)
with Francesca French (1871–1960)

On the threshold of the desert:
A ray of the rising sun touched the scalloped ridge of ice-fields in
the Tibetan Alps and threw a veil of pink over their snowy slopes,
but the great mass of the mountain range was still in the grip of that
death-like hue which marks the last resistance of night to the coming
day. The morning star was still visible, but it was grey dawn on the
plain below, and light was gaining rapidly. There was a strange sense
of vibration in the air, for the world was awakening and all nature
responded to the call of a new day.

At the foot of the mountain range lay the old travel road, wide
and deeply marked, literally cut to bits by the sharp nail-studded
wheels of countless caravan carts. The ruts parted and merged, then
spread again, as the eddies of a current mark the face of a river.
Over this road myriads of travellers had journeyed for thousands of
years, making of it a ceaselessly flowing stream of life, for it was the
great highway of Asia, which connected the Far East with distant
European lands.

The Story of the Young Italian

From *Tales of a Traveller, by Geoffrey Crayon, Gent., 1824*

Washington Irving (1783–1859)

Leaving the convent, where he was brought up, for the first time:
When I had nearly attained the age of sixteen, I was suffered, on one
occasion, to accompany one of the brethren on a mission to a distant
part of the country. We soon left behind us the gloomy valley in
which I had been pent up for so many years, and after a short journey
among the mountains, emerged upon the voluptuous landscape that
spreads itself about the Bay of Naples. Heavens! How transported
was I, when I stretched my gaze over a vast reach of delicious sunny
country, gay with groves and vineyards; with Vesuvius rearing its
forked summit to my right; the blue Mediterranean to my left, with
its enchanting coast, studded with shining towns and sumptuous
villas; and Naples, my native Naples, gleaming far, far in the
distance.

Good God! was this the lovely world from which I had been
excluded! I had reached that age when the sensibilities are in all their
bloom and freshness. Mine had been checked and chilled. They
now burst forth with the suddenness of a retarded spring. My heart,
hitherto unnaturally shrunk up, expanded into a riot of vague, but
delicious emotions. The beauty of nature intoxicated, bewildered me.
The song of the peasants; their cheerful looks; their happy avocations;
the picturesque gayety of their dresses; their rustic music; their
dances; all broke upon me like witchcraft. My soul responded to the
music; my heart danced in my bosom. All the men appeared amiable,
all the women lovely.

Antwerp

From *Little Travels and Roadside Sketches, 1840*

William Makepeace Thackeray (1811–1863)

As many hundreds of thousands of English visit this city (I have met at least a hundred of them in this half-hour walking the streets, 'Guide-book' in hand), and as the ubiquitous Murray has already depicted the place, there is no need to enter into a long description of it, its neatness, its beauty, and its stiff antique splendour. The tall pale houses have many of them crimped gables, that look like Queen Elizabeth's ruffs. There are as many people in the streets as in London at three o'clock in the morning; the market-women wear bonnets of a flower-pot shape, and have shining brazen milk-pots, which are delightful to the eyes of a painter. Along the quays of the lazy Scheldt are innumerable good-natured groups of beer-drinkers (small-beer is the most good-natured drink in the world); along the barriers outside of the town, and by the glistening canals, are more beer-shops and more beer-drinkers. The city is defended by the queerest fat military. The chief traffic is between the hotels and the railroad. The hotels give wonderful good dinners, and especially at the 'Grand Laboureur' may be mentioned a peculiar tart, which is the best of all tarts that ever a man ate since he was ten years old. A moonlight walk is delightful. At ten o'clock the whole city is quiet; and so little changed does it seem to be, that you may walk back three hundred years into time, and fancy yourself a majestical Spaniard, or an oppressed and patriotic Dutchman at your leisure.

Service With a Smile

From *The Road to Oxiana, 1937* | Robert Byron (1905–1941)

IRAK: Baghdad (115 ft.), September 27th

If anything on earth could have made this place attractive by contrast, it was the journey that brought us here. We travelled in a banana-shaped tender on two wheels, which was attached to the dickey of a two-seater Buick and euphemistically known as the aero-bus. A larger bus, the father of all motor-coaches, followed behind. Hermetically sealed, owing to the dust, yet swamped in water from a leaky drinking-tank, we jolted across the pathless desert at forty miles an hour, beaten upon by the sun, deafened by the battery of stones against the thin floor, and stifled by the odour of five sweating companions. At noon we stopped for lunch, which was provided by the company in a cardboard box labelled 'Service with a Smile'. It will be Service with a Frown if we ever run transport in these parts. Butter-paper and egg-shells floated away to ruin the Arabian countryside. At sunset we came to Rutbah, which had been surrounded, since I lunched there on my way to India in 1929, by coolie lines and an encampment: the result of the Mosul pipe-line. Here we dined; whiskies and sodas cost six shillings each. At night our spirits lifted; the moon shone in at the window; the five Irakis, led by Mrs Mullah, sang.

London

John Davidson (1857–1909)

Athwart the sky a lowly sigh
    From west to east the sweet wind carried;
The sun stood still on Primrose Hill;
    His light in all the city tarried:
The clouds on viewless columns bloomed
Like smouldering lilies unconsumed.

'Oh sweetheart, see! how shadowy,
    Of some occult magician's rearing,
Or swung in space of heaven's grace
Dissolving, dimly reappearing,
Afloat upon ethereal tides
St. Paul's above the city rides!'

A rumour broke through the thin smoke
    Enwreathing abbey, tower, and palace,
The parks, the squares, the thoroughfares,
    The million-peopled lanes and alleys,
An ever-muttering prisoned storm,
The heart of London beating warm.

A Roving Disposition

From *The Coral Island, 1857* | R. M. Ballantyne (1835–1894)

Roving has always been, and still is, my ruling passion, the joy of my heart, the very sunshine of my existence. In childhood, in boyhood, and in man's estate, I have been a rover; not a mere rambler among the woody glens and upon the hilltops of my own native land, but an enthusiastic rover throughout the length and breadth of the wide, wide world.

It was a wild, black night of howling storm, the night in which I was born on the foaming bosom of the broad Atlantic Ocean. My father was a sea-captain; my grandfather was a sea-captain; my great-grandfather had been a marine. Nobody could tell positively what occupation *his* father had followed; but my dear mother used to assert that he had been a midshipman, whose grandfather, on the mother's side, had been an admiral in the royal navy. At any rate we knew that, as far back as our family could be traced, it had been intimately connected with the great watery waste. Indeed this was the case on both sides of the house; for my mother always went to sea with my father on his long voyages, and so spent the greater part of her life upon the water.

Thus it was, I suppose, that I came to inherit a roving disposition.

How the Camel Quest Began

From *The Lost Camels of Tartary, 1998* | John Hare (1934–2022)

30 September

'Walk?' exclaimed Professor Yuan. 'Where to?'

I got out of the jeep and pointed towards a barrier of sand dunes that stretched out interminably in front of us.

'There,' I said. 'I want to walk there.'

'Impossible,' came the reply. 'We can't walk over those dunes.'

I could understand his reluctance. We were tired, dirty and thirsty and had been travelling for hours through the Chinese Desert of Lop, described by Marco Polo as 'fearful' and the scholar and traveller, Hsuan Tsang, as the 'haunt of poisonous imps and fiends'. Finally, we'd reached the truly formidable range of the Kum Tagh sand dunes, spreading 400 kilometres east to west and forming a forbidding barrier south of the dry lake of Lop Nur. Admittedly, it didn't look inviting, but I was undeterred.

The Professor and his team followed reluctantly, muttering and grumbling at my utter stupidity. I closed my ears to their mumbled protests and, as though mindlessly possessed, strode on ahead. We tramped on through a howling, dusty gale for about five kilometres, then, just as I rounded a massive dune, I saw the most extraordinary sight. Standing directly in front of me was a wild camel. The beast didn't move and at first I thought that it must be sick and dying. Moments later, I spotted what looked like a discarded sack at its feet. It was a young camel, no more than a few hours old. A female had just given birth.

The camel calf struggled unsteadily to its feet and began to suckle. All the disappointment and hardships of the previous weeks were forgotten as we watched, completely absorbed by the miracle of new life in one of the most desolate places on earth. We knew that there was no recorded witness of such a scene.

'You must have second sight,' whispered the Professor.

I had nothing of the sort. It was just another inexplicable link in a chain of events that had propelled me into the desert to search for the Wild Bactrian camel.

OCTOBER

A Road Through the Forest

The Crescent Lake

From *The Gobi Desert, 1942* | Mildred Cable (1878–1952)
with Francesca French (1871–1960)

I sat for long hours in my sand chair by the Crescent Lake and reflected on the teaching of those desert experiences, the illusive mirage, the tormenting bitter water, the sweet water of the karez channel and the invigorating water of the living spring. Then slowly the lovely lake at my feet recaptured my attention, seeming to say, 'Now consider what lies before your eyes.' So I dismissed all thought of desert rigours and yielded myself to the charm of the moment.

The whole scene, from the brilliant glazed-tiled roofs, the light loggia, the golden sand, the silver trees, the fringe of green sedge, and the delicate hues of wheeling pigeons, was reflected in the still water as sharply as in a mirror.

In Eighty Days

From *Around the World in Eighty Days, 1873* | Jules Verne (1828–1905)

Translated by George Makepeace Towle (1841–1893)

Wednesday 2nd October, 1872

'That is true, gentlemen,' added John Sullivan. 'Only eighty days, now that the section between Rothal and Allahabad, on the Great Indian Peninsula Railway, has been opened. Here is the estimate made by the *Daily Telegraph*:–

From London to Suez via Mont Cenis and Brindisi, by rail and steamboats	7 days
From Suez to Bombay, by steamer	13 "
From Bombay to Calcutta, by rail	3 "
From Calcutta to Hong Kong, by steamer	13 "
From Hong Kong to Yokohama (Japan), by steamer	6 "
From Yokohama to San Francisco, by steamer	22 "
From San Francisco to New York, by rail	7 "
From New York to London, by steamer and rail	9 "
Total	80 days

'Yes, in eighty days!' exclaimed Stuart, who in his excitement made a false deal. 'But that doesn't take into account bad weather, contrary winds, shipwrecks, rail-way accidents, and so on.'

'All included,' returned Phileas Fogg.

An Intense Fascination

From *A Lady's Life in the Rocky Mountains, 1879*

Isabella Bird (1831–1904)

October 3.

This is surely one of the most entrancing spots on earth. Oh, that
I could paint with pen or brush! From my bed I look on Mirror Lake,
and with the very earliest dawn, when objects are not discernible,
it lies there absolutely still, a purplish lead color. Then suddenly
into its mirror flash inverted peaks, at first a dawn darker all round.
This is a new sight, each morning new. Then the peaks fade, and
when morning is no longer 'spread upon the mountains,' the pines
are mirrored in my lake almost as solid objects, and the glory steals
downwards, and a red flush warms the clear atmosphere of the
park, and the hoar-frost sparkles and the crested blue-jays step forth
daintily on the jewelled grass. The majesty and beauty grow on me
daily. As I crossed from my cabin just now, and the long mountain
shadows lay on the grass, and form and color gained new meanings,
I was almost false to Hawaii; I couldn't go on writing for the glory
of the sunset, but went out and sat on a rock to see the deepening
blue in the dark canyons, and the peaks becoming rose color one by
one, then fading into sudden ghastliness, the awe-inspiring heights of
Long's Peak fading last. Then came the glories of the afterglow, when
the orange and lemon of the east faded into gray, and then gradually
the gray for some distance above the horizon brightened into a cold
blue, and above the blue into a broad band of rich, warm red, with an
upper band of rose color; above it hung a big cold moon. This is the
'daily miracle' of evening, as the blazing peaks in the darkness
of Mirror Lake are the miracle of morning. Perhaps this scenery
is not lovable, but, as if it were a strong stormy character, it has an
intense fascination.

A Unique Arrangement

From *Through Khiva to Golden Samarkand, 1925*

Ella Christie (1861–1949)

Lines of green and gold, and gold and green, beyond which the walls and minarets of Khiva appeared in sight. Can that be really Khiva? I was forced to say. The scene filled one with a thrill of satisfaction. All past difficulties and discomforts were forgotten, and future ones unthought of – the goal was reached. As we neared the town, a building, whose foundations were little more than laid, showed itself just outside one of the gates. Anything of a modern nature seemed so surprising – its purpose, as I afterwards learned, not less so, being a post office and fever hospital combined; surely an absolutely unique arrangement either in the history of post offices or hospitals. There were no postal arrangements of any kind, nor of course a telegraph, yet that town of 60,000 inhabitants seemed to have prospered notwithstanding its lack of either.

4 October

Where go the Boats?

Robert Louis Stevenson (1850–1894)

Dark brown is the river.
    Golden is the sand.
It flows along for ever,
    With trees on either hand.

Green leaves a-floating,
    Castles of the foam,
Boats of mine a-boating –
    Where will all come home?

On goes the river
    And out past the mill,
Away down the valley,
    Away down the hill.

Away down the river,
    A hundred miles or more,
Other little children
    Shall bring my boats ashore.

The Need to Cross the Channel

From *The Scarlet Pimpernel*, 1905 | Baroness Orczy (1865–1947)

[Sir Andrew] 'I am sorry to say we cannot cross over to-night.'

'Not cross over to-night?' she [Lady Blakeney] repeated in amazement. 'But we must, Sir Andrew, we must! There can be no question of cannot, and whatever it may cost, we must get a vessel to-night.'

But the young man shook his head sadly.

'I am afraid it is not a question of cost, Lady Blakeney. There is a nasty storm blowing from France, the wind is dead against us, we cannot possibly sail until it has changed.'

Marguerite became deadly pale. She had not foreseen this. Nature herself was playing her a horrible, cruel trick. Percy was in danger, and she could not go to him, because the wind happened to blow from the coast of France.

'But we must go! – we must!' she repeated with strange, persistent energy, 'you know, we must go! – can't you find a way?'

'I have been down to the shore already,' he said, 'and had a talk to one or two skippers. It is quite impossible to set sail to-night, so every sailor assured me. No one,' he added, looking significantly at Marguerite, '*no one* could possibly put out of Dover to-night.'

Marguerite at once understood what he meant. *No one* included Chauvelin as well as herself.

Finding Xanadu

From *In Xanadu, 1989* | William Dalrymple (1965–)

The next morning the alarm went off, as usual, at five-thirty.
Thousands of miles away in East Anglia the Cambridge term was
about to begin. Everyone would be rushing off to Heffer's to buy
their textbooks, Lever-Arch files and file paper. We should have been
there too; instead we were in the middle of Mongolia and had twelve
hours to find Xanadu.

. . . .

I took out the phial of oil from my waistcoat pocket and, with Lou
two steps behind, we very slowly climbed up the ramp. At the top
I knelt before the place where the throne of the Khan used to stand.
I unscrewed the phial then tipped the oil onto the ground. For a
second it floated on the surface, then it slowly began to sink into
the earth, leaving only a glistening patch on the mud where it had
fallen. Then, in the drizzle, halfway across the world from Cambridge
Louisa and I recited in unison the poem that had immortalized the
palace in whose wreckage we stood:

Kubla Khan

Samuel Taylor Coleridge (1772–1834)

Lines 1–11

In Xanadu did Kubla Khan
A stately pleasure-dome decree:
Where Alph, the sacred river, ran
Through caverns measureless to man
    Down to a sunless sea.
So twice five miles of fertile ground
With walls and towers were girdled round:
And there were gardens bright with sinuous rills,
Where blossomed many an incense-bearing tree;
And here were forests as ancient as the hills,
Enfolding sunny spots of greenery.

The Totems at Kitwancool

From *Klee Wyck, 1941*

Emily Carr, 'Klee Wyck' or 'Laughing One' (1871–1945)

I stood before the tall, cold woman. She folded her arms across her body and her eyes searched my face. They were as expressive as if she were saying the words herself instead of using the hero's tongue.

'My mother-in-law wishes to know why you have come to our village.'

'I want to make some pictures of the totem poles.'

'What do you want our totem poles for?'

'Because they are beautiful. They are getting old now, and your people make very few new ones. The young people do not value the poles as the old ones did. By and by there will be no more poles. I want to make pictures of them, so that your young people as well as the white people will see how fine your totem poles used to be.'

. . . .

The sun enriched the old poles grandly. They were carved elaborately and with great sincerity. Several times the figure of a woman that held a child was represented. The babies had faces like wise little old men. The mothers expressed all womanhood – the big wooden hands holding the child were so full of tenderness they had to be distorted enormously in order to contain it all. Womanhood was strong in Kitwancool.

Signs of Land

From *The Journal of Columbus's First Voyage 1492–1493*

Christopher Columbus (1451–1506)

Wednesday, 10th of October.

The course was W.S.W., and they went at the rate of 10 miles an hour, occasionally 12 miles, and sometimes 7. During the day and night they made 59 leagues, counted as no more than 44. Here the people could endure no longer. They complained of the length of the voyage. But the Admiral cheered them up in the best way he could, giving them good hopes of the advantages they might gain from it. He added that, however much they might complain, he had to go to the Indies, and that he would go on until he found them, with the help of our Lord.

Thursday, 11th of October.

The course was W.S.W., and there was more sea than there had been during the whole of the voyage. They saw sandpipers, and a green reed near the ship. Those of the caravel *Pinta* saw a cane and a pole, and they took up another small pole which appeared to have been worked with iron; also another bit of cane, a land-plant, and a small board. The crew of the caravel *Niña* also saw signs of land, and a small branch covered with berries. Everyone breathed afresh and rejoiced at these signs.

The Test of a Voyage

From *The Cruise of the Snark, 1911* | Jack London (1876–1916)

In 1906 Jack and his wife Charmian set out on a seven year, round-the-world cruise but the voyage has to be abandoned:

A last word: the test of the voyage. It is easy enough for me or any man to say that it was enjoyable. But there is a better witness, the one woman who made it from beginning to end. In hospital when I broke the news to Charmian that I must go back to California, the tears welled into her eyes. For two days she was wrecked and broken by the knowledge that the happy, happy voyage was abandoned.

Leaving London

From *The Voyage Out, 1915* | Virginia Woolf (1882–1941)

Winding veils round their heads, the women walked on deck. They were now moving steadily down the river, passing the dark shapes of ships at anchor, and London was a swarm of lights with a pale yellow canopy drooping above it. There were the lights of the great theatres, the lights of the long streets, lights that indicated huge squares of domestic comfort, lights that hung high in air. No darkness would ever settle upon those lamps, as no darkness had settled upon them for hundreds of years. It seemed dreadful that the town should blaze for ever in the same spot; dreadful at least to people going away to adventure upon the sea, and beholding it as a circumscribed mound, eternally burnt, eternally scarred. From the deck of the ship the great city appeared a crouched and cowardly figure, a sedentary miser.

Leaning over the rail, side by side, Helen said, 'Won't you be cold?' Rachel replied, 'No … How beautiful!' she added a moment later. Very little was visible – a few masts, a shadow of land here, a line of brilliant windows there. They tried to make head against the wind.

'It blows – it blows!' gasped Rachel, the words rammed down her throat. Struggling by her side, Helen was suddenly overcome by the spirit of movement, and pushed along with her skirts wrapping themselves round her knees, and both arms to her hair.

The Winds of Fate

Ella Wheeler Wilcox (1850–1919)

One ship drives east and another drives west
With the self-same winds that blow;
   'Tis the set of the sails
    And not the gales
That tells them the way to go.

Like the winds of the sea are the winds of fate
As we voyage along through life;
   'Tis the set of the soul
    That decides its goal
And not the calm or the strife.

Moving On

From *Walden, 1954* | Henry David Thoreau (1817–1862)

I left the woods for as good a reason as I went there. Perhaps it
seemed to me that I had several more lives to live, and could not
spare any more time for that one. It is remarkable how easily and
insensibly we fall into a particular route, and make a beaten track
for ourselves. I had not lived there a week before my feet wore a path
from my door to the pond-side; and though it is five or six years
since I trod it, it is still quite distinct. It is true, I fear that others
may have fallen into it, and so helped to keep it open. The surface
of the earth is soft and impressible by the feet of men; and so with
the paths which the mind travels. How worn and dusty, then, must
be the highways of the world, how deep the ruts of tradition and
conformity! I did not wish to take a cabin passage, but rather to go
before the mast and on the deck of the world, for there I could
best see the moonlight amid the mountains. I do not wish to go
below now.

14 October

Impossible

From *Around the World in Seventy-Two Days, 1890*

Nellie Bly (1864–1922)

I approached my editor rather timidly on the subject. I was afraid
that he would think the idea too wild and visionary.

. . . .

'I want to go around in eighty days or less. I think I can beat Phileas
Fogg's record. May I try it?'

To my dismay he told me that in the office they had thought of
this same idea before and the intention was to send a man. However
he offered me the consolation that he would favor my going, and
then we went to talk with the business manager about it.

'It is impossible for you to do it,' was the terrible verdict. 'In the
first place you are a woman and would need a protector, and even if it
were possible for you to travel alone you would need to carry so much
baggage that it would detain you in making rapid changes. Besides
you speak nothing but English, so there is no use talking about it; no
one but a man can do this.'

'Very well,' I said angrily, 'Start the man, and I'll start the same
day for some other newspaper and beat him.'

'I believe you would,' he said slowly. I would not say that this had
any influence on their decision, but I do know that before we parted
I was made happy by the promise that if any one was commissioned
to make the trip, I should be that one.

The Palace of Prester John

From *Travels, 1356/1366: The version of the Cotton Manuscript in modern spelling, London, 1900*

Sir John Mandeville (c. 1300–1371)

He dwelleth commonly in the city of Susa. And there is his principal palace, that is so rich and so noble, that no man will trow it by estimation, but he had seen it. And above the chief tower of the palace be two round pommels of gold, and in everych of them be two carbuncles great and large, that shine full bright upon the night. And the principal gates of his palace be of precious stone that men clepe sardonyx, and the border and the bars be of ivory. And the windows of the halls and chambers be of crystal. And the tables whereon men eat, some be of emeralds, some of amethyst, and some of gold, full of precious stones; and the pillars that bear up the tables be of the same precious stones. And the degrees to go up to his throne, where he sitteth at the meat, one is of onyx, another is of crystal, and another of jasper green, another of amethyst, another of sardine, another of cornelian, and the seventh, that he setteth on his feet, is of chrysolite. And all these degrees be bordered with fine gold, with the tother precious stones, set with great pearls orient. And the sides of the siege of his throne be of emeralds, and bordered with gold full nobly, and dubbed with other precious stones and great pearls. And all the pillars in his chamber be of fine gold with precious stones, and with many carbuncles, that give great light upon the night to all people. And albeit that the carbuncles give light right enough, natheles, at all times burneth a vessel of crystal full of balm, for to give good smell and odour to the emperor, and to void away all wicked airs and corruptions. And the form of his bed is of fine sapphires, bended with gold, for to make him sleep well and to refrain him from lechery; for he will not lie with his wives, but four sithes in the year, after the four seasons, and that is only for to engender children.

The Listeners

Walter de la Mare (1873–1956)

'Is there anybody there?' said the Traveller,
    Knocking on the moonlit door;
And his horse in the silence champed the grasses
    Of the forest's ferny floor:
And a bird flew up out of the turret,
    Above the Traveller's head:
And he smote upon the door again a second time;
    'Is there anybody there?' he said.
But no one descended to the Traveller;
    No head from the leaf-fringed sill
Leaned over and looked into his grey eyes,
    Where he stood perplexed and still.
But only a host of phantom listeners
    That dwelt in the lone house then
Stood listening in the quiet of the moonlight
    To that voice from the world of men:
Stood thronging the faint moonbeams on the dark stair,
    That goes down to the empty hall,

Hearkening in an air stirred and shaken
    By the lonely Traveller's call.
And he felt in his heart their strangeness,
    And their stillness answering his cry,
While his horse moved, cropping the dark turf,
    'Neath the starred and leafy sky;
For he suddenly smote on the door, even
    Louder and lifted his head: –
'Tell them I came, and no one answered,
    That I kept my word,' he said.
Never the least stir made the listeners,
    Though every word he spake
Fell echoing through the shadowiness of the still house
    From the one man left awake:
Ay, they heard his foot upon the stirrup,
    And the sound of iron on stone,
And how the silence surged softly backward,
    When the plunging hoofs were gone.

The Canary Islands

From *Personal Narrative of Travels to the Equinoctial Regions of America During the Years 1799–1804*, published 1807–1834 | Alexander von Humboldt (1769–1859)

Translated by Thomasina Ross (1795–1875)

The current drew us toward the coast more rapidly than we wished. As we advanced, we discovered at first the island of Forteventura, famous for its numerous camels; and a short time after we saw the small island of Lobos in the channel which separates Forteventura from Lancerota. We spent part of the night on deck. The moon illumined the volcanic summits of Lancerota, the flanks of which, covered with ashes, reflected a silver light. Antares threw out its resplendent rays near the lunar disk, which was but a few degrees above the horizon. The night was beautifully serene and cool. Though we were but a little distance from the African coast, and on the limit of the torrid zone, the centigrade thermometer rose no higher than 18°. The phosphorescence of the ocean seemed to augment the mass of light diffused through the air. After midnight, great black clouds rising behind the volcano shrouded at intervals the moon and the beautiful constellation of the Scorpion. We beheld lights carried to and fro on shore, which were probably those of fishermen preparing for their labours. We had been occasionally employed, during our passage, in reading the old voyages of the Spaniards, and these moving lights recalled to our fancy those which Pedro Gutierrez, page of Queen Isabella, saw in the isle of Guanahani, on the memorable night of the discovery of the New World.

Four Hours From the Summit

From *A Short Walk in the Hindu Kush*, 1958

Eric Newby (1919–2006)

The moment where Eric Newby and Hugh Carless meet Wilfred
Thesiger is one of the most amusing endings to a book and is
probably one of the most-quoted pieces of travel writing. This
gives a better idea of their great achievement:

The ridge became more and more narrow and eventually we emerged
onto a perfect knife edge. Ahead, but separated from us by two
formidable buttresses, was the summit, a simple cone of snow as
high as Box Hill.

We dug ourselves a hole in the snow and considered our position.
Below us on every side mountains surged away it seemed for ever;
we looked down on glaciers and snow-covered peaks that perhaps no
one has ever seen before, except from the air. To the west and north
we could see the great axis of the Hindu Kush and its southward
curve, away from the Anjuman Pass around the northern marches
of Nuristan. Away to the east-north-east was the great snow-covered
mountain we had seen from the wall of the east glacier, Tirich Mir,
the 25,000 foot giant on the Chitral border, and to the south-west
the mountains that separated Nuristan from Paryshir.

Our own immediate situation was no less impressive. A stone
dropped from one hand would have landed on one of the upper
glaciers of the Chamar Valley, while from the other it would have
landed on the east glacier.

A Sleeping-sack

From *Travels with a Donkey in the Cévennes, 1879*

Robert Louis Stevenson (1850–1894)

It was already hard upon October before I was ready to set forth, and at the high altitudes over which my road lay there was no Indian summer to be looked for. I was determined, if not to camp out, at least to have the means of camping out in my possession; for there is nothing more harassing to an easy mind than the necessity of reaching shelter by dusk, and the hospitality of a village inn is not always to be reckoned sure by those who trudge on foot. A tent, above all for a solitary traveller, is troublesome to pitch, and troublesome to strike again; and even on the march it forms a conspicuous feature in your baggage. A sleeping-sack, on the other hand, is always ready – you have only to get into it; it serves a double purpose – a bed by night, a portmanteau by day; and it does not advertise your intention of camping out to every curious passer-by. This is a huge point. If a camp is not secret, it is but a troubled resting-place; you become a public character; the convivial rustic visits your bedside after an early supper; and you must sleep with one eye open, and be up before the day. I decided on a sleeping-sack; and after repeated visits to Le Puy, and a deal of high living for myself and my advisers, a sleeping-sack was designed, constructed, and triumphantly brought home.

This child of my invention was nearly six feet square, exclusive of two triangular flaps to serve as a pillow by night and as the top and bottom of the sack by day. I call it 'the sack,' but it was never a sack by more than courtesy: only a sort of long roll or sausage, green waterproof cart-cloth without and blue sheep's fur within. It was commodious as a valise, warm and dry for a bed. There was luxurious turning room for one; and at a pinch the thing might serve for two. I could bury myself in it up to the neck; for my head I trusted to a fur cap, with a hood to fold down over my ears and a band to pass under my nose like a respirator; and in case of heavy rain I proposed to make myself a little tent, or tentlet, with my waterproof coat, three stones, and a bent branch.

Sea-Fever

John Masefield (1878–1967)

I must go down to the seas again, to the lonely sea and the sky,
And all I ask is a tall ship and a star to steer her by,
And the wheel's kick and the wind's song and the white sail's
    shaking,
And a grey mist on the sea's face and a grey dawn breaking.

I must go down to the seas again, for the call of the running tide
Is a wild call and a clear call that may not be denied;
And all I ask is a windy day with the white clouds flying,
And the flung spray and the blown spume, and the sea-gulls crying.

I must go down to the seas again, to the vagrant gypsy life,
To the gull's way and the whale's way where the wind's like a whetted
    knife;
And all I ask is a merry yarn from a laughing fellow-rover,
And a quiet sleep and a sweet dream when the long trick's over.

Pyrates Infesting the West-Indies

From *A General History of the Pyrates, from the first Rise and Settlement in the Island of Providence, to the present Time. With the remarkable Actions and Adventures of the two female Pyrates Mary Read and Anne Bonny, 1724*

Captain Charles Johnson: identity unknown. Thought by some to be a pseudonym for Daniel Defoe (*c.* 1660–1731) or the journalist and printer Nathaniel Mist (d. 1737)

Why they are more numerous than in any other Parts of the World: *First*, Because there are so many uninhabited little Islands and *Keys*, with Harbours convenient and secure for cleaning their Vessels, and abounding with what they often want, Provision; I mean Water, Sea-Fowl, Turtle, Shell, and other Fish; where, if they carry in but strong Liquor, they indulge a Time, and become ready for new Expeditions before any Intelligence can reach to hurt them.

It may here perhaps be no unnecessary Digression, to explain upon what they call Keys in the *West-Indies*: These are small sandy Islands, appearing a little above the Surf of the Water, with only a few Bushes or Weeds upon them, but abound (those most at any Distance from the Main) with Turtle, amphibious Animals, that always chuse the quietest and most unfrequented Place, for laying their Eggs, which are to a vast Number in the Seasons, and would seldom be seen, but for this, (except by Pyrates:) Then Vessels from *Jamaica* and the other Governments make Voyages, called Turtling, for supplying the People, a common and approved Food with them. I am apt to think these *Keys*, especially those nigh

Islands, to have been once contiguous with them, and separated by Earthquakes (frequently there) or Inundations, because some of them that have been within continual View, as those nigh *Jamaica*, are observed within our Time, to be entirely wasted away and lost, and others daily wasting. There are not only of the Use above taken Notice of to Pyrates; but it is commonly believed were always in buccaneering pyratical Times, the hiding Places for their Riches, and often Times a Shelter for themselves, till their Friends on the Main, had found Means to obtain Indemnity for their Crimes; for you must understand, when Acts of Grace were more frequent, and the Laws less severe, these Men continually found Favours and Incouragers at *Jamaica*, and perhaps they are not all dead yet; I have been told many of them still living have been of the same Trade, and left it off only because they can live as well honestly, and gain now at the hazard of others Necks.

Stanzas from the Grande Chartreuse

Matthew Arnold (1822–1888)

Verses 1–3

Through Alpine meadows soft-suffused
With rain, where thick the crocus blows,
Past the dark forges long disused,
The mule-track from Saint Laurent goes.
The bridge is cross'd, and slow we ride,
Through forest, up the mountain-side.

The autumnal evening darkens round,
The wind is up, and drives the rain;
While, hark! far down, with strangled sound
Doth the Dead Guier's stream complain,
Where that wet smoke, among the woods,
Over his boiling cauldron broods.

Swift rush the spectral vapours white
Past limestone scars with ragged pines,
Showing – then blotting from our sight! –
Halt – through the cloud-drift something shines!
High in the valley, wet and drear,
The huts of Courrerie appear.

A Creole in Constantinople

From *Wonderful Adventures of Mrs Seacole in Many Lands*, 1857 | Mary Seacole (1805–1881)

I do not think that Constantinople impressed me so much as I had expected; and I thought its streets would match those of Navy Bay not unfairly. The caicques, also, of which I had ample experience – for I spent six days here, wandering about Pera and Stamboul in the daytime, and returning to the *Hollander* at nightfall – might be made more safe and commodious for stout ladies, even if the process interfered a little with their ornament. Time and trouble combined have left me with a well-filled-out, portly form – the envy of many an angular Yankee female – and, more than once, it was in no slight danger of becoming too intimately acquainted with the temperature of the Bosphorus. But I will do the Turkish boatmen the justice to say that they were as politely careful of my safety as their astonishment and regard for the well-being of their caicques (which they appear to love as an Arab does his horse, or an Esquimaux his dogs, and for the same reason perhaps) would admit. Somewhat surprised, also, seemed the cunning-eyed Greeks, who throng the streets of Pera, at the unprotected Creole woman, who took Constantinople so coolly (it would require something more to surprise her); while the grave English raised their eyebrows wonderingly, and the more vivacious French shrugged their pliant shoulders into the strangest contortions. I accepted it all as a compliment to a stout female tourist, neatly dressed in a red or yellow dress, a plain shawl of some other colour, and a simple straw wide-awake, with bright red streamers. I flatter myself that I woke up sundry sleepy-eyed Turks, who seemed to think that the great object of life was to avoid showing surprise at anything; while the Turkish women gathered around me, and jabbered about me, in the most flattering manner.

Keeping Off Demons

From *Eothen, 1844* | A. W. Kinglake (1809–1891)

We had ridden on for some two or three hours – the stir and bustle of our commencing journey had ceased, the liveliness of our little troop had worn off with the declining day, and the night closed in as we entered the great Servian forest. Through this our road was to last for more than a hundred miles. Endless, and endless now on either side, the tall oaks closed in their ranks and stood gloomily lowering over us, as grim as an army of giants with a thousand years' pay in arrear. One strived with listening ear to catch some tidings of that forest-world within – some stirring of beasts, some night-bird's scream, but all was quite hushed, except the voice of the cicalas that peopled every bough, and filled the depths of the forest through and through, with one same hum everlasting – more stilling than very silence.

At first our way was in darkness, but after a while the moon got up, and touched the glittering arms and tawny faces of our men with light so pale and mystic, that the watchful Tatar felt bound to look out for demons, and take proper means for keeping them off; forthwith he determined that the duty of frightening away our ghostly enemies (like every other troublesome work) should fall upon the poor Suridgees, who accordingly lifted up their voices, and burst upon the dreadful stillness of the forest with shrieks and dismal howls. These precautions were kept up incessantly, and were followed by the most complete success, for not one demon came near us.

Atarantians and Atlantes

From *The Histories, 426–415 BC* | Herodotus (484 BC–c. 425 BC)

Translated by George Rawlinson (1812–1902)

Book IV, chapters 184–185

184. At a distance of ten days' journey from the Garamantians there
is again another salt-hill and spring of water; around which dwell
a people, called the Atarantians, who alone of all known nations are
destitute of names. The title Atarantians is borne by the whole race
in common; but the men have no particular names of their own. The
Atarantians, when the sun rises high in the heaven, curse him, and
load him with reproaches, because (they say) he burns and wastes
both their country and themselves. Once more at a distance of ten
days' journey there is a salt-hill, a spring, and an inhabited tract.
Near the salt is a mountain called Atlas, very taper and round; so
lofty, moreover, that the top (it is said) cannot be seen, the clouds
never quitting it either summer or winter. The natives call this
mountain 'the Pillar of Heaven;' and they themselves take their name
from it, being called Atlantes. They are reported not to eat any living
thing, and never to have any dreams.

185. As far as the Atlantes the names of the nations inhabiting the
sandy ridge are known to me; but beyond them my knowledge fails.

Reading for Train Journeys

From *The Importance of Being Earnest, 1895*

Oscar Wilde (1854–1900)

Act II

Gwendoline:

I never travel without my diary. One should always have something sensational to read in the train.

An Earthquake

From *Personal Narrative of Travels to the Equinoctial Regions of America During the Years 1799–1804*, published 1807–1834 | Alexander von Humboldt (1769–1859)

Translated by Thomasina Ross (1795–1875)

After the 28th of October, the reddish mist became thicker than it had previously been. The heat of the nights seemed stifling, though the thermometer rose only to 26°. The breeze, which generally refreshed the air from eight or nine o'clock in the evening, was no longer felt. The atmosphere was burning hot, and the parched and dusty ground was cracked on every side. On the 4th of November, about two in the afternoon, large clouds of peculiar blackness enveloped the high mountains of the Brigantine and the Tataraqual. They extended by degrees as far as the zenith. About four in the afternoon thunder was heard over our heads, at an immense height, not regularly rolling, but with a hollow and often interrupted sound. At the moment of the strongest electric explosion, at 4h 12', there were two shocks of earthquake, which followed each other at the interval of fifteen seconds. The people ran into the streets, uttering loud cries. M. Bonpland, who was leaning over a table examining plants, was almost thrown on the floor. I felt the shock very strongly, though I was lying in a hammock.

Gondolas

From *Travels in Italy, 1786–1788, published 1816, 1817*

Johann Wolfgang von Goethe (1749–1832)

Translated by A. J. W. Morrison (1806–1865)

As the first of the gondoliers came up to the ship (they come in order to convey more quickly to Venice those passengers who are in a hurry), I recollected an old plaything, of which, perhaps, I had not thought for twenty years. My father had a beautiful model of a gondola which he had brought with him [from Italy]; he set a great value upon it, and it was considered a great treat, when I was allowed to play with it. The first beaks of tinned iron-plate, the black gondola-cages, all greeted me like old acquaintances, and I experienced again dear emotions of my childhood which had been long unknown.

To *****

Thomas Hood (1799–1845)

Verses 1–2

I gaze upon a city,
A city new and strange;
Down many a wat'ry vista
My fancy takes a range;
From side to side I saunter,
And wonder where I am; –
And can *you* be in England,
And I at Rotterdam!

Before me lie dark waters
In broad canals and deep,
Whereon the silver moonbeams
Sleep, restless in their sleep:
A sort of vulgar Venice
Reminds me where I am, –
Yes, yes, you are in England,
And I'm at Rotterdam.

Comfortable Lodgings

From *Can You Forgive Her?* 1864 | Anthony Trollope (1815–1882)

Kate Vavasor, in writing to her cousin Alice, felt some little difficulty in excusing herself for remaining in Norfolk with Mrs. Greenow. She had laughed at Mrs. Greenow before she went to Yarmouth, and had laughed at herself for going there. And in all her letters since, she had spoken of her aunt as a silly, vain, worldly woman, weeping crocodile tears, for an old husband whose death had released her from the tedium of his company, and spreading lures to catch new lovers. But yet she agreed to stay with her aunt, and remain with her in lodgings at Norwich for a month.

But Mrs. Greenow had about her something more than Kate had acknowledged when she first attempted to read her aunt's character. She was clever, and in her own way persuasive. She was very generous, and possessed a certain power of making herself pleasant to those around her. In asking Kate to stay with her she had so asked as to make it appear that Kate was to confer the favour. She had told her niece that she was all alone in the world. 'I have money,' she had said, with more appearance of true feeling than Kate had observed before. 'I have money, but I have nothing else in the world. I have no home. Why should I not remain here in Norfolk, where I know a few people? If you'll say that you'll go anywhere else with me, I'll go to any place you'll name.' Kate had believed this to be hardly true. She had felt sure that her aunt wished to remain in the neighbourhood of her seaside admirers; but, nevertheless, she had yielded, and at the end of October the two ladies, with Jeannette, settled themselves in comfortable lodgings within the precincts of the Close at Norwich.

NOVEMBER

A View of Astonishing Grandeur

Returning to the Marshes in 1973

From *Return to the Marshes, 1977* | Gavin Young (1928–2001)

Amara had been Thesiger's beloved companion. I retained a vision
from all those years ago in Basra of a small slim figure smiling up at
me when Thesiger introduced us, and then just as gravely offering me
a handful of Huntley and Palmer's ginger biscuits from a silver box
on the British Consul's tea-table. After that, in obscure parts of the
Marsh, I had met him whenever I met Thesiger. They had parted for
ever at Basra Airport in 1958. I had not seen Amara since 1956.

. . . .

Then I saw Amara. His face was suddenly illuminated by a leap of
flame from an open fire (it was warm weather and they had been
sitting round their tea out-of-doors). It was a long, lined, rather worn
face, with a day's stubble and a neat black moustache. He was
now taller and, like me, a good deal older. I knew him at once from
his eyes; deep-set, rather sad, or, at least, resigned-looking eyes.
But I knew he had not recognized me, despite his murmur and
handshake of welcome. At that moment he was turning away to see
to the tea for us.

'Amara,' I called in English, 'Amara, you bloody boy, damn and
blast it!' It was the only English Amara had ever known. It had
been Thesiger's shout of protest in the stress of doctoring if Amara
dropped the syringe or handed him the wrong medicine-bottle.
It had soon become a joke-phrase to all our Marsh friends. When
Amara heard it now, he stood stock-still with his back to me. Then
he wheeled round, eyes wide, and an expression of astonishment and
gladness that I shall never forget.

'Sahib!' He came back to me in two strides, swiftly grabbing my
hands. 'Oh, it's a long time, a long time,' he said.

Paper Money

From *The Travels, 1271–1295, published* c. *1300* | Marco Polo
(1254–1324), co-written by Rustichello da Pisa (fl. late 13th century)
Translated as *The Book of Ser Marco Polo, the Venetian*, 1871 by
Colonel Henry Yule (1820–1889)

The Emperor's Mint then is in this same City of Cambaluc, and the
way it is wrought is such that you might say he hath the Secret of
Alchemy in perfection, and you would be right! For he makes his
money after this fashion.

He makes them take of the bark of a certain tree, in fact of the
Mulberry Tree, the leaves of which are the food of the silkworms, –
these trees being so numerous that whole districts are full of them.
What they take is a certain fine white bast or skin which lies between
the wood of the tree and the thick outer bark, and this they make
into something resembling sheets of paper, but black. When these
sheets have been prepared they are cut up into pieces of different
sizes. The smallest of these sizes is worth a half tornesel; the next,
a little larger, one tornesel; one, a little larger still, is worth half a
silver groat of Venice; another a whole groat; others yet two groats,
five groats, and ten groats. There is also a kind worth one Bezant of
gold, and others of three Bezants, and so up to ten. All these pieces
of paper are issued with as much solemnity and authority as if they
were of pure gold or silver; and on every piece a variety of officials,
whose duty it is, have to write their names, and to put their seals.
And when all is prepared duly, the chief officer deputed by the Kaan
smears the Seal entrusted to him with vermilion, and impresses it on
the paper, so that the form of the Seal remains printed upon it in red;
the Money is then authentic. Any one forging it would be punished
with death. And the Kaan causes every year to be made such a vast
quantity of this money, which costs him nothing, that it must equal
in amount all the treasure in the world.

Long Skirts

From 'On Horse Back – Saddle Dash, No. I',
Christian Recorder, November 3, 1866

Edmonia Goodelle Highgate (1844–1870)

Oh, how independent one feels in the saddle! One thing, I can't imagine why one needs to wear such long riding skirts. They are so inconvenient when you have to ford streams or dash through briers. Oh, fashion, will no Emancipation Proclamation free us from thee!

3 November

The First Description of the Mountain Later Called Everest

From *Himalayan Journals, 1855* | Joseph Dalton Hooker (1817–1911)

November 1848

From the summit of Tonglo I enjoyed the view I had so long desired of the Snowy Himalaya; Sikkim being on the right, Nepal on the left, and the plains of India to the southward; and I procured a set of compass bearings, of the greatest use in mapping the country. In the early morning the transparency of the atmosphere renders this view one of astonishing grandeur. Kinchinjunga bore nearly due north, a dazzling mass of snowy peaks, intersected by blue glaciers, which gleamed in the slanting rays of the rising sun, like aquamarines set in frosted silver. From this the sweep of snowed mountains to the eastward was almost continuous as far as Chola, following a curve of 150 miles, and enclosing the whole of the northern part of Sikkim, which appeared a billowy mass of forest-clad mountains. On the north-east horizon rose the Donkia mountain (23,176 feet), and Chumulari (23,929). Though both were much more distant than the snowy ranges, being respectively eighty and ninety miles off, they raised their gigantic heads above, seeming what they really are, by far the loftiest peaks next to Kinchinjunga; and the perspective of snow is so deceptive, that though from forty to sixty miles beyond, they appeared as though almost in the same line with the ridges they overtopped. Of these mountains, Chumulari presents many attractions to the geographer, from its long disputed position, its sacred character, and the interest attached to it since Turner's mission to Tibet in 1783. It was seen and recognised by Dr. Campbell, and measured by Colonel Waugh, from Sinchul, and also from Tonglo, and was a conspicuous object in my subsequent journey to Tibet. Beyond Junnoo, one of the western peaks of Kinchinjunga, there was no continuous snowy chain; the Himalaya seemed suddenly to decline into black and rugged peaks, till in the far north-west it rose again in a white mountain mass of stupendous elevation at eighty miles distance, called, by my Nepal people, 'Tsungau.'

Ulysses

Alfred, Lord Tennyson (1809–1892)

Lines 1–23

It little profits that an idle king,
By this still hearth, among these barren crags,
Match'd with an aged wife, I mete and dole
Unequal laws unto a savage race,
That hoard, and sleep, and feed, and know not me.

I cannot rest from travel: I will drink
Life to the lees: All times I have enjoy'd
Greatly, have suffer'd greatly, both with those
That loved me, and alone, on shore, and when
Thro' scudding drifts the rainy Hyades
Vext the dim sea: I am become a name;
For always roaming with a hungry heart
Much have I seen and known; cities of men
And manners, climates, councils, governments,
Myself not least, but honour'd of them all;
And drunk delight of battle with my peers,
Far on the ringing plains of windy Troy.
I am a part of all that I have met;
Yet all experience is an arch wherethro'
Gleams that untravell'd world whose margin fades
For ever and forever when I move.
How dull it is to pause, to make an end,
To rust unburnish'd, not to shine in use!

A Rewarding Vision

From *Seven Pillars of Wisdom, 1926* | T. E. Lawrence (1888–1935)

Auda marshalled us for the road, and led us up the last mile of soft heath-clad valley between the rounded hills. It was intimate and homelike till the last green bank; when suddenly we realized it was the last, and beyond lay nothing but clear air. The lovely change this time checked me with amazement; and afterwards, however often we came, there was always a catch of eagerness in the mind, a pricking forward of the camel and straightening up to see again over the crest into openness.

Shtar hill-side swooped away below us for hundreds and hundreds of feet, in curves like bastions, against which summer-morning clouds were breaking: and from its foot opened the new earth of the Guweira plain. Aba el Lissan's rounded limestone breasts were covered with soil and heath, green, well watered. Guweira was a map of pink sand, brushed over with streaks of watercourses, in a mantle of scrub: and, out of this, and bounding this, towered islands and cliffs of glowing sandstone, wind-scarped and rain-furrowed, tinted celestially by the early sun.

After days of travel on the plateau in prison valleys, to meet this brink of freedom was a rewarding vision, like a window in the wall of life. We walked down the whole zigzag pass of Shtar, to feel its excellence, for on our camels we rocked too much with sleep to dare see anything. At the bottom the animals found a matted thorn which gave their jaws pleasure; we in front made a halt, rolled on to sand soft as a couch, and incontinently slept.

At Last

From *Journals, 1805* |

Meriwether Lewis (1774–1809) and William Clark (1770-1838)

Clark: November 7th Thursday 1805

Great joy in camp. We are in view of the ocean, this great Pacific
Ocean which we been so long anxious to see, and the roaring or
noise made by the waves breaking on the rocky shores (as I suppose)
may be heard distinctly.

Those Glorious Islands

From *À La Recherche du Temps Perdu: À l'Ombre des Jeunes Filles en Fleurs, 1918* | Marcel Proust (1871–1922)

Translated as *Remembrance of Things Past: Within a Budding Grove* by K. C. Scott Moncrieff (1889–1930)

When Swann had said to me, in Paris one day when I felt particularly unwell: 'You ought to go off to one of those glorious islands in the Pacific; you'd never come back again if you did.' I should have liked to answer: 'But then I shall not see your daughter any more; I shall be living among people and things she has never seen.' And yet my better judgment whispered: 'What difference can that make, since you are not going to be affected by it? When M. Swann tells you that you will not come back he means by that that you will not want to come back, and if you don't want to that is because you will be happier out there.'

The Train

John Davidson (1857–1909)

Verses 1–5

A monster taught
To come to hand
Amain,
As swift as thought
Across the land
The train.

The song it sings
Has an iron sound;
Its iron wings
Like wheels go round.

Crash under bridges,
Flash over ridges,
And vault the downs;
The road is straight –
Nor stile, nor gate;
For milestones – towns!

Voluminous, vanishing, white,
The steam plume trails;
Parallel streaks of light,
The polished rails.

Oh, who can follow?
The little swallow,
The trout of the sky:
But the sun
Is outrun,
And Time passed by.

The Famous Meeting

From *How I Found Livingstone: Travels, Adventures and Discoveries in Central Africa, 1872* | Sir Henry Morton Stanley (1841–1904)

Ujiji, near Lake Tanganyika, 10 November 1871

I did that which I thought was most dignified. I pushed back the crowds, and, passing from the rear, walked down a living avenue of people, until I came in front of the semicircle of Arabs, in the front of which stood the white man with the grey beard. As I advanced slowly towards him I noticed he was pale, looked wearied, had a grey beard, wore a bluish cap with a faded gold band round it, had on a red-sleeved waistcoat, and a pair of grey tweed trousers. I would have run to him, only I was a coward in the presence of such a mob – would have embraced him, only, he being an Englishman, I did not know how he would receive me; so I did what cowardice and false pride suggested was the best thing – walked deliberately to him, took off my hat, and said:

'Dr. Livingstone, I presume?'

'Yes,' said he, with a kind smile, lifting his cap slightly.

I replace my hat on my head, and he puts on his cap, and we both grasp hands, and I then say aloud:

'I thank God, Doctor, I have been permitted to see you.'

He answered, 'I feel thankful that I am here to welcome you.'

Forestalled From an Easy-chair

From *Missionary Travels and Researches in South Africa,*
1857 | Dr David Livingstone (1813–1873)

Old news:

Amongst other things, I discovered that my friend, Sir Roderick
Murchison, while in his study in London, had arrived at the same
conclusion respecting the form of the African continent as I had
lately come to on the spot; and that, from the attentive study of the
geological map of Mr. Bain and other materials, some of which were
furnished by the discoveries of Mr. Oswell and myself, he had not
only clearly enunciated the peculiar configuration as an hypothesis in
his discourse before the Geographical Society in 1852, but had even
the assurance to send me out a copy for my information! There was
not much use in nursing my chagrin at being thus fairly 'cut out' by
the man who had foretold the existence of the Australian gold before
its discovery, for here it was, in black and white. In his easy-chair he
had forestalled me by three years, though I had been working hard
through jungle, marsh, and fever, and, since the light dawned on
my mind at Dilolo, had been cherishing the pleasing delusion that
I should be the first to suggest the idea that the interior of Africa was
a watery plateau of less elevation than flanking hilly ranges.

The Storytellers

From *In Arabian Nights: In Search of Morocco Through its Stories and Storytellers, 2008* | Tahir Shah (1966–)

On our childhood travels to Morocco, my father used to say that to understand a place you had to look beyond what the senses show you. He would tell us to stuff cotton in our nostrils, to cover our ears and close our eyes. Only then, he would say, could we absorb the essence of the place. For children the exercise of blocking the senses was confusing. We had a thousand questions, each one answered with another question.

At dusk one evening we arrived at Fès. As usual the family was squeezed into our old Ford estate car, vinyl suitcases loaded on the roof, the gardener at the wheel. That evening I caught my first sight of the massive medieval city walls. There were figures moving beside them in hooded robes, carts laden with newly slaughtered sheep, and the piercing sound of a wedding party far away.

The car stopped and we all trooped out.

In the twilight my father pointed to a clutch of men huddled on the ground outside the city's grand Imperial Gate.

'They're gamblers,' said my mother.

'No, they're not,' my father replied. 'They are the guardians of an ancient wisdom.'

I asked what he meant.

'They are the storytellers,' he said.

Departure From Damascus

From *Travels in Arabia Deserta*, 1888 |

C. M. Doughty (1843–1926)

The new dawn appearing we removed not yet. The day risen the tents were dismantled, the camels led in ready to their companies, and halted beside their loads. We waited to hear the cannon shot which should open that year's pilgrimage. It was near ten o'clock when we heard the signal gun fired, and then, without any disorder, litters were suddenly heaved and braced upon the bearing beasts, their charges laid upon the kneeling camels, and the thousands of riders, all born in the caravan countries, mounted in silence. As all is up the drivers are left standing upon their feet, or sit to rest out the latest moments on their heels: they with other camp and tent servants must ride those three hundred leagues upon their bare soles, although they faint; and are to measure the ground again upward with their weary feet from the holy places. At the second gun, fired a few moments after, the Pasha's litter advances and after him goes the head of the caravan column: other fifteen or twenty minutes we, who have places in the rear, must halt, that is until the long train is unfolded before us; then we strike our camels and the great pilgrimage is moving. There go commonly three or four camels abreast and seldom five; the length of the slow-footed multitude of men and cattle is near two miles, and the width some hundred yards in the open plains. The hajjàj were this year by their account (which may be above the truth) 6,000 persons; of these more than half are serving men on foot; and 10,000 of all kinds of cattle, the most camels, then mules, hackneys, asses and a few dromedaries of Arabians returning in security of the great convoy to their own districts. We march in an empty waste, a plain of gravel, where nothing appeared and never a road before us.

Columbus Discovers Himself

John Agard (1949–)

Sailing interior seas is a risky enterprise.

Who knows what Other dwells
under the skin's uncharted skies?

What manner of fauna and flora
will the blood's Sargasso deliver?

The brain's treacherous horizon ahoy.
The tierra incognita of self-discovery.

O mapless mariner lost in his inner Indies.

A Footprint in the Sand

From *Robinson Crusoe, 1719* | Daniel Defoe (1660–1731)

It happened one day, about noon, going towards my boat, I was exceedingly surprised with the print of a man's naked foot on the shore, which was very plain to be seen on the sand. I stood like one thunderstruck, or as if I had seen an apparition. I listened, I looked round me, but I could hear nothing, nor see anything; I went up to a rising ground to look farther; I went up the shore and down the shore, but it was all one; I could see no other impression but that one. I went to it again to see if there were any more, and to observe if it might not be my fancy; but there was no room for that, for there was exactly the print of a foot, toes, heel, and every part of a foot:– how it came thither I knew not, nor could I in the least imagine; but after innumerable fluttering thoughts, like a man perfectly confused and out of myself, I came home to my fortification, not feeling, as we say, the ground I went on, but terrified to the last degree, looking behind me at every two or three steps, mistaking every bush and tree, and fancying every stump at a distance to be a man. Nor is it possible to describe how many various shapes my affrighted imagination represented things to me in, how many wild ideas were found every moment in my fancy, and what strange, unaccountable whimsies came into my thoughts by the way.

Armenian Churches

From *The Crossing Place, 1993* | Philip Marsden (1961–)

Continuing north, around the lower slopes of Mount Ararat, I came
to the ruins of the Armenian city of Ani. Its extraordinary thousand-
year-old cathedral, in a no-man's land between Turkish and Soviet
borders, was open to the sky, shelter for three ill-looking sheep.
A long way up the gorge near Digor, I found an Armenian church
so perfect in its design that at first I did not notice its collapsing roof,
nor the gaps in its walls.

. . . .

Some years later:

Against the pale pink cliff behind it, the pale pink ashlar of
Goshavank monastery almost disappeared. Its tight cluster of
buildings seemed hidden, camouflaged. But nothing could disguise
its austere genius. I spent a whole morning there, alone, under its
spell. Completed in the thirteenth century, Goshavank was among
the last of the great Armenian monasteries.

. . . .

Empty though they were, the buildings had remained intact and
ordered, an oasis of calm in a dangerous world. I'd half forgotten its
strange spirit, the spirit of Ani and Digor and Aghtamar. Too long in
the diaspora had cast doubt on my impressions – too many miles and
too many books. After several years' gap, I was now back within sixty
miles of Ani, convinced now that there *was* something extraordinary
about these churches, that in them burned the same fuse that coursed
through Armenian history, both brilliant and explosive.

The Aurora Borealis

From *The Note-Books, 1912* | Samuel Butler (1835–1902)

I saw one once in the Gulf of the St. Lawrence off the island of Anticosti. We were in the middle of it, and seemed to be looking up through a great cone of light millions and millions of miles into the sky. Then we saw it farther off and the pillars of fire stalked up and down the face of heaven like one of Handel's great basses.

In front of my room at Montreal there was a verandah from which a rope was stretched across a small yard to a chimney on a stable roof over the way. Clothes were hung to dry on this rope. As I lay in bed of a morning I could see the shadows and reflected lights from these clothes moving on the ceiling as the clothes were blown about by the wind. The movement of these shadows and reflected lights was exactly that of the rays of an Aurora Borealis, minus colour. I can conceive no resemblance more perfect. They stalked across the ceiling with the same kind of movement absolutely.

A City

From *Lawless Roads, 1939* | Graham Greene (1904–1991)

How to describe a city? Even for an old inhabitant it is impossible;
one can present only a simplified plan, taking a house here, a park
there as symbols of the whole. If I were trying to describe London
to a foreigner, I might take Trafalgar Square and Piccadilly Circus,
the Strand and Fleet Street, the grim wastes of Queen Victoria Street
and Tottenham Court Road, villages like Chelsea and Clapham and
Highgate struggling for individual existence, Great Portland Street
because of the secondhand cars and the faded genial men with old
school ties, Paddington for the vicious hotels ... and how much
would remain left out, the Bloomsbury square with its inexpensive
vice and its homesick Indians and its sense of rainy nostalgia, the
docks ...?

The Tide Rises, the Tide Falls

Henry Wadsworth Longfellow (1807–1882)

The tide rises, the tide falls,
The twilight darkens, the curlew calls;
Along the sea-sands damp and brown
The traveller hastens toward the town,
    And the tide rises, the tide falls.

Darkness settles on roofs and walls,
But the sea, the sea in the darkness calls;
The little waves, with their soft, white hands,
Efface the footprints in the sands,
    And the tide rises, the tide falls.

The morning breaks; the steeds in their stalls
Stamp and neigh, as the hostler calls;
The day returns, but nevermore
Returns the traveller to the shore,
    And the tide rises, the tide falls.

Railway Stations

From *Chai, Chai, 2009* | Bishwanath Ghosh (1970–)

Railway stations in India stand like fiercely independent states within cities and towns, insulated from the local flavour, as if they are territories of a common colonial master sitting in Delhi, which they are anyway.

Such is their sameness that if you were to ignore the yellow slab and all other signboards that identify a railway station, you would barely know where you are. All you would know is that you are in a country where tea is available round the clock and whose inhabitants have two primary occupations – travelling and waiting.

20 November

The Poles

From *The Blazing World, 1666* | Margaret Cavendish (1623–1673)

On kidnapping a virtuous young Lady:

When he fancied himself the happiest man of the world, he proved to be the most unfortunate; for Heaven frowning at his theft, raised such a tempest, as they knew not what to do, or whither to steer their course; so that the vessel, both by its own lightness, and the violent motion of the wind, was carried as swift as an arrow out of a bow, towards the North Pole, and in a short time reached the Icy Sea, where the wind forced it amongst huge pieces of ice; but being little, and light, it did by the assistance and favour of the Gods to this virtuous Lady, so turn and wind through those precipices, as if it had been guided by some experienced pilot, and skilful mariner: but alas! those few men which were in it, not knowing whither they went, nor what was to be done in so strange an adventure, and not being provided for so cold a voyage, were all frozen to death; the young Lady only, by the light of her beauty, the heat of her youth, and protection of the gods, remaining alive: neither was it a wonder that the men did freeze to death; for they were not only driven to the very end or point of the Pole of that world, but even to another Pole of another world, which joined close to it; so that the cold having a double strength at the conjunction of those two Poles, was insupportable: at last, the boat still passing on, was forced into another world; for it is impossible to round this world's globe from Pole to Pole, so as we do from East to West; because the Poles of the other world, joining to the Poles of this, do not allow any further passage to surround the world that way; but if any one arrives to either of these Poles, he is either forced to return, or to enter into another world.

Sound Advice

From *'The Little Governess', Bliss and Other Stories, 1920*

Katherine Mansfield (1888–1923)

Oh, dear, how she wished that it wasn't night-time. She'd have
much rather travelled by day, much much rather. But the lady at the
Governess Bureau said: 'You had better take an evening boat and
then if you get into a compartment for 'Ladies Only' in the train
you will be far safer than sleeping in a foreign hotel. Don't go out of
the carriage; don't walk about the corridors and *be sure* to lock the
lavatory door if you go there.'

Arab Love-Song

Francis Thompson (1859–1907)

The hunchèd camels of the night*
Trouble the bright
And silver waters of the moon.
The Maiden of the Morn will soon
Through Heaven stray and sing,
Star gathering.
Now while the dark about our loves is strewn,
Light of my dark, blood of my heart, O come!
And night will catch her breath up, and be dumb.

Leave thy father, leave thy mother
And thy brother;
Leave the black tents of thy tribe apart!
Am I not thy father and thy brother,
And thy mother?
And thou – what needest with thy tribe's black tents
Who hast the red pavilion of my heart?

*Cloud-shapes often observed by travellers in the East.

Rather a Heavy Sea

From *American Notes, 1842* | Charles Dickens (1812–1870)

It is the third morning. I am awakened out of my sleep by a dismal
shriek from my wife, who demands to know whether there's any
danger. I rouse myself, and look out of bed. The water-jug is plunging
and leaping like a lively dolphin; all the smaller articles are afloat,
except my shoes, which are stranded on a carpet-bag, high and dry,
like a couple of coal-barges. Suddenly I see them spring into the air,
and behold the looking-glass, which is nailed to the wall, sticking
fast upon the ceiling. At the same time the door entirely disappears,
and a new one is opened in the floor. Then I begin to comprehend
that the state-room is standing on its head.

Before it is possible to make any arrangement at all compatible
with this novel state of things, the ship rights. Before one can say
'Thank Heaven!' she wrongs again. Before one can cry she *is* wrong,
she seems to have started forward, and to be a creature actually
running of its own accord, with broken knees and failing legs,
through every variety of hole and pitfall, and stumbling constantly.
Before one can so much as wonder, she takes a high leap into the
air. Before she has well done that, she takes a deep dive into the
water. Before she has gained the surface, she throws a summerset.
The instant she is on her legs, she rushes backward. And so she goes
on staggering, heaving, wrestling, leaping, diving, jumping, pitching,
throbbing, rolling, and rocking: and going through all these
movements, sometimes by turns, and sometimes altogether: until one
feels disposed to roar for mercy.

A steward passes. 'Steward!' 'Sir?' 'What *is* the matter? What *do*
you call this?' 'Rather a heavy sea on, sir, and a head-wind.'

Duties

From *The English Governess at the Siamese Court*, 1870

Anna Leonowens (1834–1914)

'I have sixty-seven children,' said his Majesty, when we had returned to the Audience Hall. 'You shall educate them, and as many of my wives, likewise, as may wish to learn English. And I have much correspondence in which you must assist me. And, moreover, I have much difficulty for reading and translating French letters; for the French are fond of using gloomily deceiving terms. You must undertake; and you shall make all their murky sentences and gloomily deceiving propositions clear to me. And, furthermore, I have by every mail foreign letters whose writing is not easily read by me. You shall copy on round hand, for my readily perusal thereof.'

Nil desperandum; but I began by despairing of my ability to accomplish tasks so multifarious. I simply bowed, however, and so dismissed myself for that evening.

A Flame of Hope Smothered

From *Twelve Years a Slave, 1853* | Solomon Northup (1807–after 1857)

Vessels run up the Rio Teche to Centreville. While there, I was bold
enough one day to present myself before the captain of a steamer, and
beg permission to hide myself among the freight. I was emboldened
to risk the hazard of such a step, from overhearing a conversation, in
the course of which I ascertained he was a native of the North. I did
not relate to him the particulars of my history, but only expressed
an ardent desire to escape from slavery to a free State. He pitied me,
but said it would be impossible to avoid the vigilant custom house
officers in New-Orleans, and that detection would subject him to
punishment, and his vessel to confiscation. My earnest entreaties
evidently excited his sympathies, and doubtless he would have
yielded to them, could he have done so with any kind of safety.
I was compelled to smother the sudden flame that lighted up my
bosom with sweet hopes of liberation, and turn my steps once more
towards the increasing darkness of despair.

The French Language

From *Paris and the Parisians in 1835, 1836*

Fanny Trollope (1779–1863)

I suppose that, among all people and at all times, a certain portion
of what we call slang will insinuate itself into familiar colloquial
intercourse, and sometimes even dare to make its unsanctioned
accents heard from the tribune and the stage. It appears to me,
I confess, that France is at present taking considerable liberties with
her mother-tongue. But this is a subject which requires for its grave
discussion a native critic, and a learned one too. I therefore can
only venture distantly and doubtingly to allude to it, as one of the
points at which it appears to me that innovation is visibly and audibly
at work.

I know it may be said that every additional word, whether
fabricated or borrowed, adds something to the riches of the
language; and no doubt it does so. But there is a polished grace,
a finished elegance in the language of France, as registered in the
writings of her Augustan age, which may well atone for the want of
greater copiousness, with which it has been sometimes reproached.
To increase its strength, by giving it coarseness, would be like
exchanging a high-mettled racer for a dray-horse. A brewer would
tell you, that you gained in power what you lost in grace: it may be
so; but there are many, I think, even in this age of operatives and
utilitarians, who would regret the change.

Hill Difficulty

From *The Pilgrim's Progress, 1678* | John Bunyan (1628–1688)

I beheld, then, that they all went on till they came to the foot of the
Hill Difficulty; at the bottom of which was a spring. There were also
in the same place two other ways besides that which came straight
from the gate; one turned to the left hand, and the other to the right,
at the bottom of the hill; but the narrow way lay right up the hill,
and the name of the going up the side of the hill is called Difficulty.
Christian now went to the spring, and drank thereof, to refresh
himself [Isa. 49:10], and then began to go up the hill, saying, –

> 'The hill, though high, I covet to ascend,
> The difficulty will not me offend;
> For I perceive the way to life lies here.
> Come, pluck up heart, let's neither faint nor fear;
> Better, though difficult, the right way to go,
> Than wrong, though easy, where the end is woe.'

The other two also came to the foot of the hill; but when they saw
that the hill was steep and high, and that there were two other ways
to go, and supposing also that these two ways might meet again, with
that up which Christian went, on the other side of the hill, therefore
they were resolved to go in those ways. Now the name of one of these
ways was Danger, and the name of the other Destruction. So the
one took the way which is called Danger, which led him into a great
wood, and the other took directly up the way to Destruction, which
led him into a wide field, full of dark mountains, where he stumbled
and fell, and rose no more.

Escaping the Weather

From *A Thousand Miles up the Nile, 1877*

Amelia Edwards (1831–1892)

We intended, of course, to go up the Nile; and had any one ventured to inquire in so many words what brought us to Egypt, we should have replied: – 'Stress of weather.'

For in simple truth we had drifted hither by accident, with no excuse of health, or business, or any serious object whatever; and had just taken refuge in Egypt as one might turn aside into the Burlington Arcade or the Passage des Panoramas – to get out of the rain.

And with good reason. Having left home early in September for a few weeks' sketching in central France, we had been pursued by the wettest of wet weather. Washed out of the hill-country we fared no better in the plains. At Nismes it poured for a month without stopping. Debating at last whether it were better to take our wet umbrellas back at once to England, or push on farther still in search of sunshine, the talk fell upon Algiers – Malta – Cairo; and Cairo carried it. Never was distant expedition entered upon with less premeditation. The thing was no sooner decided than we were gone. Nice, Genoa, Bologna, Ancona flitted by, as in a dream; and Bedreddin Hassan when he woke at the gates of Damascus was scarcely more surprised than the writer of these pages, when she found herself on board the 'Simla,' and steaming out of the port of Brindisi.

Here, then, without definite plans, outfit, or any kind of Oriental experience, behold us arrived in Cairo on the 29th of November 1873, literally and most prosaically in search of fine weather.

My Heart's in the Highlands

Robert Burns (1759–1796)

My heart's in the Highlands, my heart is not here;
My heart's in the Highlands, a-chasing the deer;
Chasing the wild-deer, and following the roe,
My heart's in the Highlands, wherever I go.
Farewell to the Highlands, farewell to the North,
The birth-place of valour, the country of worth;
Wherever I wander, wherever I rove,
The hills of the Highlands for ever I love.

Farewell to the mountains, high-cover'd with snow;
Farewell to the straths and green valleys below;
Farewell to the forests and wild-hanging woods;
Farewell to the torrents and loud-pouring floods.
My heart's in the Highlands, my heart is not here;
My heart's in the Highlands, a-chasing the deer;
Chasing the wild-deer, and following the roe,
My heart's in the Highlands, wherever I go.

DECEMBER

An Entanglement of Grand Wild Mountains

An Ulterior Motive

From *Mrs. General Talboys: Tales of all Countries, Second Series, 1863* | Anthony Trollope (1815–1882)

Why Mrs. General Talboys first made up her mind to pass the winter of 1859 at Rome I never clearly understood. To myself she explained her purposes, soon after her arrival at the Eternal City, by declaring, in her own enthusiastic manner, that she was inspired by a burning desire to drink fresh at the still living fountains of classical poetry and sentiment. But I always thought that there was something more than this in it. Classical poetry and sentiment were doubtless very dear to her; but so also, I imagine, were the substantial comforts of Hardover Lodge, the General's house in Berkshire; and I do not think that she would have emigrated for the winter had there not been some slight domestic misunderstanding.

'S-t-e-a-m-boat a-comin'!

From *Life on the Mississippi, 1883* | Mark Twain (1935–1910)

The town drunkard stirs, the clerks wake up, a furious clatter of drays follows, every house and store pours out a human contribution, and all in a twinkling the dead town is alive and moving. Drays, carts, men, boys, all go hurrying from many quarters to a common centre, the wharf. Assembled there, the people fasten their eyes upon the coming boat as upon a wonder they are seeing for the first time. And the boat *is* rather a handsome sight, too. She is long and sharp and trim and pretty; she has two tall, fancy-topped chimneys, with a gilded device of some kind swung between them; a fanciful pilot-house, a glass and 'gingerbread', perched on top of the 'texas' deck behind them; the paddle-boxes are gorgeous with a picture or with gilded rays above the boat's name; the boiler deck, the hurricane deck, and the texas deck are fenced and ornamented with clean white railings; there is a flag gallantly flying from the jack-staff; the furnace doors are open and the fires glaring bravely; the upper decks are black with passengers; the captain stands by the big bell, calm, imposing, the envy of all; great volumes of the blackest smoke are rolling and tumbling out of the chimneys – a husbanded grandeur created with a bit of pitch pine just before arriving at a town; the crew are grouped on the forecastle; the broad stage is run far out over the port bow, and an envied deckhand stands picturesquely on the end of it with a coil of rope in his hand; the pent steam is screaming through the gauge-cocks, the captain lifts his hand, a bell rings, the wheels stop; then they turn back, churning the water to foam, and the steamer is at rest. Then such a scramble as there is to get aboard, and to get ashore, and to take in freight and to discharge freight, all at one and the same time; and such a yelling and cursing as the mates facilitate it all with! Ten minutes later the steamer is under way again, with no flag on the jack-staff and no black smoke issuing from the chimneys. After ten more minutes the town is dead again, and the town drunkard asleep by the skids once more.

Long Trip

Langston Hughes (1901–1967)

The sea is a wilderness of waves,
A desert of water.
We dip and dive,
Rise and roll,
Hide and are hidden
On the sea.
  Day, night,
  Night, day,
The sea is a desert of waves,
A wilderness of water.

A Taxi Driver

From *In Patagonia, 1977* | Bruce Chatwin (1940–1989)

In search of Bill Philips:

At half past nine the bus stopped at the small town where I hoped
to find Bill Philips. His grandfather was a pioneer in Patagonia and
he still had cousins there. The town was a grid of one-storey brick
houses and shops with an overhanging cornice. In the square was
a municipal garden and a bronze bust of General San Martín, the
Liberator. The streets around the garden were asphalted but the
wind blew in sideways and coated the flowers and the bronze with
white dust.

Two farmers had parked their pick-ups outside the bar and were
drinking vino rosado. An old man huddled over his maté kettle.

. . . .

An old woman gave me a leathery sandwich and a coffee. Naturally,
she said, I could leave my bag while I tried to find Señor Philips.

'It is far to Señor Philips. He lives up in the sierra.'

'How far?'

'Eight leagues. But you may find him. Often he comes to town
in the morning.'

I asked around but no one had seen the gringo Philips that
morning. I found a taxi and haggled over the price. The driver was a
thin, cheerful type, Italian I guessed. He seemed to enjoy bargaining
and went off to buy gasoline. I looked General San Martín over and
humped my bag onto the sidewalk. The taxi drove up and the Italian
jumped out excitedly and said:

'I've seen the gringo Philips. There, walking this way.'

He didn't mind losing the fare and refused to be paid. I was
beginning to like the country.

A Sleeping Bag

From *A Ride to Khiva, 1876* | Frederick Burnaby (1842–1885)

The Russian Frontier, 1875

The customs' examination was easily got through. The only part of my luggage which puzzled the douane officer was the sleeping-bag. He smelt it suspiciously, the waterproof cloth having a strong odour. 'What is it for?' 'To sleep in.' He put his nose down again, and apparently uncertain in his own mind as to what course to pursue, called for another official, who desired me to unroll it. 'And you sleep in that big bag?' was the question. 'Yes.' 'What extraordinary people the English are!' observed the man who had inspected my transport, and, sotto voce 'he must be mad;' when the other bystanders drew back a little, thinking that possibly I was dangerous as well.

Romantick but True

From *Oroonoko, or the Royal Slave, 1688* | Aphra Behn (1640–1689)

Epistle Dedicatory to the Right Honourable, the Lord Maitland:
If there be anything that seems Romantick I beseech your Lordship
to consider these Countries do, in all things, so far differ from ours
that they produce unconceivable Wonders, at least, so they appear to
us, because New and Strange. What I have mentioned I have taken
care shou'd be Truth, let the Critical Reader judge as he pleases.

Shipwrecked on a Pacific Island

From *The Coral Island, 1857* | R. M. Ballantyne (1835–1894)

This was now the first time that I had looked well about me since landing, as the spot where I had been laid was covered with thick bushes, which almost hid the country from our view. As we now emerged from among these and walked down the sandy beach together, I cast my eyes about, and, truly, my heart glowed within me and my spirits rose at the beautiful prospect which I beheld on every side. The gale had suddenly died away, just as if it had blown furiously till it dashed our ship upon the rocks, and had nothing more to do after accomplishing that. The island on which we stood was hilly, and covered almost everywhere with the most beautiful and richly coloured trees, bushes, and shrubs, none of which I knew the names of at that time, except, indeed, the cocoa-nut palms, which I recognised at once from the many pictures that I had seen of them before I left home. A sandy beach of dazzling whiteness lined this bright green shore, and upon it there fell a gentle ripple of the sea. This last astonished me much, for I recollected that at home the sea used to fall in huge billows on the shore long after a storm had subsided. But on casting my glance out to sea the cause became apparent. About a mile distant from the shore I saw the great billows of the ocean rolling like a green wall, and falling with a long, loud roar, upon a low coral reef, where they were dashed into white foam and flung up in clouds of spray. This spray sometimes flew exceedingly high, and, every here and there, a beautiful rainbow was formed for a moment among the falling drops. We afterwards found that this coral reef extended quite round the island, and formed a natural breakwater to it. Beyond this the sea rose and tossed violently from the effects of the storm; but between the reef and the shore it was as calm and as smooth as a pond.

Arriving at the Astana

From *My Life in Sarawak, 1913* |

Margaret, Lady Brooke, Ranee of Sarawak (1849–1936)

When we stepped on land, all the people came forward and shook hands with the Rajah, who presented them to me. It took about ten to fifteen minutes to shake hands with them all.

Then a strange thing happened, for which I was not prepared. A very picturesque old man, rather taller than the other Malays, dressed in a jacket embroidered with gold, black trousers with a gold band, his head enveloped in a handkerchief tied in a jaunty fashion, with two ends standing up over his left ear, came forward with a large yellow satin umbrella, fringed all round, which he opened with great solemnity and held over the Rajah's head. His name was Subu, and, as I learned, he occupied a great position in Sarawak: that of Umbrella Bearer to the Rajah and Executioner to the State. The Rajah trudged forward, the umbrella held over him, up the steps from the landing-place, and across the broad gravel path, lined with a guard of honour, leading to the house. At the entrance the umbrella was folded up with great reverence by Subu, who carried IT back to ITS home the other side of the river. I followed with the principal European officer present, and the other people who had met us came after us, up the path, and on to the verandah of the Astana.

The Bistro

From *Down and Out in Paris and London, 1933*

George Orwell (1903–1950)

Life in the quarter. Our *bistro*, for instance, at the foot of the Hôtel des Trois Moineaux. A tiny brick-floored room, half underground, with wine-sodden tables, and a photograph of a funeral inscribed '*Crédit est mort*'; and red-sashed workmen carving sausage with big jack-knives; and Madame F., a splendid Auvergnat peasant woman with the face of a strong-minded cow, drinking Malaga all day 'for her stomach'; and games of dice for *apéritifs*; and songs about 'Les Fraises et Les Framboises', and about Madelon, who said, '*Comment épouser un soldat, moi qui aime tout le regiment?*'; and extraordinary public love-making. Half the hotel used to meet in the bistro in the evenings. I wish one could find a pub in London a quarter as cheery.

Perfection

From *Erewhon, 1872, 1901* | Samuel Butler (1835–1902)

I reached my destination in one of the last months of 1868, but I
dare not mention the season, lest the reader should gather in which
hemisphere I was.

. . . .

The part known to Europeans consisted of a coast-line about eight
hundred miles in length (affording three or four good harbours),
and a tract of country extending inland for a space varying from
two to three hundred miles, until it a reached the offshoots of an
exceedingly lofty range of mountains, which could be seen from far
out upon the plains, and were covered with perpetual snow. The coast
was perfectly well known both north and south of the tract to which
I have alluded, but in neither direction was there a single harbour for
five hundred miles, and the mountains, which descended almost into
the sea, were covered with thick timber, so that none would think of
settling.

With this bay of land, however, the case was different. The
harbours were sufficient; the country was timbered, but not too
heavily; it was admirably suited for agriculture; it also contained
millions on millions of acres of the most beautifully grassed country
in the world, and of the best suited for all manner of sheep and
cattle. The climate was temperate, and very healthy; there were no
wild animals, nor were the natives dangerous, being few in number
and of an intelligent tractable disposition.

The Jim Crow Car

From *My Bondage and My Freedom*, 1855

Frederick Douglass (1818–1895)

The custom of providing separate cars for the accommodation of colored travelers, was established on nearly all the railroads of New England, a dozen years ago. Regarding this custom as fostering the spirit of caste, I made it a rule to seat myself in the cars for the accommodation of passengers generally. Thus seated, I was sure to be called upon to betake myself to the '*Jim Crow car.*' Refusing to obey, I was often dragged out of my seat, beaten, and severely bruised, by conductors and brakemen.

. . . .

After many battles with the railroad conductors, and being roughly handled in not a few instances, proscription was at last abandoned; and the 'Jim Crow car' – set up for the degradation of colored people – is nowhere found in New England. This result was not brought about without the intervention of the people, and the threatened enactment of a law compelling railroad companies to respect the rights of travelers. Hon. Charles Francis Adams performed signal service in the Massachusetts legislature, in bringing this reformation; and to him the colored citizens of that state are deeply indebted.

The Lines at Mugby Junction

From *Mugby Junction: Barbrox Brothers, 1866*

Charles Dickens (1812–1870)

There were so many lines. Gazing down upon them from a bridge at the Junction, it was as if the concentrating companies formed a great industrial exhibition of the works of extraordinary ground-spiders that spun iron. And then so many of the lines went such wonderful ways, so crossing and curving among one another, that the eye lost them. And then some of them appeared to start with the fixed intention of going five hundred miles, and all of a sudden gave it up at an insignificant barrier, or turned off into a workshop. And then others, like intoxicated men, went a little way very straight, and surprisingly slewed round and came back again. And then others were so chock-full of trucks of coal, others were so blocked with trucks of casks, others were so gorged with trucks of ballast, others were so set apart for wheeled objects like immense iron cotton-reels; while others were so bright and clear, and others were so delivered over to rust and ashes and idle wheelbarrows out of work, with their legs in the air (looking much like their masters on strike), that there was no beginning, middle, or end, to the bewilderment.

Venice

From *Venice, 1960* | Jan Morris (1926–2020)

In Venice the Orient began. Marco Polo was a Venetian and Venetian merchants, searching for new and profitable lines of commerce, travelled widely throughout central Asia. Decked in Oriental fineries, Venice became the most flamboyant of all cities – 'the most triumphant Citie I ever set eyes on', wrote de Commynes in 1495. She was a place of silks, emeralds, marbles, brocades, velvets, cloth of gold, porphyry, ivory, spices, scents, apes, ebony, indigo, slaves, great galleons, Jews, mosaics, shining domes, rubies, and all the gorgeous commodities of Arabia, China and the Indies. She was a treasure-box. Venice was ruined, in the long run, by the Muslim capture of Constantinople in 1453, which ended her supremacy in the Levant; and by de Gama's voyage to India in 1498, which broke her monopoly of the Oriental trade: but for another three centuries she retained her panache and pageantry, and she keeps her gilded reputation still.

13 December

High Spirits

From *A Time of Gifts, 1977* | Patrick Leigh Fermor (1915–2011)

December 1933

My spirits, already high, steadily rose as I walked. I could scarcely believe that I was really there; alone, that is, on the move, advancing into Europe, surrounded by all this emptiness and change, with a thousand wonders waiting. Because of this, perhaps, the actual doings of the next few days emerge from the general glow in a disjointed and haphazard way. I halted at a signpost to eat a chunk of bread with a yellow wedge of cheese sliced from a red cannon ball by a village grocer. One arm of the signpost pointed to Amsterdam and Utrecht, the other to Dordrecht, Breda and Antwerp and I obeyed the latter. The way followed a river with too swift a current for ice to form, and brambles and hazel and rushes grew thick along the banks. Leaning over a bridge I watched a string of barges gliding downstream underneath me in the wake of a stertorous tug bound for Rotterdam, and a little later as island as slender as a weaver's shuttle divided the current amid-stream. A floating reed-fringed spinney, it looked like a small castle with a steeply-pitched shingle roof and turrets with conical tops emerged romantically from the mesh of the branches. Belfries of a dizzy height were scattered haphazard across the landscape. They were visible for a very long way, and, in the late afternoon, I singled one of them out for a landmark and goal.

Sight of the Antarctic Peninsula

From *Ice Bird, 1975* | David Lewis (1917–2002)

'Land is Brabant or Anvers Island. My bet (before working sight)
is Anvers':
Now I really did appreciate the magnificent panorama – sixty miles
of ice cap and glacier topped by serrated summits two miles high.
A truly enormous berg appeared to be grounded off what I (correctly)
took to be Cape Alberto de Monaco, the south-west corner of Anvers,
that we were slowly nearing, and which we must round to reach
Palmer. The Anvers snowfields appeared, for all the world, like level
sheets of fog, filling and hiding the valleys, above which soared
the lofty summits, culminating in 9,000-foot Mount Français, the
highest point of the island.

I sat in the cockpit choked with emotion. Close alongside, parties
of penguins called 'ark, ark,' as they porpoised out of the water,
landing with a succession of little plops. I was still gazing out upon
the scene when the light began to fade with evening. The sky above
Anvers was a pastel green and the jagged Graham Coast ranger
farther southward turned pale gold. A waning moon hung over the
empty land. The ice cliffs of the great bergs turned from blue to
mauve to violet and then deep purple.

Up-Hill

Christina Rossetti (1830–1894)

Does the road wind up-hill all the way?
    Yes, to the very end.
Will the day's journey take the whole long day?
    From morn to night, my friend.

But is there for the night a resting-place?
    A roof for when the slow dark hours begin.
May not the darkness hide it from my face?
    You cannot miss that inn.

Shall I meet other wayfarers at night?
    Those who have gone before.
Then must I knock, or call when just in sight?
    They will not keep you standing at that door.

Shall I find comfort, travel-sore and weak?
    Of labour you shall find the sum.
Will there be beds for me and all who seek?
    Yea, beds for all who come.

A Greenland Christmas

From *Michel the Giant: An African in Greenland, 1981*

Tété-Michel Kpomassie (1941–)

Translated by James Kirkup (1918–2009)

For days now the village had been talking about nothing but *Jul* – Yule, or Christmas. Apparently it was the country's biggest festival.

The preparations began on Friday, December 17, when the villagers scrubbed their houses using bucketfuls of melted ice. Though I never saw one of these people having a thorough wash all winter, they were nevertheless determined to make their houses spick and span for this great occasion. When you think of the effort it takes to get water – the number of trips to the bay to break the ice, the amount of coal needed to melt it – you begin to have some idea of the importance of Christmas here.

The Time Traveller

From *The Time Machine, 1895* | H. G. Wells (1866–1946)

As I took hold of the handle of the door I heard an exclamation, oddly truncated at the end, and a click and a thud. A gust of air whirled round me as I opened the door, and from within came the sound of broken glass falling on the floor. The Time Traveller was not there. I seemed to see a ghostly, indistinct figure sitting in a whirling mass of black and brass for a moment – a figure so transparent that the bench behind with its sheets of drawings was absolutely distinct; but this phantasm vanished as I rubbed my eyes. The Time Machine had gone. Save for a subsiding stir of dust, the further end of the laboratory was empty. A pane of the skylight had, apparently, just been blown in.

I felt an unreasonable amazement. I knew that something strange had happened, and for the moment could not distinguish what the strange thing might be.

. . . .

I stayed on, waiting for the Time Traveller; waiting for the second, perhaps still stranger story, and the specimens and photographs he would bring with him. But I am beginning now to fear that I must wait a lifetime. The Time Traveller vanished three years ago. And, as everybody knows now, he has never returned.

Recollections

From *Tales of Travels, 1923* | George Curzon, 1st Marquess Curzon of Kedleston (1859–1925)

Whereas the experiences of life at home, even when they are not commonplace, are apt to fade quickly, and sometimes to be completely forgotten, the incidents of travel, a quarter or even half of a century ago, stand out indelibly as though graven in steel. Each of us has his own museum of such recollections. Among mine not the least prized are these: the music of many nightingales floating across the water from the coasts of Athos; the incredible glory of Kangchenjunga as he pierces the veils of the morning at Darjiling; the crossing of a Himalayan rope-bridge, sagging in the middle, and swaying dizzily from side to side, when only a strand of twisted twigs is stretched between your feet and the ravening torrent below; the first sight of the towered walls, *minae murorum ingentes*, of Peking; the head and shoulders of an Indian tiger emerging without a suspicion of sound from the thick jungle immediately in front of the posted sportsmen; the stupendous and terraced grandeur of Angkor Wat; the snowy spire of Teneriffe glimmering at sunrise across a hundred miles of ocean; the aethereal and ineffable beauty of the Taj.

Journeys

From *Bitter Lemons, 1957* | Lawrence Durrell (1912–1990)

Journeys, like artists are born, not made. A thousand differing
circumstances contribute to them, few of them willed or determined
by the will – whatever we may think. They flower spontaneously out
of the demands of our natures – and the best of them lead us not
only outwards in space, but inwards as well. Travel can be one of the
most rewarding forms of introspection . . .

20 December

A Wager Won

From *Around the World in Eighty Days, 1873* | Jules Verne (1828–1905)

Translated by George Makepeace Towle (1841–1893)

The drawing-room in the Reform Club, Saturday 21st December, 1872

Eight forty-five in the evening:

Phileas Fogg had won his wager, and had made his journey around the world in eighty days. To do this, he had employed every means of conveyance – steamers, railways, carriages, yachts, trading-vessels, sledges, elephants. The eccentric gentleman had throughout displayed all his marvellous qualities of coolness and exactitude. But what then? What had he really gained by all this trouble?

What had he brought back from this long and weary journey?

Nothing, say you? Perhaps so; nothing but a charming woman, who, strange as it may appear, made him the happiest of men!

Truly, would you not for less than that make the tour around the world?

Painter and Historian

From *Letters and Notes on the Manners, Customs, and Conditions of North American Indians, 1844*

George Catlin (1796–1872)

Whilst working as a painter:

A delegation of some ten or fifteen noble and dignified-looking Indians, from the wilds of the 'Far West,' suddenly arrived in the city, arrayed and equipped in all their classic beauty, – with shield and helmet, – with tunic and manteau, – tinted and tasselled off, exactly for the painter's palette!

In silent and stoic dignity, these lords of the forest strutted about the city for a few days, wrapped in their pictured robes, with their brows plumed with quills of the war-eagle, attracting the gaze and admiration of all who beheld them. After this, they took their leave for Washington City, and I was left to reflect and regret, which I did long and deeply, until I came to the following deductions and conclusions.

Black and blue cloth and civilization are destined, not only to veil, but to obliterate the grace and beauty of Nature. Man, in the simplicity and loftiness of his nature, unrestrained and unfettered by the disguises of art, Is surely the most beautiful model for the painter, – and the country from which he hails is unquestionably the best study or school of the arts in the world: such I am sure, from the models I have seen, is the wilderness of North America. And the history and customs of such a people, preserved by pictorial illustrations, are themes worthy the life-time of one man, and nothing short of the loss of my life, shall prevent me from visiting their country, and of becoming their historian.

Ozymandias

Percy Bysshe Shelley (1792–1822)

I met a traveller from an antique land
Who said: Two vast and trunkless legs of stone
Stand in the desert . . .Near them, on the sand,
Half sunk, a shattered visage lies, whose frown,
And wrinkled lip, and sneer of cold command,
Tell that its sculptor well those passions read
Which yet survive, stamped on these lifeless things,
The hand that mocked them, and the heart that fed:
And on the pedestal these words appear:
'My name is Ozymandias, king of kings:
Look on my works, ye Mighty, and despair!'
Nothing beside remains. Round the decay
Of that colossal wreck, boundless and bare
The lone and level sands stretched far away.

A Journey with Cossacks

From *My Life as an Explorer, 1925* | Sven Hedin (1865–1952)

Christmas Eve I started on a jolly journey, a wild and whizzing expedition on horseback, by sleigh, and by carriage through all of western Asia. Three Cossacks from the consulate, who had finished their term of service, were returning to Narinsk in Semiryetchensk, the Country of Seven Rivers on the Russian side, and I was going with them.

We travelled northward with our little caravan of pack-horses. The way took us through narrow valleys, in a biting cold (-4°). We crossed rivers that were only partly frozen. There the Cossacks proved invaluable. They rode out on the ice near the shore till it broke, and the horses plunged like dolphins among the ice-cakes. I often feared the animals would rip their bellies open on the sharp edges of the ice. The water reached to the middle of our saddles, and we had to balance ourselves cross-legged in order to keep our felt boots dry.

Higher up, the watercourses were frozen solid. The horses slid along and danced like maniacs, on the crystal-like surface of the ice. We crossed the Chinese border, rode through the pass of Turugart (12,740 feet), across the frozen and snow-covered lake of Chatyr-kul, and over the pass of Tash-rabat (12,900 feet). We were in a labyrinth of valleys, in an entanglement of grand wild mountains, belonging to the Tian-shan range, or the 'Celestial Mountains,' as the Chinese call them.

A Sleigh Ride

From *A Ride to Khiva, 1876* | Frederick Burnaby (1842–1885)

A well-turned-out troika with three really good horses, which get over the ground at the rate of twelve miles an hour, is a pretty sight to witness, particularly if the team has been properly trained, and the outside animals never attempt to break into a trot, whilst the one in the shafts steps forward with high action. But the constrained position in which the horses are kept must be highly uncomfortable to them. It is not calculated to enable a driver to get as much pace out of his animals as they could give him if harnessed in another manner.

Off we went at a brisk pace, the bell dangling from our horse's head collar, and jingling merrily at every stride of the team.

The sun rose high in the heavens. It was a bright and glorious morning, in spite of the intense cold, and the amount of oxygen we inhaled was enough to elevate the spirits of the most dyspeptic of mankind. Presently, after descending a slight declivity, our Jehu turned sharply to the right; then came a scramble, and a succession of jolts and jerks, as we slid down a steep bank, and we found ourselves on what appeared to be a broad high road. Here the sight of many masts and shipping which, bound in by the iron fetters of a relentless winter, would remain embedded in the ice till the ensuing spring, showed me that we were on the Volga, It was an animated spectacle, this frozen highway, thronged with peasants who strode beside their sledges, which were bringing cotton and other goods from Orenburg to the railway.

Now a smart troika would dash by us, its driver shouting as he passed, when our Jehu, stimulating his steeds by loud cries and frequent applications of the whip, would vainly strive to overtake his brother coachman. Old and young alike seemed like octogenarians. Their short thick beards and moustaches were white as hoar-frost from the congealed breath.

A Fourth Companion

From *South, 1919* | Ernest Shackleton (1874–1922)

When I look back at those days I have no doubt that Providence
guided us, not only across those snowfields, but across the storm-
white sea that separated Elephant Island from our landing place on
South Georgia. I know that during that long and racking march of
thirty-six hours over the unnamed mountains and glaciers of South
Georgia it seemed to me often that we were four, not three. I said
nothing to my companions on the point, but afterwards Worsley
said to me, 'Boss, I had a curious feeling on the march that there
was another person with us.' Crean confessed to the same idea.
One feels 'the dearth of human words, the roughness of mortal
speech' in trying to describe things intangible, but a record of our
journeys would be incomplete without a reference to a subject very
near to our hearts.

The Lure of Magic Names

From *Through Khiva to Golden Samarkand, 1925*

Ella Christie (1861–1949)

My reasons for making the journey were twofold: first, the extreme desire to see for myself what lay on that comparatively bare spot on the map east of the Caspian Sea, a stretch of some 1200 miles to the Chinese frontier; and secondly, the lure of those magic names, Bokhara and Samarkand, renowned in history as well as in the pages of classic tales and poetic fiction for chivalry and romance.

I Travelled Among Unknown Men

From *Lucy* | William Wordsworth (1770–1850)

I travelled among unknown men,
   In lands beyond the sea;
Nor, England! did I know till then
   What love I bore to thee.

'Tis past, that melancholy dream!
   Nor will I quit thy shore
A second time; for still I seem
   To love thee more and more.

Among thy mountains did I feel
   The joy of my desire;
And she I cherished turned her wheel
   Beside an English fire.

Thy mornings showed, thy nights concealed
   The bowers where Lucy played;
And thine is, too, the last green field
   Which Lucy's eyes surveyed.

The Land's End

From *Rambles Beyond Railways, 1851* | Wilkie Collins (1824–1889)

The Land's End! There is something in the very words that stirs us all. It was the name that struck us most, and was best remembered by us, as children, when we learnt our geography. It fills the minds of imaginative people with visions of barrenness and solitude, with dreams of some lonely promontory, far away by itself out in the sea – the sort of place where the last man in England would be most likely to be found waiting for death, at the end of the world! It suggests even to the most prosaically constituted people, ideas of tremendous storms, of flakes of foam flying over the land before the wind, of billows in convulsion, of rocks shaken to their centre, of caves where smugglers lurk in ambush, of wrecks and hurricanes, desolation, danger, and death. It awakens curiosity in the most careless – once hear of it, and you long to see it – tell your friends that you have travelled in Cornwall, and ten thousand chances to one, the first question they ask is:– 'Have you been to the Land's End?'

And yet, strange to say, this spot so singled out and set apart by our imaginations as something remarkable and even unique of its kind, is as a matter of fact, not distinguishable from any part of the coast on either side of it, by any local peculiarity whatever. If you desire really and truly to stand on the Land's End itself, you must ask your way to it, or you are in danger of mistaking any one of the numerous promontories on the right hand and the left, for your actual place of destination.

A Man Sees England on the Morrow of the Revolution

From *News from Nowhere, 1890* | William Morris (1834–1896)

As he sat in that vapour-bath of hurried and discontented humanity, a carriage of the underground railway, he, like others, stewed discontentedly, while in self-reproachful mood he turned over the many excellent and conclusive arguments which, though they lay at his fingers' ends, he had forgotten in the just past discussion.

. . . .

'If I could but see a day of it,' he said to himself; 'if I could but see it!'

As he formed the words, the train stopped at his station, five minutes' walk from his own house, which stood on the banks of the Thames, a little way above an ugly suspension bridge. He went out of the station, still discontented and unhappy, muttering 'If I could but see it! if I could but see it!' but had not gone many steps towards the river before (says our friend who tells the story) all that discontent and trouble seemed to slip off him.

It was a beautiful night of early winter, the air just sharp enough to be refreshing after the hot room and the stinking railway carriage. The wind, which had lately turned a point or two north of west, had blown the sky clear of all cloud save a light fleck or two which went swiftly down the heavens. There was a young moon halfway up the sky, and as the home-farer caught sight of it, tangled in the branches of a tall old elm, he could scarce bring to his mind the shabby London suburb where he was, and he felt as if he were in a pleasant country place – pleasanter, indeed, than the deep country was as he had known it.

Song of the Open Road

Walt Whitman (1819–1892)

Lines 1–7

Afoot and light-hearted, I take to the open road,
Healthy, free, the world before me,
The long brown path before me, leading wherever I choose.

Henceforth I ask not good-fortune – I myself am good-fortune,
Henceforth I whimper no more, postpone no more, need nothing,
Done with indoor complaints, libraries, querulous criticisms,
Strong and content I travel the open road.

Further Reading

Each anthology is dependent upon the whim of its compiler, but this one would have been poorer without inspiration, literary prompting and reminders from the following:

Benedict Allen, *The Faber Book of Exploration,* Faber and Faber, 2004

Paul Fussell, *The Norton Book of Travel,* W. W. Norton, 1987

Tim Hannigan, T*he Travel Writing Tribe*, Hurst & Co, 2021

Robin Hanbury-Tenison, *The Oxford Book of Exploration,* Oxford University Press, 2010

Alexander Maitland, *Exploring the World,* Weidenfeld and Nicolson, 2022

Eric Newby, *A Book of Travellers' Tales,* William Collins, 1985

John Julius Norwich, *A Taste for Travel: An Anthology,* Macmillan, 1985

Peter Whitfield, *Travel: A Literary History,* Bodleian Library, 2011

Index

Sources

John Agard, 'Jet-lagged Prophets' from *We Brits* (Bloodaxe Books, 2006), 'Columbus Discovers Himself' from *Travel Light, Travel Dark* (Bloodaxe Books, 2013), reproduced with permission of Bloodaxe Books. www.bloodaxebooks.com

Benedict Allen, *Explorer* and *The Skeleton Coast,* reproduced with kind permission of Benedict Allen.

Sybille Bedford, *A Visit to Don Otavio,* © The Estate of Sybille Bedford, with permission of Eland Publishing. US rights, Inkwell Management.

Michael Bond, *A Bear Called Paddington,* © The Estate of Michael Bond 1958, HarperCollins Publishers UK.

W. E. Bowman, *The Ascent of Rum Doodle,* © The Estate of William Ernest Bowman 1956, Penguin Random House.

Bill Bryson, *The Lost Continent,* © Bill Bryson 1989, Penguin Random House.

Mildred Cable and Francesca French, *The Gobi Desert,* © The Estate of Francesca French 1942, Hodder & Stoughton.

Bruce Chatwin, *The Songlines* and *In Patagonia,* © The Estate of Bruce Chatwin 1987 and 1977, Penguin Random House.

Apsley Cherry-Garrard, *The Worst Journey in the World,* © The Estate of Apsley Cherry-Garrard 1922, Penguin Random House.

William Dalrymple, *In Xanadu,* © William Dalrymple 1989, HarperCollins Publishers UK.

Nick Danziger, *Danziger's Travels*, © Nick Danziger 1987, HarperCollins Publishers UK.

Walter de la Mare, 'The Listeners', reproduced with permission of The Literary Trustees of Walter de la Mare and the Society of Authors as their representative.

Lawrence Durrell, *Bitter Lemons*, reproduced by permission of Faber & Faber Ltd.

Lauren Elkin, *Flâneuse*, © Lauren Elkin 2016, Penguin Random House.

Patrick Leigh Fermor, *A Time of Gifts*, © The Estate of Patrick Leigh Fermor 1977, Hachette UK.

Peter Fleming, *News from Tartary* and *Brazilian Adventure*, © The Estate of Peter Fleming 1933, Hachette UK.

Bishwanath Ghosh, *Chai, Chai*, © Bishwanath Ghosh 2009, Tranquebar Press.

Graham Greene, *Lawless Roads*, © The Estate of Graham Greene 1939, Penguin Random House.

Robin Hanbury-Tenison, *A Ride Along the Great Wall*, reproduced with kind permission of Robin Hanbury-Tenison. *Jake's Escape*, © Robin Hanbury-Tenison 2013, Penguin Random House.

John Hare, *The Lost Camels of Tartary* and 'A Life Well Lived', last words to Kate Rae, reproduced with kind permission of Kate Rae.

Norman Lewis, *A Dragon Apparent, Naples '44* and *In Sicily*, © The Estate of Norman Lewis, with permission of Eland Publishing.

John Lewis-Stempel, *La Vie: A Year in Rural France*, © John Lewis-Stempel 2023, Penguin Random House.

Rose Macaulay, *The Towers of Trebizond*, © The Estate of Rose Macaulay 1956, Folio Society.

Tim Mackintosh-Smith, *Travels with a Tangerine: A Journey in the Footnotes of Ibn Battutah*, © Tim Mackintosh-Smith 2001, Hachette UK.

Ella Maillart, *Forbidden Journey*, © The Estate of Ella Maillart 1937, Read and Co Books.

Philip Marsden, *The Crossing Place*, © Philip Marsden 1993, HarperCollins Publishers UK.

John Masefield, 'Sea-Fever' from *Collected Poems*, 1938. Copyright The Estate of John Masefield.

Peter Mayle, *A Year in Provence*, © The Estate of Peter Mayle 1989, Penguin Random House.

Jan Morris, *Venice*, reproduced by permission of Faber & Faber Ltd.

Dervla Murphy, *Full Tilt: Ireland to India with a Bicycle*, © The Estate of Dervla Murphy 1965, Hachette UK.

Eric Newby, *A Short Walk in the Hindu Kush*, © The Estate of Eric Newby 1958, HarperCollins Publishers UK.

John Julius Norwich, *A Taste for Travel*, © John Julius Norwich 1986.

Redmond O'Hanlon, *In Trouble Again*, © Redmond O'Hanlon 1988, Penguin Random House.

Noo Saro-Wiwa, *Looking for Transwonderland: Travels in Nigeria*, © Noo Saro-Wiwa 2012, Granta.

Tahir Shah, *In Arabian Nights: In Search of Morocco Through its Stories and Storytellers*, © Tahir Shah 2008, Penguin Random House.

Mark Staples, *The Books that Bind*, reproduced with kind permission of Mark Staples.

Freya Stark, *The Valleys of the Assassins*, © The Estate of Freya Stark 1934, Hachette UK.

Chris Stewart, *Driving Over Lemons: An Optimist in Andalucía*, © Chris Stewart 1999, Sort Of Books.

Paul Theroux, *The Great Railway Bazaar*, © Paul Theroux 1975, Penguin Random House.

Wilfred Thesiger, *Arabian Sands*, © The Estate of Wilfred Thesiger 1959, HarperCollins Publishers UK.

Colin Thubron, *Among the Russians*, © Colin Thubron 1983, Penguin Random House.

Alexandra Tolstoy, *The Last Secrets of the Silk Road*, reproduced by permission of Profile Books.